Paschal

Paschal

Living the Dream

An Inspirational Memoir
by
James Vaughn Paschal

As told to
Mae Armster Kendall, EdD

Foreword
by
Ambassador Andrew J. Young

iUniverse, Inc.
New York Lincoln Shanghai

Paschal
Living the Dream

Copyright © 2006 by Mae A. Kendall

iUniverse books may be ordered through booksellers or by contacting:

iUniverse
2021 Pine Lake Road, Suite 100
Lincoln, NE 68512
www.iuniverse.com
1-800-Authors (1-800-288-4677)

ISBN-13: 978-0-595-37453-3 (pbk)
ISBN-13: 978-0-595-67503-6 (cloth)
ISBN-13: 978-0-595-81846-4 (ebk)
ISBN-10: 0-595-37453-0 (pbk)
ISBN-10: 0-595-67503-4 (cloth)
ISBN-10: 0-595-81846-3 (ebk)

Printed in the United States of America

This is the historical epic of James and Robert Paschal, two black brothers from McDuffie County and Atlanta, Georgia. These two stalwart men of color, fighting against the debilitating odds of a sharecropping life, became millionaires, philanthropists, world-renowned restaurant/hotel owners, and leaders in the struggle for civil rights.

To the everlasting memory of my beloved brother Robert, and to Phyllis, my precious wife of fifty-eight blessed years. Without her encouragement and her belief that I had history to share, this story might have never been told. She kept urging me onward.

James Paschal

To my husband, Charles, who, through my writing of this book, now clearly sees—though understandably sometimes grudgingly and, at intervals, "through a glass darkly"—that much patience, love, prayer, and generosity are prerequisites for the completion of such passionate, necessary, and committed endeavors. He has given all from the heart.

Dr. Mae Kendall

Contents

Foreword. xvii

Timeline xix

Prologue 1
- *Robert Goes Home*. 2
- *"An Evening Honoring Robert and James Paschal"* 4
- *And I Must Carry On*. 8

CHAPTER 1   Paschal Who? 10
- *Just Looking Back Is a Glorious Blessing* 12

CHAPTER 2   Humble Beginnings. 17
- *Living in Thomson and McDuffie County* 20
- *Held Together by a Deep Love* 21
- *Meeting Up Face-to-Face with Cotton*. 24

CHAPTER 3   Cotton Fields. 27
- *Calling on the Lowly but Highly Feared Boll Weevil* 30

CHAPTER 4   Beyond McDuffie County. 34
- *Getting an Education* 37

CHAPTER 5   Visions Abroad 40
- *My Dreams Outdistanced My Age* 43
- *Family Life*. 46

CHAPTER 6   Turning Points 51
- *Finding Jesus, the Old-Time Way*. 52
- *Baptized* 54

CHAPTER 7   Out of the Country, into the City 57
- *My Vegetable Sales*. 65
- *Robert, Stretching Out His Arms*. 66

CHAPTER 8   Promises to Keep 70
- *Not Getting Blown Upside Down, Nor Sideways* 76

CHAPTER 9   No Conflict of Mission 78
- *Staying the Course* 79
- *James' Place* 80
- *Claimed by the United States Army*. 84

CHAPTER 10   On to Other Things. 86
- *A Rose from the Gardens of Homewood* 90

CHAPTER 11   Atlanta 96
- *A True Beginning: Building on Principle* 97
- *The Paschal Creed* 99
- *Laying the Foundation, Brick by Brick* 101

CHAPTER 12   A New Life 105
- *And We Continued Growing*. 106
- *Bringing Curtis Home*. 111

CHAPTER 13   More to Come 114
- *La Carrousel Is Born* 118

CHAPTER 14   Trying Times 123
- *Prying Open Immovable Doors* 126
- *Building More Worthy Spaces* 128
- *Freedom's Chapters Continued*. 133

CHAPTER 15   Adventures 137

CHAPTER 16   Home 143
- *The Abundant Life* 146
- *Growing Up Paschal* 149
- *Her Great Gifts* 149

CHAPTER 17   Castleberry Hill 152
- *And They All Came Back*. 155

Epilogue. 209

The Paschal Formula for Success 211

Reflections. 215

Quotes from "An Evening Honoring Robert and James Paschal" 223

Full Text of Articles and Remarks 227

Afterword 237

Selected Bibliography 241

Index 243

Acknowledgments

Soon after beginning the research necessary to create an authentic "An Evening Honoring Robert and James Paschal," it became very clear to me that the histories of Atlanta, Georgia; the United States; and black America have again been cheated. I felt deeply ashamed that not one of us—historians, educators, politicians, community leaders, or relatives—had taken the time to formally recognize or record the remarkable lives of Robert and James Paschal. Thus began this exciting journey backward into the unheralded existence of two remarkable men who have enriched us all.

Once they began, encouragement and inspiration flowed like waves rolling in from a restless sea. The number of people to whom I would become forever indebted, if I were to complete the project, became real. It is impossible to thank every person who helped make this book a reality. Some people, however, stand out.

Thank you to:

- James V. Paschal, for finally leading us on this triumphant excursion as well as for yielding, giving in, and allowing us to move you toward opening the closets of your private and very personal experiences. We shall all be blessed.

- Mrs. Phyllis "Phil" Paschal, wife of James Paschal, for helping me convince him that his and his brother's lives—their courage, determination, endurance, and giving ways—held a story that simply had to be told. To Phil, I give my deepest gratitude and appreciation for helping me pound away at James Paschal until he gave in and agreed to tell the story of the Paschal brothers.

- Mrs. Gussie "Sister Gussie" Grant, the last living Paschal sister. Mr. James told me, "Sister Gussie remembers much more of the details about our lives than I do." From the date of my first telephone call, Sister Gussie, along with the enthusiastic help of her daughter, Ms. Beatrice Grant, shared generously. In our frequent exchanges between my home in Atlanta and theirs in Bethlehem, Pennsylvania, precious childhood memories flowed freely across the miles.

- Andrew J. Young, an old friend of forty-five years, former mayor of Atlanta, and beloved, world-renowned ambassador. His vibrant, warm contribution to this book as well as his continued words of encouragement shall remain priceless.

- Dr. Herman "Skip" Mason, professor and archivist at Morehouse College; owner of Digging It Up, Inc., an African-American research and consulting firm, and minister in the Christian Methodist Episcopal Church, for his encouragement and assistance. He wrote (and his company produced) the documentary, *Fried Chicken, Jazz, Politics: The Life and Legacy of the Paschal Brothers.* The moving videography was shown on giant screens at the "Evening Honoring Robert and James Paschal." Skip pushed me onward, responded to my every call, and shared news clippings, pictures, opinions, and ideas.

- The following all helped me keep this project moving forward when surgeries sidetracked me for an extended period: Dr. Mary S. Harris, PhD, president of Bio Technical Communications, Inc.; Lee Davidson Wilder, consultant and writer; Dr. Lucinda Ross Sullivan, PhD, educator.

Grateful appreciation to…

- Every single individual who responded to my call to share their special, unforgettable memories of "stopping by Paschal's."

Special thanks and appreciation to…

- My friend, Dr. Joyce Essien, MD, for introducing me to Carol Gee, author of *The Venus Chronicles* and *Diary of a Flygirl Wannabe,* who guided me to consultant publisher, Kelley Alexander.

- Kelley Alexander, up-and-coming president/CEO of InnerLight Publishing. Her profound, warm, quasi-effusive, but very professional approach has allowed me to draw upon her intelligence, wit, and strength in her continued support of this project.

- Lynn Wheeldin Suruma, I offer my personal and professional gratitude as well as respect for her professional input and scrutiny. All of which have all been priceless.

Foreword

Every sociopolitical or religious movement has a place of meeting—an "upper room," a pub of Patrick Henry, a gathering place where ideas are allowed to flow freely, a place of restoration and renewal, a sanctuary where one can return time and again when struggles in the outside world wear you down.

Paschal Brothers restaurant was the place for the Civil Rights Movement of the 1960s and the "sacramental meal" we shared together. It was the place for the South's best fried chicken, greens, black-eyed peas, cornbread, lettuce and tomato salad, sweet-iced tea, and homemade peach cobbler and ice cream. This was comfort food, food for the soul and body. This provided the energy and spirit that gave birth to freedom.

James Paschal's presence always welcomed individuals and groups. Brother Robert moved in and out of the kitchen, assuring quality control of food and ambience. To Sister Ora Belle Sherman, everyone was "sweetheart."

People met formally and informally at Paschal's to learn the day's agenda and get field reports from all over the South and the nation. Someone was always coming in with reports from Mississippi, Montgomery, Nashville, North Carolina, or Charleston. Before CNN and *Jet* covered the Movement, you could get news every morning at Paschal's. We could argue about what it all meant over grits and eggs, sausage and biscuits, pancakes, waffles, and always, fried chicken—breakfast, lunch, dinner, and late night.

During construction of Atlanta's burgeoning black housing market, Q. V. Williamson and John Calhoun would hold forth at one corner table while John Cox, Jesse Hill, and Leroy Johnson plotted the politics. The pastors gathered to share their sermons of last Sunday and next Sunday. Artists circulated, trading beautiful sketches for meals and rent money. As the happy hour at La Carrousel began, soft lights and good jazz saw the gathering of the soon-to-become racial joint venture business deals that would drive the city's economy for fifty years.

Even before there were black mayors to enforce it, enlightened business deals grew out of friendships made at Paschal's to the tunes of Billy Taylor, Ahmad Jamal, Hugh Masakela, Nina Simone, and the Murdock Jazz Quintet. Everybody played Paschal's La Carrousel and offered great music, **which built trust and** lasting friendships. These friendships enabled Herman Russell, then a small but reliable drywall contractor, to build America's largest black business ventures, starting out with a young John Portman, a white boy from the south side of town who envisioned the tall buildings and empires that have become Atlanta.

Muhammad Ali was locked out of the boxing ring because of his stand on Vietnam, but Leroy Johnson and Jesse Hill got Lester Maddox to form a boxing commission to create a fight in Atlanta. Hank Aaron and the Braves along with athletes from all over the sports world made Paschal's a home away from home. The brightest and the best from the AU Center made Paschal's a constant fashion show after school, after church...after everything.

Paschal's has been there, a center of soul-food fame and finance, thanks to the Paschal brothers. They would not franchise their restaurant because this was family, but they expanded to the world's busiest airport and now a new facility on Northside Drive. The tradition continues!

Andrew Young

Timeline

1908: Robert Paschal is born September 14 in McDuffie County, Georgia.

1922: James Vaughn Paschal is born October 8 in McDuffie County, Georgia.

1930: The Paschal family moves from McDuffie County to the city of Thomson.

1934: Robert leaves for Atlanta, Georgia.

1937: James opens his first store, "James' Place."

1941: James graduates from McDuffie County Training School and is inducted into the United States Army.

1943: James leaves Atlanta for Cleveland, Ohio.

1945: James begins work as a Pullman porter.

1946: James meets Phyllis Johnson, his future wife.

1947: Robert and James open Paschal's Restaurant on West Hunter Street. James and Phyllis marry on June 8.

1959: New Paschal's Restaurant opens across the street at 837 West Hunter Street (now Martin Luther King Drive). Phyllis and James adopt a son, Curtis Alston Paschal. United States Supreme Court issues ruling in Brown vs. Board of Education.

1960: Paschal brothers build the lounge, La Carrousel.

1964: Civil Rights Act becomes law.

1965: Civil Rights demonstration now known as Bloody Sunday, a march from Montgomery to Selma, Alabama, ends on the Edmund Pettus Bridge on March 7. Groundbreaking ceremonies for the new Paschal's Motor Hotel take place on August 3.

1967: Paschal's Motor Hotel opens for business. (Until 1996, Paschal's Hotel becomes the place for many civil rights and political decisions.)

1968: Dr. Martin Luther King Jr. leads the Poor People's Campaign and is assassinated on April 4.

1969: James Paschal elected to the board of directors of the Atlanta chapter of the Georgia Restaurant Association, becoming the first black man so designated.

1978: The Paschals, jointly with Dobbs House, Inc., form Dobbs-Paschal Midfield Corporation and win the bid for the Hartsfield International Airport Concessions contract with the City of Atlanta. James Paschal is the executive vice president of this joint venture, again becoming the first black to hold such a high-level position.

1980: Dobbs-Paschal's, the principal concessionaire at the Atlanta Airport until 1995, is responsible for leasing space to all sub-concessionaires in the passenger terminal, including Paschal's Concessions, Inc.

1984: Morris Brown College awards James Paschal an honorary doctor of laws degree.

1995: Paschal's sells its original complex to Clark Atlanta University. The sale is finalized in 1996, and the facility becomes the Paschal Center at Clark Atlanta University.

1997: Robert H. Paschal dies on Thursday, February 27. On March 4, "An Evening Honoring Robert and James Paschal" is held at the Georgia World Congress Center in Atlanta with more than 1,400 in attendance.

2002:   New Paschal's Restaurant opens on March 11 in Atlanta's historic Castleberry Hill.

2005:   James Paschal awarded the Phi Beta Sigma Lifetime Achievement Award for Business.

        October third, James Paschal's wife of fifty-eight years, Phyllis, passed away.

        November eighth, Atlanta Convention and Visitors Bureau selects James and Robert Paschal to be inducted into the Atlanta Hospitality and Tourism Hall of Fame.

Prologue

March 4, 1997, 7:00 PM

The early spring evening was perfect. Night seemed to have crept beautifully and cloud-free into the spaces of a yellow- and orange-hued brightly glowing sunset. The weather was beyond pleasing with its cool, velvety smooth breeze. I could feel a special vibrancy and expectation for what soon would be a glorious occasion: "An Evening Honoring Robert and James Paschal."

"Hold up, man!" shouted a middle-aged, balding, slightly fleshy man of average height. Dressed in black tie and waving his arms, he ran past our chauffeured limousine. Our driver had just stepped out and opened our door. The man hailed another up ahead.

"Hey, man! Wait! This is going to be rich stuff tonight! I can just taste it in my bones." He did a little dance movement and then caught up to the older, rotund man. "Let's go through this door! I see some mighty fine dolls in my view!"

As they proceeded through the massive entrance doors of Atlanta's Georgia World Congress Center, I overheard the other man respond, "Yeah, I sure do believe ya! Ummm Uh! Fine thing, this Paschal night!"

I did not recognize either of them, but their exchange was an appropriate forecast of the beautiful memories that would be packed into the next few hours.

My longtime friend and business neighbor, Juanita Sellers Stone of Sellers Brothers Funeral Home, had dispatched one of the longest, most glistening, black limousines I had ever seen to our home. The "Evening" was black tie. My wife, Phyllis, was beautiful in her formal evening suit of dark blue raw silk, which complemented her golden beige complexion and mixed gray hair.

1

When our car pulled up to the World Congress Center, our eyes met in stark disbelief. We could see a seemingly unending stream of men and women who were dressed to kill, an occasional small child, and a sizeable number of teenagers. All were smiling, talking, and laughing. The crowd moved quickly through every door and into the cavernous entry halls. For one moment, I was nearly overcome. I wish Robert could have been there to share this awesome night and these heartfelt expressions of love.

Robert Goes Home

There were a lot of things right with the world in which my brother and I had grown up. But then, there were also far too many things that were wrong. We wanted to live long enough to make some of those things right.
(James Paschal, March 2001)

My brother, Robert H. Paschal, died on Thursday, February 27, 1997. The following Monday, March 3, the day before "An Evening Honoring Robert and James Paschal," we buried him after a joyful and thankful praise service. The "home-going" services for Robert had been so eloquent and beautiful that it seemed nearly extraordinary. It was a conscious sharing, touching, and lasting testimony to the infinite capacity of loved ones and friends to go on giving of themselves. Our entire family was filled with peaceful mourning and the sad, but beautiful, acceptance of God's comforting will for Robert H. Paschal.

Robert had been eighty-eight years old when he died. Cancer had so ravished his body that the deterioration imposed upon his already slender frame had rendered him gaunt, darkened, speechless, and unable to eat or drink. For a time, he had just been wasting away. The "good-bye, I am tired of suffering" look in his eyes made his death an almost welcomed, compassionate companion.

For fifty years, Robert had been my inseparable business partner. I stood helplessly beside his bed, watching as death crept silently into his hospice room. I held his hand in mine as he coughed, slipping into oblivion. Within our feelings of hurt, sadness, and longing for his life, peacefulness found its resting place. We knew we had to release him to eternity. My wife and I had been there for Robert, as had his daughter, Corliss, and son, Thaddeus. Robert's dear wife, Florine, had preceded him in death some years earlier.

I had planned, ordered, and overseen every detail to give Robert the highest possible level of comfort while he was suffering. We watched him bravely endure every agonizing pain that cancer inflicted upon him. After he went, our sense of loss was so deep; however, our souls were satisfied. We knew Robert had gone in peace. We each said our private good-byes and watched as the ritual of death silenced his labored breathing. Finally, his suffering ceased.

At once sad, ordered, and jubilant, Robert's funeral service was worthy of his life. Mourners turned out in the hundreds—black, white, red, yellow, brown—from the very poor to those of us who believe ourselves to be "in charge and living large." The love, respect, sympathy, and caring was evident.

Organist Mrs. Ethel Harvey played a medley of Robert's favorite hymns as the processional, extending the full length of the entrance to the stage, filed reverently into the Martin Luther King Jr. International Chapel, situated on the campus of Atlanta's Morehouse College. Under the outstretched arms of the imposing statue of Dr. King outside the chapel entrance, throngs had come to celebrate my brother's life. The building was filled to capacity.

The renowned Reverend Dr. Joseph Lowery, then president of the Southern Christian Leadership Conference (SCLC), delivered the eulogy in his own country preacher style. His sermon was biblical, urbane, humorous, and "down home."

> Bob [was] a vibrant, energetic, creative, culinary artist…[C]hallenge Bob about the origin of some of the delicacies from the Paschal's kitchen; [he] would laughingly reflect about how he gave his mother some of the credit for his own conjured-up recipe.
> Bob's cooking capabilities really came about as the result of his poking around in the kitchen alongside his mother, Mrs. Lizzie Paschal, and his learning experiences after he arrived and remained in Atlanta. He learned well, and he taught well all of those whom he trained. Of course, that did not include his brother James. Brother James handled the management section of the business. James was never accused of being blessed with a mind to cook. Bob was satisfied to let his younger brother handle the business end of their partnership. (The complete text of Reverend Lowery's eulogy is available in the Reflections section.)

I struggled to fight back tears. Robert had worked so hard and faced so much prejudice and hatred. He had fought hard to remain good, kind, and noble. I wanted him to hear how that desire had been given life, fruit, and joy. I wanted Robert to hear the words, which may have soothed his aching heart when he watched our mother pull heavy, full crocus sacks down row after endless long row, up and down acres and acres of cotton fields. A poetic piece of Atlanta's history was about to be physically laid to rest. I sincerely believed, within the closeted depths of our hearts, we all knew Robert's spirit and his history would never die.

"An Evening Honoring Robert and James Paschal" had been arranged and prepared before Robert's death. The only missing link was a "go" signal from our family; the entire family was looking to me for decisive leadership. Would we—could we—bear to say yes? At a pivotal instant, I seemed to hear Robert's voice, "Hell, yeah! In the name of all things, James Paschal, you will—you must—move forward."

Family accord was never more solid, but we requested the event be "In Memoriam" to Robert H. Paschal. One of the lead planners of the gala had told me, "People are working and running around and feeling good, as though ecstatically preparing for the second coming of the Lions of Judah. And, Mr. Paschal," she declared, "people are coming from all across the nation."

"An Evening Honoring Robert and James Paschal"

When Phyllis and I arrived at the gala and got out of our car, what we saw deeply shook us. Eagerly and joyfully, we started walking toward the massive doorways and through the growing crowd. A woman's voice called, "We love you, Mr. Paschal. You and your brother have given so much to so many." I squeezed Phyl's hand, and we walked slowly through the door.

As we entered the World Congress Center, I looked left toward the grand escalators, which led to the ballroom. They were packed with smiling, talkative, well-dressed men, women, and children of different races. I wanted to stretch out my arms, surround each one, and pull them collectively into one big bear hug. Instead, as we glided upward on the escalator, I just placed my arm around Phyl's waist and whispered, "Can you believe this?" Phyllis whispered back, "Yes, I truly do believe this evening. You and Robert have always shared and shown such giving spirits."

As we neared the top of the escalator, we could hear the sounds of many cheerful voices and laughter coming from the grand lobby entrance to the Tom Murphy Ballroom. I could immediately see the focus of the lively, happy exchanges. We approached the smiling crowd. In the style of Moses parting the Red Sea, they lovingly and obligingly beckoned us through so we both could see and take it all in. I was almost humbled to tears.

An awe-inspiring photographic exhibit was directly in front of us, a chronology of many of the significant Paschal events. There were lively scenes of many of the notable jazz stars, politicians, community leaders, businessmen, and just plain folks. A huge ladder, more than six feet high and five feet wide, was lined with pictures, plaques, proclamations, and other Paschal artifacts. Photographer Susan J. Ross, a City of Atlanta official, had constructed this extensively researched, well-organized documentary.

The display was drawing admiring and very vocal throngs who pointed to specific pictures, plaques, and other memorabilia, which depicted so many unforgettable events in our lives. There were photos of us at our first little "Chicken Shack," of groundbreaking ceremonies, of the construction of the hotel, and so much more. Phyllis and I were nearly speechless. Almost at the same time, we said, "Gosh! Wouldn't Robert have loved this!"

"There you are!" Louise Hollowell, wife of Donald Hollowell, rushed over with her husband behind her. She threw both arms around my neck. "This is so long overdue. You and Robert have been great shining lights to all of us who are here tonight and to thousands of others who are not here. What a happy night!" As we joined the crowds moving into the ballroom, Louise held my hand tightly. Phyllis and I felt more and more rushes of excitement. As we stepped through the doors to join other family members who had gathered to greet us inside the rear of the ballroom, we heard choruses of "thank you" and "hello."

What a touching scene. The sight humbled us, and the crowd was enormous! Phil and I had been asked to wait for our special ushers, two lovely young ladies in glittering formal gowns, who would escort us to our seats at the head table.

The honorable ambassador and former mayor of Atlanta, Andrew Young, had traveled from Johannesburg, South Africa, to co-emcee the gala. Entertainers, ministers, civil rights leaders, businessmen, dignitaries, community advocates, just plain folks, and Paschal family and friends (more than 1,400 attendees) were sharing memories and a special history together.

Numerous greeters slowed the march toward the head table. We observed people, almost proudly, dabbing and mopping away at tear-filled eyes. One very close friend, Mrs. Malinda King O'Neal, ran up to us and locked arms with Phil and me. An attractive, warm, loving businesswoman, she stood on tiptoe to plant big kisses on our cheeks. For more than thirty years, she had operated her successful printing business next door to Paschal's on West Hunter Street.

Andrew Young and his wife, Carolyn, soon joined us. So did the family of Mrs. Coretta Scott King, Mrs. Christine King Farris, sister of Dr. Martin Luther King Jr., and her family; former Atlanta Mayor Maynard Holbrook Jackson and his wife, Valerie; Mr. Robert T. Bryant, vice chairman of Carson Pirie Scott; and Jesse Hill, retired CEO of Atlanta Life Insurance Company, and his wife, Azira.

Mrs. Ora Belle Sherman, Paschal's chief hostess for almost forty years, was ushered into the ballroom. She could not stop giggling. Mrs. Sherman had made a name for herself at Paschal's as one of the country's most renowned hostesses. Dark brown, attractive, neat, and slight, Mrs. Sherman, now eighty,[1] was always dressed and made up to perfection. Her "sugar-dripping voice" greeted and seated thousands of greats, near-greats, and non-greats who had passed through Paschal's.

Gracefully beautiful people moved to their seats as if moving down the runway of a Paris fashion house. The massive ballroom sparkled with laughter as friends, who had not seen each other for years, fellowshipped and openly wrapped each other in loving, tearful embraces. As the happy crowd mixed and moved, back and forth to assigned locations, full-color images of the Paschal years were projected on the back, sides, and front of the ballroom and across strategically placed, giant-sized screens. The experience was sensational.

Recording artist Jean Carne sang in perfect splendor. With deeply moving candor, she said, "It was at Paschal's that I got my first images of the power and fervor of artistic delivery. Paschal's has been indelibly stamped in my mind and on my life."

Attendees' ages ranged from elementary school children to Atlanta friend and treasure, ninety-five-year-old Mrs. Anne Nixon Cooper.[2] One young mother, an attractive classroom teacher, told me that she wanted her two children, ages eight and ten, to learn and live these lessons in courage, service, and success. So many others came that evening because, as one speaker related, "We all just belong here. We had to be here, we needed to be here."

---

1. Mrs. Ora Belle Sherman passed away on January 23, 2004. She was eighty-seven years old.
2. Mrs. Anne Nixon Cooper celebrated her 104th birthday on January 1, 2006.

Maynard Jackson, the former mayor of Atlanta, rose from his seat.

"Everyone in this hall tonight owes some part of their well-being to Robert and James Paschal," he said. "They either gave you a job, a needed few bucks, a few nights of bedding down at Paschal's Hotel, a free meeting place for a civil rights gathering, or—quietly and often—anonymously paid your tuition at the Atlanta University Center."

Sounds of Billy Eckstine, Duke Ellington, Curtis Mayfield, Ramsey Lewis, Aretha Franklin, and other music notables floated across the ballroom. Herman Mitchell and the All-Star Trio played and sang many of the "oldies but goodies." It was hard to be still, keep calm, and just listen.

Correspondences were read from President Bill Clinton and Georgia Congressman John Lewis, who had also been a vital part of "stopping by Paschal's." Lewis's message stated how he had joined with Dr. Martin Luther King Jr., Andrew Young, Dr. Ralph David Abernathy, and others at Paschal's in the fight for racial equality.

Emcees Andrew Young, the U.S. Ambassador to the U.N., and Jesse Hill, Atlanta business and civic icon as well as retired head of Atlanta Life Insurance Company, took the podium. Andy's voice resonated:

> In spite of an absolutely daunting flight plan, I knew I simply had to be here. Because I, like so many others of you in this room, owe much of the richness, meaning, success, and safety of the Civil Rights Movement and my own success to the overflowing generosity and love of James and Robert Paschal.
>
> The Paschal brothers were there for me when I ran for and won the 5th District Seat for the United States Congress. They were there for me each time I ran for mayor of the City of Atlanta and for governor of Georgia. It was Ralph David Abernathy, who said, 'No doubt, the walls of America will be changed in Paschal's.'
>
> James and Robert Paschal brought with them to Atlanta everything it took to help make a great Atlanta even greater. All that could possibly have been given has been given. Every year, after our marches, we would gather at Paschal's for our family meals. Coretta would invite various celebrities, and they would come. We started out, and our gatherings numbered about fifteen or twenty. Our crowd soon grew to over 150. We could all feel that deep, inner spirit. Robert and James Paschal poured forth from their broad and loving hearts, a special kind of bravery, love, and compassion; a sincere and public kind of caring this city had never seen before from two brothers—black or white. And they never asked for nor did they expect anything in return. (The complete text of Andrew Young's remarks is available in the Reflections section.)

Jesse Hill was the soul of generosity:

> Anyone in the hall who truly knows me...know[s] how the Paschal brothers were a cosmic power in my own self-actualization...
> When the...climate of downtown Atlanta was filled with racial divisiveness and when downtown Atlanta was a heatedly unwelcome territory for our black brothers and sisters, Robert and James Paschal always stepped forward as our two great Hannibal warriors of our time. They often had to help us keep cool heads and fearless hearts.
> What for many of us were fearful and trembling times, Robert and James Paschal stood bravely there. With arms outstretched, they were steadfast beacons of love, hope, and black power. They were examples of colorless power. It was these stalwart, humble, two, strong, black brothers who offered themselves and their place, Paschal's. What was to become nationally known and recognized as "The Place," Paschal's was a courageous, open, resilient citadel, a safe haven in Atlanta for blacks. And then, there were also those whites who, at such a time, owned the courage to assemble, to meet together prayerfully and politically, with black folks. We are here simply to say a real, long overdue and grand thanks to Robert and James Paschal. (The complete text of Jesse Hill's remarks are available in the Reflections section.)

And I Must Carry On

The evening was unmatched and powerful in its supremely touching and human fullness. Robert and I had never perceived our sharing as anything special. Sharing and giving had been our way of life. Our parents, Henry and Lizzie Paschal, never had much. However, what our family had was always shared with others.

Joy, sorrow, love, excitement, and sincere expressions of thanks filled every corner of the gathering. Grown men laughed and cried. At the close of the gala, people lingered as if they thought the captivating spirit of the evening might not follow them home. But people gradually left. It was as if all the magic and miracles of the unforgettable moments had taken hold, becoming forever emblazoned in our souls.

As a clan forever united, the crowd gradually dwindled slowly. Some held hands; some said blessings and good-byes. Others hugged, kissed, and bade farewell; while others simply left the room in tearful silence. As we exited the ballroom, I could have sworn I heard someone humming "Amazing Grace."

So many had given so much to make this evening special. It was as if a tremendous wave was lifting me, sweeping me forward. I knew God would continue lighting my pathway, giving me directions. Whenever fatigue, disappointment, hurt, family needs, or anything negative sought to impede or block our progress, Robert and I would say, "Remember, we Paschals, all of us, are thoroughbreds."

History moves on. Despite my yearning for Robert, the threads remain unbroken.

1

Paschal Who?

...When the [Paschal] brothers and Dobbs House Inc., inked a contract with the city for joint operation of all retail operations in the new Atlanta airport—a deal expected to put a whopping $1 billion into the coffers of Paschal and Dobbs House over the next fifteen years—the resounding question in the boardrooms of the nation's business moguls was, "Paschal who?"[1]

Our families must have read and reread that magazine story more than 100 times. We just kept looking at each other, crying, laughing, and quietly thanking God. It was not surprising that, if and when the name Paschal was mentioned in the conference rooms of the white and powerful, they would most likely retort, "Paschal who?"

They could not know. It had taken us years to become what we had struggled to make our business and personal reputations become. It had taken us McDuffie County, Thomson, Georgia, brothers' years of labor, determination, slaps in our faces, painful sacrifices, unbending love, respect, and giving to reach even small milestones. How could they have known that we (two black men) had so many muddy and sometimes alligator-infested rivers to cross?

Many times, we waded, swam, fought, and gulped high waters. However, with blessed help from the Almighty and Paschal values, we fought our way

---

1.   "The Paschals of Atlanta: Selling Southern hospitality pays off for hardworking brothers," *Ebony*, November 1979, 63–66.

across and around those rivers. Swimming often became exhausting. Our arms got tired, our hearts became heavy, and our bodies numbed. However, God's boundless love continued filling our souls, and we continued stroking. The team of Robert and James Paschal—the cotton picker, the busboy, and the Pullman porter—was wonderfully blessed.

In the years between 1947 and 1995, "Stopping by Paschal's" was the regular, common declaration by newcomers, native Atlantans, celebrities, and a variety of visitors throughout much of Atlanta. Each, with his or her own special flavor, played a major part in giving life to the Paschal history in Atlanta. It took us nearly twenty years to reach the heights of our dreams and goals, but time did not stop us or blur our vision. Those awesome years gave life, deep feelings, and lasting memories.

Throngs stopped by every day of the week and for special celebratory occasions. During the fight for civil rights, brave and determined men and women, often in lonely quests for victory, stopped by the original Paschal's on Atlanta's old West Hunter Street, now named Martin Luther King Jr. Drive. Dr. Ralph David Abernathy of the Southern Christian Leadership Conference (SCLC) and his lieutenants named Paschal's "The Place." In an article featuring Dr. Abernathy, the author wrote:

> 'Historians [said Abernathy] may well recall that the Paschal's Motor Hotel was used often as the war room for a nonviolent revolution.' It was almost as if he were in his own pulpit preaching about 'those golden streets' and the glory of 'the promised land.' Slowly and distinctly, Rev. Ralph David Abernathy spoke solemn words of praise. But the awe he inspired was not for the hereafter, it was for Paschal's Motor Hotel which is very much here and now—an establishment he described as 'a living monument to black capitalism.'
> Abernathy spoke passionately of an establishment he described as the center for more than a decade of 'a glorious campaign to build a new America, an America free of racism, war, and poverty,' an establishment described by his friend, Julian Bond, as simply 'The Place.'
> 'I consider Paschal's…the finest black-owned and operated restaurant and hotel in the country,' Dr. Abernathy began in an eloquent tribute which almost became a premature eulogy for a meeting place which has meant so much to all Americans of good will. 'Since its inception, SCLC has used Paschal's for retreats and executive meetings. A new America has been mapped within the walls of Paschal's Motor Hotel.'[2]

---

2.   Gene Stephens (photograph by Clinton Davis), *Pride*, 1972.

Inside Paschal's, many people learned that the price of freedom includes responsibility and service to others. Some seemed to have felt that ownership in the battle (and credit for the winning of those battles) grew out of simply being in the crowd. Real soldiers in the Movement lived the truth. They were the thousands who prayed and marched, went to jail and were beaten, were spat upon, pushed to the ground, and stomped upon.

When the many voices of the different races of people and many dedicated souls, young and old, raised the declaration of "stopping by Paschal's," it often had a central political and social meaning as well as deep implications for our future. For those vibrant voices and sacrificial bodies who were in the thick of the battles for the liberation and deliverance of the many, "stopping by Paschal's" was either a call to social and artistic enrichment or a political call to action. These men and women of the Movement did not just stop by Paschal's. They teamed, planned, gathered to pray, march, sit-in, share encouragement, and sing songs of the Movement.

These times will be revisited repeatedly. Each has its own song and verse. They stay in my mind, happily surrounding me. They will not let go, and I will not let go.

Robert and I were born poor, but, by the will of God, we enjoyed a span of time (more than fifty years) in which our dreams were abundantly fulfilled. We struggled hard and long to shake off the shackles of an early life of sharecropping and poverty. We knew it would not be easy to build a spotless record of offering the best in good food and building community faith and trust in our quality of service. Although often brutal, sharecropping had not claimed us or wilted our dreams. Neither were we left with hatred in our hearts. Rather, we had been lifted above it all. The harder the times, the harder we worked to free ourselves and the more deeply and vividly we dreamed. God has so graciously allowed us to fully live out our dreams.

Just Looking Back Is a Glorious Blessing

Our greatest triumph was that blessed January 1947, the formal opening of our first Paschal's Restaurant. Robert had come to Atlanta in 1934. It had been thirteen years since he had left Thomson to begin a new life in Atlanta. That little restaurant, seating only forty people, endowed us with a resiliency of spirit and offered us personal, historical, and spiritual connections with so many souls that grew deep, as Langston Hughes said, "like the rivers."

It was tough for us when our crowds began swelling, but we hung in there. After testing and tasting and holding onto many of the recipes we had enjoyed as children from Momma Lizzie Paschal's kitchen stove, we agreed that what we really needed was a specialty dish. As a result, Robert's soon-to-become famous fried chicken was born.

We already knew the crunchy, crusty, light brown appearance and unique taste of Robert's fried chicken would, if further perfected, grow in popularity. It did...and very fast. He proved he had learned well from our momma's kitchen. Learning how to offer the country's best fried chicken would not be a problem. He just needed to come to the "what" in his mixture of seasonings. Like a scientist in his lab, Robert tested his blends of spices and seasonings until he was satisfied that he had hit upon the taste that meant something deliciously fit only for his fried chicken.

Robert's carefully selected, plump, best-looking chickens were always properly cut up and fried to a succulent, tasty light brown. Only he seemed to know exactly how long to leave the chicken in the deep frying pans after the birds had marinated sufficiently in his carefully guarded secret combination of spices and seasonings. That chicken quickly began to make a name for itself and was consistently praised and sought after. Atlanta University Center students formed lines around our serving counters. Many families and scores of other patrons soon began making Robert's fried chicken a Sunday dinner must. Every Sunday, they came in larger and larger numbers. All over Atlanta, everybody sang the praises of Paschal's fried chicken.

Climbing up the rough sides of many mountains, our fierce determination and commitment to offer the very best in hospitality services had indeed delivered us. The continued prayers, encouragement, and faith of our loved ones and friends surrounded us. We could hear the constant voices of our beloved parents telling us, "You two are Paschal thoroughbreds." We knew we could not fail. Our belief in God, our hard work, and our will to catch a grip and hold on would not let us think of quitting.

When that crowd of more than 1,400 well-wishers so passionately honored Robert and me, I began feeling a deep sense of an unpaid debt. During the evening, one acquaintance said it would be sad, pitiful, and unfair if I did not leave some recorded history of Paschal's. Another said, "You owe it to your brother, your family, to all of us who were there, and to generations to come who were not there." I at least owed them and my family. Although it took me a while to decide, in my heart that very night, I think I knew I had to do something.

I then had a fervent encounter with the late Honorable Maynard Holbrook Jackson, Atlanta's first black mayor. Maynard had played a vital role in the political, social, and economic mosaic that had become Paschal's. During one of his last visits to the new Paschal's Restaurant, he tightly gripped and shook my hand. In his uniquely booming voice, he said, "I hear you listened! Thank God, the book is coming! Good! You two brothers have shown unsurpassed love for this city and your fellow human beings. You have history in your bones. Hurry up and tell your story!"

I had already begun to literally hear the clear, defining voices of so many that had been passionate and dedicated partners and colleagues in the Paschal history. Many in the 1940s and 1950s had licked their fingers clean after feasting on one of our now-famous fifty-two cent fried chicken sandwiches. Others pleaded for an opportunity to revisit our history. They had been there, so many people from very diverse backgrounds. All had played a grand, vital part in the making and fulfilling of our lives. Each had given so much of himself.

During the frightening days of the Movement, quiet gatherings between blacks and whites were held at Paschal's. At our place, those whites who fearlessly joined the Movement often braved the wrath of family and friends to become partners in waging war against hatred and racial segregation. Black, brown, and white people, young and old, had marched hand in hand and had locked arms to sit in at "whites only" lunch counters. They had joined together to raise their sometimes trembling voices in singing "We Shall Overcome" and other songs in the long, dangerous fight for freedom. They had been jailed and labeled troublemakers. They regularly sought out Paschal's for food, sleep, or be bonded out of jail. One friend said,

> James, we are calling out for you to write this book because so many of us want to be heard through you. We all gave so much. We submitted our bodies to be battered. We shed briny tears in the fight against Jim Crow…We stepped forward. We lent strength and daring and love and fortitude. We all still hold membership in this heritage. We all fought gallantly to usher in the tumbling down of the vicious and insidious walls of racial injustices.

These warriors spoke fervently in a kind of choral richness of their fights and the need to fight. They spoke of the issues, frustrations, infinite hopes, and dreams realized and deferred. So many others, from every diverse group imaginable (the laborers, the construction workers, the teachers, the students, the preachers, the farmers, and Paschal employees), voiced support and encouragement from across America. Some even offered personal narratives. The seeming significance of Paschal's in their varied lives and American history drove me onward toward offering this work.

Even though many battles have been won and our fights have earned some gains, much remains to be done. Unfortunately, our world still needs healing. It is severely pained with the agony and grief resulting from hatred, quests for power, racism, and humankind's inhumanity to one another. So much hope and belief in the ability of America and the rest of the world to heal was generated in the dining rooms and meeting rooms of the old Paschal's on West Hunter Street.

Robert and I only prayed to be able to share unconditional love and our blessed abundance as well as stand strong and immovable in the fight for the civil rights of our people, all people. However, this book is also the story of family and their enduring love, even when hours away from home often became much too long. It is about home, heritage, and good manners. It is about love for people and wanting to serve. It is about driving and working hard to succeed. It is about being taught to give. Much credit must be given to our family members who, in those early childhood and teenage years of building Paschal's, toiled alongside us and helped make our business ventures the successes they all became.

Others may gain insight into holding onto their dreams, visions, hopes, and desires to become successful. A life does not have to fit the mold of another life. The common and basic elements of a deep belief in self, family, a superior being, and steady hard work toward a goal will spell success. Where one begins in life does not have to hinder where, how high, how far one goes, or how successful one becomes.

If telling this story about what had to happen for Robert and James Paschal to make useful contributions to the lives of others inspires, then I am blessed to be able to share. If our accomplishments are deemed valid to others, I am pleased to share. If the story of our lives can shake and motivate a single young person into firmly believing that any person in this world can successfully conquer and overcome any earthly adversity and if that person is willing to go under, around, or over whatever stands in the way of success, then I will tell our story. If I can cause one person to see and feel the need to cultivate, build, and nurture friendships, instead of accumulate enemies, my sharing is worth this effort. I have enjoyed more than eighty years on this beautiful earth. I believe the positive substance and blessed length of my existence is largely due to the basics by which I have tried to live: give me just a few minutes with my worst enemy, and I will make that enemy my friend.

Today, I am blessed to enjoy the abundances of life. However, I cannot ever—nor do I want to—forget or ignore my past. Doing so would be engaging in the unforgivable act of murdering my precious history. All generations, those present and yet to be born, need to know of the bloody, often brutal past of people of color all over this world. It was—and still is—shameful. Hating a person, given to the universe by God Almighty, simply because he was born with skins of hue seems anti-God. However, it was a time upon which we should all continue to reflect and build. It is a time about which we should continue to pray. It is a time for which we should continue to seek forgiveness for our enemies and for all of us.

2

Humble Beginnings

I came into this blessed, beautiful world at a time when conditions in American society were much sicker than they are now, when people of color were subjected to cruel, inhumane conditions. White folks happily piled upon black folks (coloreds or niggers, as we were often called), the shameful shackles of sharecropping. No one in government tried stopping them. They were happy partners in this new slavery.

Don't get me wrong. My father and mother always told us some white folks did not agree with the way colored folks were treated. However, many were just too scared to step forth and say no to whites in power. These whites were often members of the dreaded Ku Klux Klan or had friends, family, or business connections with this group. Nevertheless, as we grew older, all of the Paschal children got to know and feel the sympathy of some of those good white folks.

I was born in rural McDuffie County in northeast Georgia. I was named James Vaughn Paschal. I am told I was born on October 8, 1922. We lived in a three-bedroom, unpainted clapboard shack. My father, Henry Paschal, was a hardworking, honest, uneducated sharecropper. I was born into the especially hard life of digging in the black, rough, unyielding soil of dirt farming. Yes, I know the pain, sweat, drudgery, and shame of backs bent low for hours while plucking the white man's cotton.

My father was married twice. My mother, Lizzie Paschal, was his second wife. She bore him seven children: four boys (Gilmer, Hodges, Robert, and I) and three girls (Gussie, Claudie, and Annie Mae). My daddy had two children from his first marriage, Effie and Joseph.

Lizzie Paschal dearly loved *all* of her children, including the two who became her own when she married my daddy. Machines were not available for plucking the cotton from the sometimes stiff, dried, hardened cotton bolls or easing the pulling and shaking off the gritty black, dirt-tough country growth, which freely surrounded the roots of the peanut crops. However, our parents worked just as hard at home to make love and laughter alive to us, along with their passion for moving our minds—and ultimately our bodies—from those damnable cotton fields. They encouraged us to always build our own dreams and then work hard to follow them through to fulfillment. We were constantly taught to "never do anything halfway" and "whatever is worth your time is worth doing your best." Henry and Lizzie were their children's best teachers. They did not just tell us. They taught by example.

Henry Paschal was a keen, crafty, and full-producing farmer who labored in the massive, rolling cotton fields in the sharecropping style. He tilled, planted, and toiled in the soil from dawn to dusk. Still, he often declared he knew precious love and peace inside himself. He knew Lizzie Paschal was also calmly and lovingly at work. Wherever she was, she was busily taking great care to make her family's home life a centerpiece of love, hope, and unending search for survival. She wanted the best for her children. She dreamed for her family. She dreamed along with her family. She often spoke her dreams aloud. She willed her lovely, smooth soprano voice to dreams through the lilting, soft tones of "God Will Take Care of You." She then quietly placed us in the loving embrace of her close connection with God Almighty and left us there. My parents' constant hope was that we would pray every day for God to deliver us from living a sharecropper's life.

My parents never let wishing, dreaming, and believing just wither and blow away into nothingness. Holding regular, serious family meetings around the breakfast or dinner table, they, in their own humble way, breathed visions of great possibilities, spiritual hungriness, confidence, and wisdom into the very bodies and minds of their children.

"Lord, bless and guide each of these children," my mother prayed. "Let each one keep on striving to be the best they can be." The sound of her sweet voice still rings strong in my ears.

My mother was a slim woman of medium height with a full head of hair and light brown skin. Her smooth skin and high cheekbones made it seem as if she was always about to break into one of her broad smiles. Always clean and neatly dressed, even when she was bowed low over a row in a cotton field, she was fiercely devoted to cleanliness. She literally lived the saying, "Cleanliness is next to godliness." She was a loving, kind, determined, and, as needed, firm Christian mother. I never knew her to consume any drink stronger than Royal Crown Cola. She made no differences among her children. We loved each other as dearly as if we were all born of the same father and mother.

While growing up, we shared a loving, but slightly different, kind of black sharecropper's lifestyle. Our dad, who was aggressive and creative, never worked just one job. He said, "The pay is so near nothing that you gotta take in all you can to try to live a partly decent life." Because of our family's hard work, we had things other sharecroppers did not have, including horses and mowers to cut the heavy grass to help clear the fields. We grew crops others did not grow, such as fig trees, peanuts, and sweet potatoes. We grew and took good care of our fruit trees. We also took care of our soil, which was good soil.

Like most other poor black families, our family and extended families were extremely close. We had to share in whatever small fortunes came our way. We were all loved, hugged, and well-fed throughout our lives, and we protected each other. We believed, if we were going to make it safely through the dreadful years that were ahead of us, we had to be strong. We also had to work and depend on each other.

"One who loves, respects, and has a love of work will never be hungry or broke" was constantly repeated to us. Often, you may not have any cash money left, but a family's love and caring will make you rich. If God spares life, you can always work and make more money. The Paschal children latched onto—and never released—the charges we were given to keep. There was always the reminder: "You can blaze some trails of your own…Do not wait and want for anyone to give you anything…Go for what you want yourself…We believe better days are ahead…Be ready!"

Around our big, wooden, homemade dining table, that was always brimming full with fresh, painstakingly prepared meals, each Paschal child heard and saw life's great possibilities before him or her. We knew we could claim these rainbows as our own, only if we were willing to pay the price of prayer and hard work. Our parents' seeds of courage fell into receptive soil. We listened; we heard well. Each Paschal child went onto live lives of relative comfort and spiritual connectedness, while learning to share, loving and supporting our families, and serving our communities.

Living in Thomson and McDuffie County

Thomson, Georgia, may think it is very cosmopolitan today. However, when I came along, the town was purely rural, menacingly laced with acres of cotton fields. My family was on the cutting, picking, chopping, and cropping edges of those fields. We did not have much, but we did have family, hope, committed love, and an undying, deep desire to overcome. Hard work was the foundation of our lives.

Thomson is a somewhat coastal town. Located 120 miles east of Atlanta and thirty miles west of Augusta, Thomson is midway between Atlanta and the Carolinas. I said hello to our Lord's earth at a time when life was tedious or, as my parents said, "Life was 'tejus' and full of shame."

Many whites knew of (and indeed participated in) the frightening, often terrifying mistreatment of an entire race of people. Not only were the ruling classes participants in nurturing and maintaining a "boss and slave-owning mentality," they bred and unashamedly reared their children as they had been raised, to continue the traditions of hatred for black people, only because of the color of our skin. There were a few blessed, God-sent exceptions, but my daddy reminded us almost daily, "Do not get mad at the white man. Get educated, and let God Almighty be the avenger. In his own due time, he will fix it for you. When God fixes things, nothing can be done about what nor how God chooses to fix them." My daddy then sometimes led us in a family singing of "Let Jesus Fix It for You."

Back then, black people were treated as if they were almost unseen and certainly unheard, except when needed and ordered to do white folks' hard work. Socially and economically, black people were virtually invisible. Poor black people were labeled nice and sweet, based upon how hard they labored and grinned in the white man's kitchens and cotton fields. Life was rough and scary. Poor black families, the farmhands, woke with daylight and never stopped working until sundown. Saturday was a half-day of work. Sunday was most likely the same, except the rich white folks proclaimed a belief in the Almighty, no matter how hollow. This meant black families were allowed to take a church break on Sunday.

The most pretentious words spoken can never truthfully tell how hard so many black people worked to simply eke out a living. My parents and grandparents prayed unceasingly and worked every day. They were always in a hurry, never stopping. The work was backbreaking and demanding. It was honest, but degrading and never ending. Our family joined the throngs of hardworking, cotton-planting, cotton-picking, cotton-chopping, struggling black families and gave dedicated service to this often violent, intimidating period in our times. Rumors were regularly passed around about how some hard-bearing, mean old farmers beat their laborers (and sometimes their workers' children) if they felt the families were unwilling to follow orders to work harder or do as ordered.

Held Together by a Deep Love

From the first time I remember knowing myself, I knew my parents truly loved us, that is, if one could ever be thoroughly loving while knowing your life and your children's lives depended on planting, raising, and picking the cotton for wealthy, bossy, often coldhearted, white landowners. How could you live a respectable life knowing, except when you were in the fields picking cotton or slaving in their homes, you were nothing more than chattel in the eyes of those responsible for your livelihood? At the time, picking cotton or growing other crops was all most black families could do for a living.

One of my earliest memories is standing with my mother at weighing up time. My small hand is locked in hers. We stand in line in a blazing hot sun until it is her turn to place her full, heavy sack of cotton on the scale. Looking upward, I see fatigue and shame painted all over her face. Sweat rolls off her in streams. I also feel hot and ashamed. As I watch fatigue wrap itself around my mother, I push back the tears.

Monday through Saturday, as soon as the sun came up and until its brightness had hidden itself behind the horizon, I watched as my parents, like most other blacks in the South, slaved in the white man's cotton fields or in their homes. Many times, black mothers also nursed and reared the whites' children while their own babies needed a mother's nursing and nurturing. My young mind could well have been filled to the brim with hatred, but that would not do for any of my parents' brood. They grilled us, "Never allow hatred to seep into your mind, your soul, or your bloodstreams…Pray hard to be able to love everybody…Love even those who hate you…Show the world the love we have shown you…Hatred rots everything it touches."

My parents had to know the white man had truly done a job on us. I say white man because white women were often in almost equal bondage, even though I do not think they knew. If they did, they did not care. Only how they lived in the present seemed to matter. White men usually made all of the major decisions. There were always the frightening admonitions, even warnings. Almost daily, we were told to always say, "Yes, sir" and "Yes, ma'am" to whites. My daddy's voice sometimes trembled as he told his sons, "Whatever you do, please do not smile or even look at a white girl!" I thought it was so stupid. Can whites really tell your eyes, given to you by God, where to look? Yes, and they did.

While I was growing up, I would hear the grown folks whispering about black men, sometimes boys, being dragged behind cars or trucks or hung from a tree limb for simply smiling or whistling at a white girl or woman. Black folks took the abuse and the often demeaning treatment while continuing to pick in those blazing cotton fields.

The pay was pitiful. The one-hour breaks for lunch were like fleeting moments. You had to eat, pee, and rest in nearly one breath. I never wanted to nor did I ever make one single effort to pick enough cotton to break into notoriety as a cotton picker. Our parents gave their all and demanded no less from their children. The deep hatred I felt in my heart for the cotton fields when I did my limited plucking and picking was the only hint of rebellion I ever showed. I only did just enough to get by. The only words I could happily hold onto for future reference were those that spelled possibilities. Some Paschal children were better at picking than others. Robert, as it turned out, was the cotton-picking star of all the Paschal offspring.

Like thousands of others, our parents continued to march up and down through endless, hot fields of cotton, onward toward the seemingly elusive quest for freedom. In those hellish days, my mother rose with the sun, cooked breakfast for all of us, went to the cotton fields, and labored through mid-morning. She then went back to our shanty to prepare the noon meal. When she finished cooking, she rang a bell suspended from a long, skinny wooden pole that was set deep into the ground in our front yard.

The "callin' pole" had been cut and shaped from a young pine tree that had been stripped of its bark and made slick. My brothers and I thought the slickness discouraged youthful climbs up the greasy pole. The bell my mother rang could be clearly heard in the fields. Those peals happily called all pickers to a bit of rest and a table spread—even laden—with many good things to eat. For most black families, a full, varied, delicious table was one of the major highlights in an otherwise bondage way of life. With tummies always too full, everyone knew they had to return to the heat and sweat of picking cotton.

You never really wanted to go back. It had nothing to do with being smart or lazy. Between the urgent call for the needed few pennies earned at the end of the day and the white man calling you a "bunch of lazy niggers" or worse, all managed to waddle back to the fields. As I grew older, I soon learned the sadness of hearts and the piercing aching of backs really had to do with all the damnable inequities flourishing all around you. No one in power or position to make a change even cared. It seemed to me that the misery and heaviness of summertime in those burning cotton fields would never end.

Many nights, even though we were tired, sweaty, and smelly and our heads were bowed low from the backbreaking, merciless work of the day, our parents gathered us together in prayerful thanks around the evening table. Before a crumb of food was touched, tin washtubs and white enamel basins filled with warm water were worked overtime to banish most of the day's dirt and grime from our bodies. Holding hands all around the table, my daddy fervently blessed the food he said was given "to nourish our bodies." He added, "And bless the hands of dear Lizzie who fixed it."

My daddy then began his daily talk about how we had to hold onto the teachings of the Bible as well as our spiritual values, morals, and Christian beliefs. My parents truly believed in their hearts that, if we each lived a Christian life, God would deliver us from "these evils we must endure, but only for a time." My mother sometimes raised her beautiful soprano voice, singing "Jesus, Keep Me Near the Cross." We were all supposed to join in, but, even then, it was a resounding no for me. I knew then, as I know now, I was not born to sing.

They also told us to always love and care for each other as well as love and respect other people. God would bless us to be whatever we wanted to be. Our big, shabby table (but scrubbed clean) was always filled with good things to eat. My mother could somehow make the simplest morsels of food taste as if each had been carefully prepared and served up fit for a king's palate.

My mother was noted for her talents in the kitchen, especially her baking. Her tea cakes were our much-loved, prized childhood favorite. She would mix flour, country cream, milk, butter, eggs, lemon or vanilla flavoring, spices, and sugar, and when done baking, she would give them to us as a reward for being good and working hard, usually in the cotton fields or the family garden. The tea cakes were lovingly kneaded, thinly rolled out, cut into various shapes, and baked to a light, crispy, crunchy brown. They always smelled so good. All the children and anyone else around waited in mouthwatering impatience for tea cakes and glasses of fresh cold milk or big cups of warm sassafras tea.

People said my mother's pound cakes were better than anyone else's in McDuffie County or Thomson. The saying must have been true. She was regularly sought after for her cakes, cobblers, and pies. However, her pound cakes rested majestically on their own reputation. Many times, white women came searching for her cakes. Each time I heard our landowner's wife and other white women around town say, "Lizzie, I want a cake for Sunday's dinner," I was filled with rage. I never heard, "Mrs. Paschal, will you please bake me a pound cake for Sunday's dinner?" or even "Miss Lizzie." It was always just, "Lizzie, I want a cake." I concluded, unlike us, they had never been taught good manners.

My mother may have become famous around McDuffie County and Thomson for baking and selling cakes and pies, but her talents in the kitchen did not earn her enough respect to keep her out of the cotton fields. No "niggra" woman living on the boss man's property would have ever been allowed to stay at home like his wife. It would have been too much like white folks. I concluded the cotton fields were the white man's factories for black humiliations. Even the education of their black servants and their servants' children did not get any consideration. For black children, the new school year often did not begin until the very last boll of cotton had been pulled from its stem and the last bunch of peanuts had been pulled out and shaken clean of the soil holding it.

Meeting Up Face-to-Face with Cotton

I will never forget my first introduction to the cotton fields of McDuffie County. The year was 1929, and I was just turning seven years old. I was young, but I was not too young to feel the weight of the Depression years. Hard times were already hanging over families, black and white. I heard my mother and father praying almost daily, "Lord, please stand by our family. Help us through the hard days ahead." For many families, there was no work, money, food, and place to live.

Little children can tell when all is not well. You feel it inside your belly. Grown folks talked about the long food lines that were visible almost everywhere we went. Haggard-looking, hungry, smelly, hopeless lines of people begged for government handouts and pleaded for relief. My daddy said these sights were backing up humanity all over America.

The radio repeatedly reported the news about these conditions, which usually, if you were poor, knew no age or color boundaries. "But, if you were black," my daddy said, "your already pitiful state was compounded, worsened." Weeping and hunger hung over the existence of thousands of American families, that is, unless you were white and had money. This money was often gained through greed, deception, and, usually, the backs of overworked people of color. While every family in this country lived its own tales of wonder and taking risks, if you happened to have entered this world covered in a skin of color, your entire family faced special turmoil and dangers at some time. Vicious, racists acts often spelled doom and damnation for thousands of black families. Lesser spirits and weaker backs than our ancestors would have been defeated and stomped out forever.

My daddy was already dreaming big ideas of how life could be much better if he could move his family out of the country of McDuffie County into Thomson, the county seat. We often heard him say, "God surely wants me to move my family onward. He wants me to walk my family out of these wretched cotton fields and into a better life." My daddy was not a formally educated man, but he was drenched in love, kindness, common sense, determination, and Christian manhood. Like so many black folks at the time, he could not even dream about finishing high school because he had to work. Nevertheless, he never failed to tell us almost daily, "Get educated, and you can rule your own world. Get educated. It is the only answer to having a well-lived life." For himself, he could not do any better. He knew he was hopelessly chained to an uncertain life. My daddy just wanted more for his family.

In the 1920s and 1930s, slavery and sharecropping were still holding us fast. Yet, the sturdiness of our father's dreams sustained us. These noble dreams of a better life and civil rights for his children stayed steadfast in his head and soul. Unless you lived very near one, colleges were out of reach, and we did not. How would we have dreamed of affording college? But, my daddy kept hearing about jobs in Thomson. The pay was low, but it was more than the one penny per pound he was paid for picking cotton.

It does not matter to me how old I live to become. I will never forget what happened to me when it was my time to labor in the cotton fields. Nothing, absolutely nothing could have prepared me. My daddy wanted all of his children to get an early look at how the cruelty and greed of one race of people were forcefully imposed upon another. He also wanted all of us to keep a belief in our hearts in a God who never fails. So, one day just before noon, my daddy came back to our frame house where I had been left with my older sister,

Gussie. Taking me by the hand, he said, "Come with me." It was summer-time, and the sun was scorching.

3

Cotton Fields

Cotton! Cotton! Cotton! Fields and fields of cotton! Acres and rows of cotton! As far as my young eyes could see, there was cotton. In the blistering, stinging heat at high noon in a Georgia summer sun, the white, rolling rows of cotton seemed to stretch for miles. My daddy told me how he and other black men had walked for miles up and down those rows they jokingly called "cotton tunnels." They worked behind mules, guiding and moving the animals while carefully plowing the rich, black soil. In preparation for the mule's work, black men often dug, turned, and hoed the dirt. These same hands had to pick and gather the white, dried puffs of cotton. I could think only about all the cotton I had to pick with my own stinging, aching, bleeding hands.

As far as I could see in any direction, black backs were bent low, pulling, picking, and stuffing. The men wore old, often ragged, long-sleeved shirts, and denim overalls. The women wore equally old, tattered, long, cotton skirts. The women sometimes wore aprons tied around their waists to swat the insects and wipe sweat from their faces. My mother and the other women often wore long-sleeved blouses and head rags, which surely must have increased the heat's deepness and oppressiveness.

All were hunched over, as if they were to never again stand up straight. Etched in their prematurely aging faces was the hurt and fatigue of collecting the crops, which they had been driven and ordered to produce. Still, some sang. Others moaned the familiar and touching, "Come by Here, Lord, Come By Here," "Amazing Grace," and "Jesus, Keep Me Near the Cross." Others occasionally told a joke. These fleeting moments must have surely brought a bit of fun into a sea of crushing boredom, sadness, hurt, and drudgery. How could anyone sing? In years to come, the strength and incredible power of black people to hold on just a little while longer, believing everything really would soon be all right, humbled and inspired me, and allowed me to gain a deep, lasting spirit.

My father's pride in his ability to pray, keep the faith, and conquer what seemed like two-mile-long rows of cotton at one time while making hundreds of pounds every day shone through in many conversations about the white man's cotton. He often spoke of how "we Negroes were being used, bought, sold, traded, and enslaved to bring great wealth to the pockets of the white landowners." I began understanding my daddy's testimonies about his superior skills in the cotton fields. He must have offered them up to hide his disgust about the denial of his right to the rites of manhood.

Robert was only ten years old when he began plodding through McDuffie County's cotton fields. As I watched him inch painfully ahead toward his teen years, still picking cotton, his twisted face told the story. Sometimes, but not often and always quickly, I could see a fleeting bit of resignation. You know the kind. It is when you almost decide to give up, but something inside yells, "Just keep on trucking."

Robert used an old towel to flit away the swarms of flies and other insects that constantly encircled his sweating face while he dragged a big, heavy, cotton crocus sack down an endless row of cotton. The sack, which looked as if it was made from tough cotton strings, was slung from a rough, thick strap looped over his left shoulder. Either standing, bent over, or crawling on his knees, Robert picked and pulled those cotton puffs from the dried bolls with both hands. From top to bottom, his clothing was always sweaty and sticking to his body. I saw the never-ending, salty liquid running in streams down his dark, slim face. The huge sack he pulled alongside was almost full. The friction and grit from the grime, dirt, and sand often left gaping holes in his shoes, sometimes revealing bloody toes.

Our mother was always in the row of cotton next to Robert's, struggling to fill her 100-pound bag. Robert insisted that our mother pick next to him. That way, he could help her. Her sack was equal in size and weight to his. She never seemed to stop to rest, not even for a moment. She struggled to make it to the end of her own row. I could always hear her humming in her beautiful but, at times, solemn, sad soprano voice.

My mother was always "trying to make 100." Her face looked drained and beaten down. Her thin frame dragged the heavy sacks. She picked, pulled, picked, and pulled to finish. My heart stayed heavy as anger seethed and swelled within me. When I tried picking my very first crocus sack of cotton, I knew then I would never pick cotton for a living, no matter the cost.

A rapid inner uprising began as I took in everything I had learned from my first visit to a cotton field. I questioned my reasons for living. I questioned God. How could a loving God, who my parents prayed openly to and placed their total belief and trust, allow Mr. Johnnie Boyd, who owned the farm and the old house in which our family lived, make life for my family so harsh, limited, and abusive? I swore I would die before bending my back and soul to cotton fields or any other fields. However, by the age of nine, I was working hard. For a while, I dragged around cotton sacks in Thomson in those same hated cotton fields. When I was not chopping cotton, I was picking it. It was honest work, a value, which had been drummed into us. It did not matter. Although my seasons of labor in the fields of cotton were brief, I hated every single minute of it. Even as I picked, I prayed daily and repeated, "I will never pick cotton for a living."

We worked in the fields from dawn to dusk, wrapping both of our hands around those stinging cotton bolls, but it seemed the work was hardly ever done. After the cotton was picked, the painful labors of black families had only just begun. The same routine prevailed. There was washing, ironing, cleaning, cooking, and feeding hungry mouths. Moreover, there was praying for better days. We did not have any electric lights or indoor toilet. Only the whites had those provisions. As far as they were concerned, black folks were just not entitled. We washed our faces from a small, white, enamel basin. We heated water on an old wood-burning stove in an open pan, the foot tub, a small tin tub with a handle. When the biweekly time came around for bathing the whole body, you got naked and bathed in an old tin washtub, usually not well hidden. My daddy and older brothers shaved by looking in a broken piece of a mirror hung between nails on the wall in a corner of one of the bedrooms. In the spring and summer, the mirror was hung from a post on the back porch.

Meanwhile, the big man and his wife and children lived up the road in a big, white house. On so many evenings, I looked up the road toward that massive white bungalow with the green top. I could see the soft, even glow of electric lights through their beveled glass doors and polished windowpanes. I cried out of anger, disgust, and envy, but I was always careful to not let my parents see me cry because I never wanted to hurt them. The choices and conditions forced upon them caused them enough heartache. Anyway, my parents were always telling us, "Listen to us, you are as good as anybody white. And don't you ever forget it! Work hard, go to school, get your lessons, and you will be all right."

Calling on the Lowly but Highly Feared Boll Weevil

Our family lived through times when the old saying (and truth) was "Cotton is king." What they really meant was, "The men who owned the cotton were the kings." Sometimes, the lowly boll weevil brought the kings to their wealthy knees. They could not kill that pest or rid the fields of it. If that tiny brown plague decided to take up residence on their property, it was usually with deadly consequences. White people could supposedly "kill off a nigger" if they did not like the way one worked, but that boll weevil had the boss right between the legs.

Boll weevils ate and gnawed away at the soft, tender hearts of the cotton buds before the cotton could bloom and grow, leaving the buds limp, dirty, soggy, and sometimes smelly. They thrived mightily in wet, warm spring weather and traveled in waves, eating at acres of cotton. It happened all over the South.

Everyone suffered, black and white. In the 1930s, picking cotton was the main job for sharecropping families, and we always looked forward to sharing in a little money from this big pay crop. There were no machines back then, so you were not paid when you did not handpick. When you were paid, the amount was never equal to the hard work. You slaved in the cotton fields from dawn to dusk. For decades after slavery, cotton remained the largest part of the white man's crop and the black family's cursed existence.

When climate and conditions were right, black folks' labor made big bucks for those white bosses. If he did not get as much profit as he wanted, the folks who had grown the cotton for him often got little or, too often, nothing. When the boll weevils ate it all, black folks and white folks alike were left with very little. For black folks, it was sometimes nothing at all. I mean absolutely nothing. This was when hog chitterlings, neck bones, pig feet, hog kidneys, "cracklins," hog "liver and lights," and pig ears filled many poor families' plates. When a hog was killed, the white folks most always took the best, leaving us to make do with the rest.

One year, the boll weevils ate the entire crop of cotton. It was the only time I think I really saw my father shed tears. Settling up time was very near, and little or no money would be coming to our family. I had heard my parents sometimes whispering about settling up time. One day, when I was eight or nine years old, I asked, while sitting atop a cotton bale, "Daddy, what is settling up time?" Sweating and groaning, he continued pushing and praying as he loaded another cotton bale onto the bed of the hauling wagon. Suddenly, as if he was ashamed to speak the truth or say anything at all, he began talking slowly:

> Well, James, as I have told your sisters and brothers, it's hard. That is why you all have got to do more for yourselves. Settling up is when the boss man figures up how much cotton we all have picked, baled, taken to the gin, and sold for him. Then, he gets the money. After he figures out how much you owe him for rent, any food bought on credit, a few dollars borrowed, or anything else he wants to figure in your bill, he says he gives you your part of what is left. Sometimes, nothing is left. We think he makes sure he has his before he even starts thinking about what he is going to give us, no matter how hard we have worked.

I still remember how I had to fight hard, swallow hard, to hold back the tears. I remember thinking, "Good! If those bugs would eat all the damn cotton, I would never have to see another cotton field." I felt like screaming aloud and calling all the dreaded armies of boll weevils to gather together, rise up quickly, and invade every acre and cotton boll all over the South. I wanted to see armies floating over the horizons of every rolling field of cotton. Then, stark reality took hold. I felt guilty because I knew our lives and living depended largely on those miles of cotton fields.

When the crops were good, we all tried picking. Lord, I hated every cotton boll I ever touched. I was never any good at it, and I never wanted to be good at it. To this day, my sister, Gussie, teases me about how I knew how to avoid the fields. Sometimes, I hid out. She says I contrived and schemed to keep from filling up even one cotton sack.

On the other hand, Robert was a magnificent cotton picker. The poor fellow put on kneepads and picked two rows at a time. He proudly said how he would put his "double whammy" on that cotton. Robert did not just pick the cotton. He picked, packed, and baled it. Bales contained 1,000 pounds of cotton. To make a bale, the picked cotton was dragged to the packing sheds and then dumped into huge piles onto big, square sheets made from crocus sacks sewn together. Piles of cotton were rolled, packed, stacked, and jumped on until they were ready to be shaped into oblong bulks. Long strips of metal ribbons secured the bales. If you were not careful, those metal ribbons would cut into a young child's tender hands and fingers.

Teaming would always get the work done. We all helped. We stuck to the job until it was completed. After baling the cotton, the boys got atop the stacked bales. By mule and wagon, we helped haul the cotton to the gin, an old mill where the bales were weighed and sold. The landowner was always there to collect the money.

In his own way, my father always tried finding a few bright spots in the drudgery of it all. After the tiring trips to the cotton gin, my daddy took all of us, boys and girls, to a store, usually the little community lean-to that a share-cropper usually owned. He took some of his little, hard-earned money and bought cheese and crackers for us to eat on the ride home. Of course, we always had those big "belly washer" Royal Crown Colas. During those long, bumpy rides by mule and wagon toward home, he reminded us again, "Unless you children work to get all the education and know-how you can get in your heads and hearts, you will always suffer for the rest of your lives.

Every single day, in every way they could, our parents showed us that a positive nurturing of the human spirit and a belief in God would lead to our overcoming. They said, "If you can always hold onto your dignity, carry yourself in respectable, loving ways, and try offering kindness instead of anger, others will suffer for not having gotten to know you." Our white landlords could have never known what dreams danced daily, back and forth, through the heads and souls of the black sons and daughters of their sharecroppers. They may have had us tied and bound. To work inside the depths of our hearts, we knew they could never become killers of those dreams. This was during the time of the Ku Klux Klan and house burnings as well as beatings, castrations, and brutal lynchings of black men. These were frightening times when black families were seen as only a bit higher than the farm animals they had to care for, except when some white landowners wanted to take a black woman to his bed and have his way with her. While the Paschal family escaped the raw evilness of the Klan, we often heard rumors of unspeakable atrocities. Many times, we saw white landowners walk up to a horse, cow, mule, or a dog and pat and speak lovingly to the animal. They did not say one word of thanks or kindness to the black people who were the animals' caretakers.

We called the part of McDuffie County I was born in "the backside of the country." The years were hard and long. The struggles were brutal, and the cotton fields were painful. Before my father could move our family into Thomson, the 1920s and 1930s seemed to just drag on. Every black family and a few whites knew those scuffling hard times. It was a time of walking to school with holes in the soles of our shoes, if you got to go to school at all.

We may have lived in a thrown-together, three-bedroom sharecropper's house, but it was our home. Love and family pride were shared in big doses. It was a constant song:

> Home was survival. Home was where people nurtured you, cared about you, and looked out for you. Home was where family surrounded you with total love, support, and caring. Home was where we received the discipline and encouragement to soar. Home was your personal connection to community, where people who truly cared continued to lift you high above danger while guiding and teaching you.

Home was also where we were encouraged to save money, make money grow, and use money to help others. I saw little cash in our cookie jar, but we felt a deep respect for what was earned and learned. Home was where our father repeatedly told us to believe we did not have to remain forever poor. My parents pushed me toward building businesses, even beginning at the age of eight. Home is where we learned to watch how rich white folks had grown and accumulated their vast holdings of land and wealth. These lessons remained with us, sinking deeply and permanently into our bones. We did not know how lasting that education would be or how the substance of these powerful teachings would later intervene, time after time, to form the foundations of our enchanted, blessed lives. My parents often said, "You children can take the low roads to failure, or you can choose to travel the bright, shining high roads to success. Times won't be always be easy, but success will give you many more opportunities for great times in your lives. We hope we have given you what you need—the love, Christian training, values, and encouragement. Always stay on the straight and narrow pathways, and you will have blessed, lasting results."

4

Beyond McDuffie County

Robert and I dreamed to be real men, to play our part in helping to shape and form our family's peace. Our hopes began taking shape many decades ago in the midst of the leftovers from the evils of slavery, which had held on all over this land, like the bark on a cypress tree. The lingering ghosts of the Confederacy of McDuffie County and thousands of other enclaves of hatred and racism made us strong runners, sprinting toward better lives.

Whatever dreams Robert and I may have had, whatever large ideas we may have created in our minds, and whatever legacies the Paschal ancestors may have bequeathed had their beginnings in Thomson and McDuffie County. However, we were not alone in adding a black chapter to Thomson's historical records. There were many others, including "Blind Willie," the phenomenal blues singer and guitarist whose "career stretched from the ragtime era to playing for tips on the streets of Atlanta."[1] I will certainly bet there are Thomson residents, black and white, who think themselves well-versed but do not know who Blind Willie was or he was a Thomson native.

Today, Thomson and McDuffie County are far different from the places into which I was born, grew up, and formed life's initial impressions. Whites in McDuffie County and all over the South, without conscience or fear of prosecution, could lynch, hang, beat, or castrate black men. They could rape black women and inflict other violent, indecent acts upon innocent black people. These times shaped the lives of my entire family. Early on, Robert and I

---

1. Bill Orsinski, "Main Street," *The Atlanta Journal*-Constitution, 20 December 1998.

began forming our hopes for the abundant possibilities, which we believed were beyond McDuffie County. Our childhood years and impressions were formed and imprinted and could have been forever engulfed by the attitudes and behaviors of those of the times. We could well have been satisfied with just ordinary lives.

The ruling classes had become accustomed to the slavery and sharecropper mentality that supported the basic, accepted laws of the land at that time, especially in the South. Glib, often cold, ruthless, and uncaring, most whites saw us as animals needing to be disciplined. For many of them, this meant being beaten into obedience and submission.

People who held power were often tenacious in holding onto the goodness of the master/slave relationship for as long as the law allowed. They were the law, and that was that. Indeed, they often saw themselves as protectors, that is, guardians of the happy, unlearned slaves. They believed God had decreed the slave master as being called upon to enslave and protect an ignorant, helpless people. How dumb!

A few, better-educated Southern whites knew the enslavement of an entire people was wrong, though they often feared (and rightly so) for their own safety. These whites, often covertly, did good, humane deeds for our family and many other black families. Robert and I were the beneficiaries of these kindnesses.

Even in Thomson and McDuffie County, some whites secretly taught their black servants about books and reading. Others taught their servants how to write and count money. Some shared pictures of their travels, which let us know there was indeed another world out there. A few even paid their servants a little more than the going rate of twenty-five or fifty cents per day for domestic labor. Moreover, they were brave enough to not look the other way when good, solid black families were treated with less respect than the master's animals. Unfortunately, there were just too few of them though.

These whites placed themselves in great jeopardy when they allowed themselves to be drawn into the fight for civil rights. Often, their own families, friends, and even acquaintances were at risk. Entire families were known to have had their bank loans declared due—in full—when they were not yet due. Others faced eviction. Some were clubbed or had their lives threatened. Some were publicly ostracized. Those who did help continually fueled the dreams of freedom for so many black folks.

Our family gladly accepted help from whites who were brave enough to offer assistance. Those were joyfully rich moments. When my daddy was finally convinced he must move us out of the country and into the real city limits of Thomson for us to have a better life, while sharecropping on less acreage and seeking additional work in town, the Knox family offered him a job. The Knox family became prominent players in our family's ability to forge steadily ahead. As a result, our parents began blazing secret pathways, sometimes carving out permanent black-white alliances.

As we worked, Robert and I observed the white folks' moneymaking hunger. We noticed how they organized and managed their businesses, even their feudal approaches to sharecropping. We swore to never bastardize the human spirit or deny anyone their rightful place in the order of anything good. We began dreaming about the far-reaching possibilities of success. We pledged kindness, fair play, and sharing. We also promised, as a family, to try to get as much education as possible and never allow ourselves to be banished into ignorance and poverty. That Paschal spirit sprang up within us and grew, taking hold in our hearts and minds. Our parents struggled to plant their brood's feet solidly on a journey toward a bright, sunny future. My mother said, "Take on the world…Make your presence felt…Become glowing, good examples for what is right…Make change and reform happen, and make them last in your own world."

Robert and I felt swept straight forward. Like so many other black children of the era, we let nothing stop us, blow us sideways, or tie us down. Growing up Southern, black, and male and having to struggle for merciful lives only emboldened us. Our family orders were clear. We had to be rough, tough, determined thoroughbreds, but we also had to be generous and considerate.

Nature's beauty had always blessed Thomson. In 1913, Thomson was named the Camellia City of the South because of its "ideal climate conditions and the perfect combination of soils of various types that make up McDuffie County." Without fail, the entire area shows itself off every spring. Thousands of camellias bloom in an array of colors, and the earth becomes vibrantly alive as azaleas, dogwoods, irises, spirea, roses, and other flowers burst forth in incomparable colors. Located fifteen minutes outside of Thomson are the beautiful waters of the Thurmond-Clarks Hill Lake, which was created from the damming of the Savannah River.

The area was always reaching out to all to partake of its natural blessings, if you were white. Even into the 1950s, black folks were barred from recreational facilities. They could only watch and yearn silently as whites played, worked, and bossed in the plushest of comforts. Thomson and McDuffie County now brags on itself, inviting any and all who want to enjoy "country living, city style." My hometown now even claims to celebrate its diversity. Thanks be to God!

Robert and I knew very well that we had to explore the unexplored. Never in their rarest of dreams had our parents envisioned the depths of the valleys below, but they wanted so much for us to build onward and upward. So, he and I set out to face bright successes and, if need be, dark disappointments as well. We knew they would come, and they did. For a time, they far outnumbered the successes. Then, there was the pressing urgency to launch the great escape from McDuffie County. It was always as if he and I each felt a call to more deeply know the unseen rivers. With a burning surety, we felt and knew it was preordained that we would be successful. When the inevitable was upon us, we would know.

Getting an Education

Like thousands of other children of color, our schooling was usually set in a shack of a one-room schoolhouse, especially through the elementary grades and, frequently, through junior and senior high school. There was often only one teacher for all grades. If there were any books at all, they were the white children's used, usually ragged leftovers.

We had been told to be good and get our lessons. I soon learned being good meant getting good grades, speaking well (like the well-educated white folks), and not sassing or acting smart with the teacher. I was in the fourth grade when I saw what acting smart could really do to you. Matthew Taylor, a boy in my fourth-grade class, decided he was going to act brash and rough when our teacher asked him to sit down and study his spelling. In a very loud, ugly voice, he told her, "I am sitting down, but I already know my spelling!" In those days, teachers did not have to get permission to paddle your behind and they did not bother taking you to the principal's office. They took care of the problem in the classroom, which is what happened that day. A leather strap came out from the teacher's desk drawer. It looked like the one my daddy used to sharpen his shaving razor. Matthew was whacked about four times. He hurried to his seat and was never heard from again that day or many more after that. Our teacher was so strict that we knew not one giggle had better be heard.

Black children did not get indoor toilets. The antiquated outdoor privy was the norm, which made winters especially harsh. White children rode buses to school and attend sports events. Frequently, they rode right pass black children, who either had to trudge along on foot or were sometimes able to get a mule and wagon ride, that is, if we were to get to school or school functions at all. I can still see their mean, mocking faces as they rode past us in the big, yellow school buses. They sometimes threw rocks, big spit-wads, or even chicken or pork chop bones out of the bus windows at us.

In spite of the humiliation and indignation we endured, I look back with appreciation and pride in the days I spent in those one-room classrooms. We had some dedicated, hardworking teachers. Many took those old books and strive to make getting educated real for all of us. Those black teachers made you learn. We had to learn to read as well as recite multiplication tables and division by heart. We had to learn to spell, and we had spelling bees. We learned geography, health, science, and arithmetic.

A few teachers had managed to travel outside of Thomson. They came back to our otherwise drab classrooms and make our hearts yearn for those far-away places, places foreign to our limited, underexposed imaginations. I remember several of my teachers. (One from Atlanta really fueled my desire to see Atlanta and the world.) They shared their worn collections of black-and-white pictures. They questioned us, taught us new words, and told us how far away from Thomson these places were located. They made us write stories about what we had seen and what we wanted most out of life. Then we had to share our written stories.

Mrs. Clara West was one of my teachers. She loved to travel. She returned to the classroom after her summer vacation and made our hearts take flight. She was a skinny, tall, attractive, brown-skinned woman. Always immaculately dressed, everything matched. Looking good and dressing well in those days just went along with being a teacher. She pulled down an old map and guided us through places we never thought it would ever be possible to see.

Mrs. West shared and repeated her experiences with some successful man or woman of color she had met who had reached some level of achievement. She taught us all she knew about black history because nothing in our history books even hinted at black people's contributions to this country. A word was never said about the crafts and skills our ancestors had brought with them from Africa. The books said nothing about the blacksmiths, welders, carpenters, housepainters, inventors, singers, dancers, and musicians. They did not mention our passionate, moving histories.

When I think back on how I was educated, I remember doing just as my parents taught us. Be respectful of your teachers. Listen carefully. Try to learn all you can. During that time, teachers were loved, respected, and idolized. Despite the barriers we faced, the Paschal children were good students. We learned well and made good grades. We would not allow our fears and the uncertainties of the times to block our will to do well. Our parents always made sure we stayed in school, regardless of what work had to be done. Studying, working hard, doing our best, and holding on were the family rules. My sisters and brothers also attended primary and secondary school in McDuffie County. Years later, I received additional training in Cleveland, Ohio.

5

Visions Abroad

My father was a real man, that is, as much of a man as the times and conditions allowed a black man to be. Although we lived in a white man's house and worked his land, my father still took his duties and responsibilities as a man to heart. Sheltering, clothing, feeding, and comforting his wife and brood of children was a serious matter for him. He did his best and passed on to his male offspring just what it truly means to be a real man and a good provider. Despite our early lot in life, my daddy struggled to ensure everyone in his household always had everything they needed to live with an inner sense of plenty. He never wanted us to feel we were less than anyone else just because we were poor.

My daddy was not an educated man. I think he only went to the fifth grade, but he wanted his children to go much farther in life. He wanted us to work hard and pray for a change in the kinds of lives we were forced to live in McDuffie County. So many times, his eyes filled with water as he talked to us about the kinds of lives we would have to live if we did not work our brains:

> Work hard. Do better than your Momma and I could do. You can either work hard and make better lives for yourselves, stand up, hold onto your dreams, and nurse your vision, or you can forever have the white man standing on your throat. If you do that, you will be hurting so bad that you will not be able to think for yourself. You will be in such pain that you can only breathe when that white man says breathe, and you will be too weak to stand up and be a better man or woman when God delivers you.

My daddy's life was a long and sometimes sad and tiring season. He worked in the cotton fields and in town. He lived well his own belief in being the best of whatever you must be for that particular period in your life. He believed fully in the heavenly call and the infinite ordering of one's eternal destiny, down to the last person born on this earth. "God intended for each of us to help make life better for each other. That is why God gave to each of us a brain."

My daddy did everything. He ran that white man's big farm as well as planted, cultivated, and weeded fields of cotton. At times, we helped out, but they never kept us out of school to do the white man's bidding.

My parents sometimes talked about their own childhoods. It hurt the heart to hear about some of the mean things that happened when they were children growing up on the white folks' farms. They said their parents had to work so hard that they rarely had time to go hunting or fishing. They seldom had time to go to church, especially during harvest. The very folks they cooked, cleaned, and raised little babies for often called them "niggers" or "niggras." Many times, they were ordered to work on because "these crops gotta be gathered," even when they had already put in a hard, full day of work. They really wanted us to understand where we had come from.

With our parents' help, we soon became very good at almost everything we attempted. We fed and milked the cows, horses, and chickens. We picked buckets of beans, apples, pears, and plums. We learned to do it all. My daddy's picture-perfect corn had been planted so straight and waved so prettily in the wind that, when other people passing our fields inquired what kind of corn-dropping machine my daddy used, he loved to say, "My little daughter, Gussie, is my corn dropper."

Our hands were called the "cotton grabbers." We were also the needed tractors, pitchforks, hoes, rakes, and shovels of record. It still seems to me that most all of our childhood summers and, often, early falls were filled with picking cotton, chopping cotton, or shaking Georgia dirt from peanuts or gathering other crops. Those summers were fiery hot, which covered the body, burning us to the bone and hanging heavily in the mind. We were sweaty, stinging and stinky. The heat alone made you want to throw up.

The more our parents worked, the prouder we became that we could help them. My daddy plowed, planted, watered, and prayed for seasonal rains. He sometimes worked beyond quitting time, even as he would send us home for rest periods. He worked for fourteen or fifteen hours nearly every day except Sunday. Many times, he could not even take a Saturday off because he worked if the white man needed him. He did not have choice or decision in the matter because that same white man owned the land and house (or shack) we occupied.

Farmwork, yard work, and even housework became a familiar part of the day for us. We tried hard to find some fun in our labor. Along with my younger brother, Hodges, and some of our friends, I often took care of the year-round rabbit boxes, which were made to trap wild rabbits. When hunting was not in season, wild rabbits made great edible, marketable game. They were considered rare delights, even for some of Thomson's elite. When we could not trap the rabbits, we grabbed our BB guns and took off through the woods. We wanted the twenty-five cents we would be paid for each critter we could collect. Our hunts were usually successful.

White people from Thomson sometimes came to our farm to get with my father to hunt birds. My daddy was a good hunter, and they knew that. Most of the time, they just wanted him along so he could pick up, store, take home, and clean whatever wild game they killed. My mother would help him clean and prepare the killed game for dinner. On one occasion, she cooked a rabbit and served it to those white men, along with the ham, chicken, and other meats she had cooked. The men thought the rabbit was chicken. They were just eating, smiling, and talking away. "Uuummm Ump!" they said as they smacked their lips. "This chicken tastes so good." We could hardly hold back our stomachs from bursting with laughter.

An old wooden barn was next to our house. It held our reserves of seasonal crops. From our garden, we gathered and stored yellow and white corn, sweet potatoes, white potatoes, peas, peanuts, and onions. Not too far from the storage barn were the stables where we kept the mules and horses. The closeness of the barn made it very easy to get the corn and hay to the stables for the animals my brothers and I had to help feed and often groom. Hunting was big and horses were highly prized, so we had to do our grooming well. We wanted all the big white folks to see how well we could polish the horses so they could see we were the best at everything we did.

We fed the animals before going to school, and we were never late for school. Often, we had to crawl out of bed before dawn. To this day, I cannot sleep late. Unless I am ill, staying in bed too long makes me mentally and physically dull. We also had three hunting dogs: two for hunting rabbits and one for hunting birds. I remember the fun we had romping through the woods and fields with them as we looked for game. We loved our pets and treated them well. They were like our brothers and sisters.

We also had a pig named Moses. A family friend religiously bought all of his fresh vegetables from our family because he said we grew the best vegetables ever tasted. As thanks for supplying his needs from our family garden, he gave us Moses. We put Moses in a pen and fed him three meals a day. We gave him the usual pig's diet of corn, but we also threw in cornbread, biscuits, oatmeal, greens, and beans. It was the same stuff we ate. That pig got so fat that he could not stand up. We children began loving Moses so much that, when hog-killing time came around, we did not want to see him get the axe. We were overruled; the grown folks decided old Moses would make some mighty fine ham and pork chops, so we had to let him go. However, I did not eat another pork chop or slice of ham that whole winter.

Many times, we may have felt as if our lives were torn into pieces by the times in which we were living. Nevertheless, so often my dad said, "Honestly, I want you all to learn as much as you can about how to live life in hard times, how things are now, what is really happening. That way, you will know and appreciate the better times when they come. I know in my heart that better times will come. Just keep working, doing your best, and praying."

My Dreams Outdistanced My Age

As far back as I can remember, I wanted to be somebody. Somehow, I always knew things were going to change for me. There would come to be a changed world out there. So often, I had seen my daddy not given the respect he deserved. I swore then I would work with a double-edged determination to be respected and find all of the good I knew God had intended for me. The harder I worked, the more self-confidence I would gain and the faster I could claim my blessed destiny. Moreover, I swore to stay honest to get it.

My childhood had many faces and memories. Some were sweet. Some were bitter. Some made me angry. However, I lived as happy a life as a young child who did not have much could live. I played, ate, climbed trees, shot marbles, and wore cutoff overalls. My childhood was blessed with love of family and friends, a love that helped to steel me and make me strong enough to stand the times.

Some eight-year-old boys were captivated by wrestling with their brothers or friends, dreaming of winning ace marble games, catching big fish, or jumping into the old swimming hole. We had a swimming hole, but I could not let swimming in a murky hole slow down my journey. I wanted more. White folks were swimming in the cool, clear waters of the Thurmond-Clarks Hill Lake. I yearned for that freedom. That lake is one of the largest inland bodies of water in the South, and we could only dream about enjoying a life of living along its shores.

My youthful dreams led me to thinking of ownership, enterprise, saving, and living anywhere I would choose to live. A billy goat was waiting in the wings for me, a goat I thought would surely be my first step into getting pockets full of money. I was still in the middle of battling through my thoughts and deciding how soon and how completely I would pursue my dreams. Robert was my sounding board. Nightly, as I lay awake wrapped in thoughts of a future where unlimited accomplishments were sure to become real, my heart pounded with childish excitement.

My brave venture began when I built a work wagon for myself. Although it was not a Red Flyer, I thought it would work for selling fresh vegetables. I could almost taste the sweetness of working hard and earning success outside of the world of Thomson. I had it all together. I would fill my little work wagon with fresh vegetables which I would purchase wholesale. Then, pulled around town by my beautiful white billy goat, I would sell my veggie collection on the streets of Thomson. There would be fresh, crispy leafy greens, including collards, mustards, and turnips in season. There would be cabbage, okra, pole beans, tomatoes, and red and green bell peppers.

I had earlier pleaded with my father to buy me my own goat. I can still recall the strange, puzzled expression on his face as he asked, "Are you sure you want a goat?"

"Oh, yes!" I enthusiastically said with a big grin covering my face.

My daddy smiled and said, "Okay." He knew a solid base of truth lies in learning through experience, unless your life was really in danger. I can still hear his chuckles as he presented me with my own billy goat and knowingly said, "Go for it!" So, happily I went.

Everything started out pretty well…for about the one or two minutes it took me to saddle up, mount my wagon, and take steering ropes in hand. I should have taken note of the goat's restlessness as I struggled to harness him to prepare for my maiden marketing voyage. From the second I tugged on the rope and said, "Go," that fat goat gave his behind a quiver and quickly became the driver of record. He went "goat crazy," seizing every possible moment to show me that it was goat, not man, who was in charge.

Billy took off, carrying me in the directions of his choice. All of which was erratic. It did not matter how much or how loudly I screamed, "Whoa!" and

"Stop! Stop!" The goat pulled while I yanked hard and furiously on the steering harness. By this time, he was truly dragging me wherever he wanted all the vegetables and us to go. Round and round and across our yard we went. We went up the street, down the street, and back across our yard. Vegetables were flying everywhere. Collard greens, pole beans, okra, plums, peppers, and tomatoes littered my trail. The load in my wagon and the weight of my body combined to wear the goat down to an eventual slow drag. The minute he came to a pace slow enough to quell the pounding of my heart, I hopped off the wagon, never to mount up again. I finally had to turn the old billy goat out to pasture. Above all though, the goat-and-wagon episode deepened my resolve. I was not about to quit.

I dropped the goat and worked hard. My mother's admonition always consoled me, "Remember, it does not matter where you come from. It is where you want to go in life that counts. You can do anything you want to do and get anything you want if you do not mind working hard for it."

Around his fourteenth or fifteenth birthday, Robert, who was ten years older than I was, took a job at the McDuddie County sawmill. He did some of just about everything the white men threw at him. Robert loaded trucks, cut lumber and logs, and then hauled the logs to be cut. He even drove the trucks full of lumber around the mill yard.

Robert did more work than most other men at the mill did, even though, by age, he was still a child. The mill bosses did not care. They just wanted the work done. It did not matter to the bosses, mill owners, state, or federal government that a child was doing the same work as the grown men. His bosses were pleased, telling him that his work was superior. The pay, although good for the times, was a pitiful one dollar per day. Robert was soon driving a sawmill truck full time. He loaded the truck with logs, drove the truck to its destination, and then unloaded.

As satisfied as he was with the mill job, his wish to do better kept whispering promises of greater possibilities in his ear. He felt Atlanta calling him, overpowering and begging him to come to test its fertile soil. Atlanta had not yet grown into the great city it is today, but we could feel the depth of a newer lure, a grander stage on which to play out our dreams.

Two other brothers, Gilmer and Hodges, had already let the happiness of moving from the country into Thomson completely wash over them. Each moved on to seek and build futures outside of our small town arena. They frequently returned to visit us, showing off the results of their move to the big city. We were never jealous of their joy because we knew we would follow if life lasted.

Hard work has always been—and remains today—the bridge that carried us across raging waters of adversity, doubt, and racism into the promised land of plenty. My siblings and I always dreamed of better times. It was not always about getting more things. It was about praying, working, and studying hard and not wasting a lifetime wishing for the lives we might have had. Robert and I held fast to a dream we fashioned, one we struggled and worked to make happen.

After driving the goat and selling vegetables did not work out for me, with great sadness and reluctance, I knew the ghosts of those hated cotton fields loomed ahead. If needed, I would attack those cotton rows with tenacity, but only for a time.

So, I returned to the joyless abundance of the cotton fields. I chopped the stuff as anger burned madly inside my chest. At the same time, I furiously harvested vegetables from my mother's garden. If there was one saving grace and tradition born out of slavery and sharecropping, it was the garden near the house.

Most often planted and tended by the women of the family, with the men handling the heaviest stuff, gardens were prized and well-tended. Most often, the big farmers and sharecroppers allowed their hands the simple, pleasurable outlets associated with planting and growing a garden. A prime reason rested in the unspoken knowledge that, anytime they had a taste for freshly grown, picture-perfect vegetables, they only had to show up and place their order. Their sharecropping hands would then set about giving them all they wanted.

Family Life

Our old, raggedy house was twelve miles outside Thomson. My daddy said that moving into town would not mean a stop to hard work. Despite all of the hard work and living poor, we found ways to enjoy family life. One of our great-aunts lived close to our house until she became ill. She then moved in with our cousin living nearby. My mother often cooked meals for them, and my siblings and I walked the meals to their house. Before her illness, my great-aunt and my mother often exchanged recipes. They cooked and tasted before publicly offering each other's jelly cakes, pound cakes, succulently divine potato pies baked in a pastry shell to die for, nutmeg- and vanilla-flavored tea cakes, and homemade, butter-drenched peanut brittle. Our entire family and plenty of close friends took part in this glorious, delicious bounty. All kinds of good eating were always available at our table.

On Saturdays, our father went into town and brought back ice and canned goods. We wrapped the ice in newspaper and crocus sacks to keep it from melting. Using an old hand-turned ice cream churn, my mother made ice cream. The canned goods were really special. They included all kinds of goodies, including pink salmon; my mother used to make delicious salmon croquettes. I watched as she crumbled the salmon, added bread crumbs or a bit of flour, eggs, seasoning, chopped celery, and chopped onion. She deep-fried and served the croquettes with buttermilk biscuits, homemade butter, fresh cane syrup, and smoked, streak of lean bacon. There was sometimes scrambled eggs, grits, or rice. There was always some kind of fresh or canned fruit. Yummy!

We grew fields of sugarcane and made our own cane syrup in a mill on our farm. The ripened sugarcane was cleaned of its sharp strips of green leaves, washed, and topped. The roots were cut off, and the cane was placed into the mill. The mill was a large, circular-shaped wooden receptacle. A big wheel rested at the center of the mill, and a mule walked round and round. As the mule pulled, turning the grinding wheel, we put the cane into the mill and watched as the sweet juice oozed from the newly cut cane. The juice was placed into a large vat and boiled until it cooked into syrup. We had fun at that time of the year because our friends, their families, and other families gathered to sip the unboiled juice and chew the sugarcane.

Once cooked to the right level of syrupy quality, the sugarcane juice was placed into heavy, darkened crock jugs. It rested there until properly aged. The dark crock jugs helped preserve the syrup's flavor and color. We waited patiently for our mother to tell us just when she would be making her delicious syrup cakes and gingerbread.

Family and friends frequently went to church together and would come home, set the big table, and enjoy the feast together. We sometimes took food to church to share with others. When there was an occasion for dinner on the grounds, everyone searched out the Paschal family's baskets and boxes. They just knew the fried chicken, potato pies, pound cakes, baked ham, potato salad, baked chicken, and delicious sage dressing would be almost toppling the Paschal tables. Eating was always one of our favorite family fun times. I only remember one grandpa, my father's daddy. Grandpa Paschal loved to eat, but it must have agreed with him. He lived to be 110 years old. My mother's father had passed away long before I was old enough to get to know him.

One time, our church, Mt. Carmel Baptist Church, put on a ticket-selling contest to determine who was our church's most popular deacon. We already knew the answer, our daddy. The deacon who could sell the most raffle tickets would be voted the most popular. Our daddy got everyone he could think of to sell tickets for him, including family, friends, and acquaintances, new and old.

Effie and Gussie wanted to help our daddy sell his tickets. They were desperately afraid, but they went ahead anyway and begged him to let them sell tickets. They told him they could sell tickets faster than Flash Gordon could fly. My daddy's love for his little girls won out over reason, and he finally said okay. Gussie and Effie were only about thirteen or fourteen years old at the time. Actually, they had played a trick. In truth, they had plotted how selling tickets would really give them a legal reason to talk to the fellows, which our daddy would not have ordinarily allowed. We always thought he knew their real reasons for wanting to help sell those 10-cent tickets.

Anyway, our daddy sold more tickets than anyone in the church. It seemed like everyone bought tickets from him. Though poor and needy, black folks always gave to the church. Often, even the widow's mite would be sacrificed to help support a church's cause. Down through history, the church has been the major nurturer and often the keeper of the souls and minds of black families and their children. Anyway, our daddy was crowned the most popular deacon in Mt. Carmel Baptist Church. We gathered around and hugged him. Gussie and Effie always took credit for helping him sell three times as many tickets as anyone else.

Those two sisters were very close in age and had a special bond. Although Effie was our sister from our father's previous marriage, she and Gussie were very similar. In fact, when Effie got married at seventeen and moved away, Gussie cried very hard. She was so angry with the fellow who became Effie's husband for taking her sister away that she cried every time Effie's name was mentioned. When Effie came home for a visit, Gussie was so glad to see her that she burst out crying. When it was time for Effie and her husband to leave, Gussie started bawling again.

Our early dreams and wishes knew no limits, but real living was another matter. Life for us knew only limitations, in all seasons. In the winter, my brothers often used axes to split pine and oak logs and chop them into wood for the fireplaces to keep warm and cook on the old, iron kitchen stove. On that four-legged stove, all of those delicious foods were simmered, fried, boiled, or baked. My mother loved to do her special kind of cooking on that wood-burning relic. At eight, nine, and ten years of age, I was still considered too small and too young to handle an axe, so I shared chores with my sisters, including milking the cows, churning the butter, and collecting eggs from the henhouse.

Until his death, Robert loved to tease me about how the snakes lay on nearby rocks and logs to shed their skins in the fall and I wanted to collect them and see if any of the white men in town would buy the snakeskins. Robert laughed and said, "You know, you were always looking to see how you could make a dollar holler. He declared that he once saw me chasing a rattler, trying to grab the snake's shedding skin. He then burst out laughing, confirming my suspicion he was telling another falsehood on me. Just as quickly though, he added, "You know, Gussie and I had to admit that you always had the bigger head for making money and closing business deals."

Dressing, like eating, always received major attention in our family. As in so many other black families, looking good reminded you that you were just as good as any white person. Our brothers said they wanted to be sure not a speck of dust touched their clothes. Robert and Gilmer stood on their bed to put on their pants, if our mother was not around. They did this, even if the floors had been scrubbed clean. They always accused me of trying to outdress all of my siblings. Gussie said, "I am afraid they could never catch up with you or match your style for dressing, James. When we went to school, you always received the prize for being the neatest dressed boy. One of your teachers, I can't remember her name, must have seen great promise in you. At the end of the school year, she had you recite a poem. You were all of eight years old when you wrote and read one of your favorite poems. I still remember it:

> When I become a man, I mean to buy a whole load of candy. And put it close beside the street, where it would be quite handy. When boys and girls go by to school, I'd call out loud and say, 'Just help yourself to the candy please...And not a cent to pay.' I'd give them lots of nuts and fruits and pumpkin pie so yellow. And all the boys and girls would say, 'Gee! What a jolly fellow.'

Robert and Gilmer never gave up. "We will live to outdo you in dressing," Gilmer once told me.

Robert and Gilmer moved to Atlanta before I did. When they came back to visit, calling themselves "the old sports," they were dressed to kill and driving their own sports cars. When they returned to Atlanta, I usually cried help-lessly. I cried tears of joy for them and of envy for myself. I cried tears of yearning for their broader world, even though I knew my time would come. However, on one visit, a tire was mounted on the back of Gilmer's car. Writ-ten on the cover of the tire were the words, "Don't Cry, Baby! I'll Be Back!" When I saw those words on that tire, that was the only time I smiled when they left.

6

Turning Points

Our family was deeply religious, and we were usually in church for the monthly Sunday service at Mt. Carmel Baptist Church. The entire Paschal family was always dressed in it Sunday best. Dress up to look your very best for praising the Lord!

In the 1930s and 1940s, it was commonplace for one circuit preacher to serve several congregations. Such was the case at our church. The three-mile country ride to church seemed just a pleasurable run around the corner. When the doors opened, we were there. We all looked forward to the "spiritual cleansings," as my father called our worship services. The rousing voices of the choir and congregation made you feel real good inside as they sang "Sweet Hour of Prayer," "Blessed Assurance," "What a Friend We Have in Jesus," "Swing Low, Sweet Chariot," "Amazing Grace," "I'll Fly Away," "Down by the Riverside," and so many other old hymns and spirituals. We wanted to hurry to Mt. Carmel to hear the amens; hallelujahs; thank you, Lords; clapping of hands; and shouts of those touched by the spirit. Even as children, we enjoyed joining in with the waving of arms and the swaying of bodies to the spirited music. Sometimes, when out of our parents' view, we snickered at the real shouters.

Our father was a deacon, and our mother sang in the senior choir. Our mother's love of music was a family treasure. She had a clear, soaring soprano voice and often sang the soprano lead. Old kerosene lanterns and lamps lit the church. I still cannot understand how the folks at the church could possibly have seen how to read the Bible or the words in their songbooks. Kerosene lamps lit our home as well. No one in power thought to bring the wiring for electricity close enough to where black folks lived, even if we could save enough money to pay for it.

On a few Sundays, there were additional numbers of extended family and friends who came to dinner, invited or not. Feasting at the Sunday dinner table was the accepted rule for many black families, although I think more people came to our house than the reverse. After the table was cleared and the dishes washed, our parents summoned everyone to gather in our living room for lively shaped note and song singing. Sunday afternoon merrymaking often filtered into the approaching nighttime. Sometimes, listening neighbors came over to just take part.

Our pastor, Reverend J. W. Harrison, and his wife often joined us. My mother always seemed to know when and how to include his old favorites. I think this was so he could join in the songfest. Proud of his bass voice, Reverend Harrison always wanted to take the lead or show the range of his deep bass notes in the harmony. Everyone always let him sing.

Finding Jesus, the Old-Time Way

Revival meetings were usually held every summer at the height of the summer heat. These weeklong services were called protracted meetings. Revival meetings were the times set aside for praying for forgiveness for your sins. Sinners, young and old, were pressed hard to seek the Lord and repent for their sinful ways. Much fervent soul-searching and asking for forgiveness had to be openly expressed. Those who were already saved knelt all around us sinners who had to sit on the mourners' bench. The mourners' bench was where one had to spend an acceptable time praying, begging, and repenting for forgiveness for whatever your young soul had done that was against God's will for your life. The special Christians prayed for the Lord to save these sinful souls, meaning all of us who were declared the candidates.

After days of praying, seeking the Lord, and confessing sins, only then could one claim to be coming through, that is, if you truly felt you had prayed hard, God had forgiven you, and you had found the Lord. Only then could you claim you were converted. Only then were you fit for a Christian existence. If you came through, could tell it, and could witness for Christ, then you had indeed gotten religion. We children often asked, "What is sinning, and what sins have we done? What is getting religion?" I am not sure we ever got the answers that could have assured us that we were or were not sinners.

While that entire part of our lives may have remained somewhat cloudy and confusing, we, the sons and daughters of Deacon Henry and Mrs. Lizzie Paschal, knew we did not have a choice. We had to believe or at least act as if we did. The whole ordeal was somewhat frightening to a young mind. However, we felt we were sinners if we did something bad. If we wanted to be saved, we had to get religion and join the church.

In this setting of deep religious faith and power, I was converted to becoming the Christian I am today. During one of those seasonal revival meetings, it happened. I sat on the mourners' bench. In the old, Southern, black church tradition, my sins were forgiven. As a shy, young boy of nine years, even though I was somewhat unsure of why, I listened with full attention to loud hand clapping, spirited singing, and shouts of hallelujah, amen, and "fire and brimstone" preaching. I shed tears of repentance for my sins. I prayed for the clear sign. I finally felt truly moved by the spirit and came through, from sin to saving.

Even today, I am still not really sure what I felt on that day during revival week. Was it truly the Holy Spirit? Was it the sagging burden of my young, sinful soul? Was it the desire to unload the weight and heaviness of a big, cotton-filled sack I had been dragging behind me? I do know the deep desire to cease picking cotton was always present and pressing at every possible opportunity.

I asked myself, "Did I dare drop my cotton sack and run—right then and there in the middle of picking—and tell my mother? Should I wait until that night at the revival meeting, where I would be prayed off the mourners' bench? If I stopped to tell about my religion, would I be seen as quitting because I was just too tired to keep up with my brother?"

The thought of hard work never pained Robert's heart. In fact, he always said, "We had to meet hard work head-on." Hard work was the rule. Robert was known to be able to rapidly suck up two rows of cotton and make it almost disappear into his sack. He finished his two rows, turned around, came back, met our mother, and helped her fill her sack before she could finish her one row. He named himself the cotton-picking machine. His energetic, simultaneous attack on two rows of cotton could make anyone who was unequal to his talents feel washed down in guilt and shame.

By the time of my saving revival, I must have been ready because I do know Jesus came into my heart that day a long time ago. I waited for evening church. On the night I came through, the revival meeting had been especially fervent, touching, and emotional. All the sisters and brothers responded loudly to the burning spirit of the Holy Ghost. All over the church, shrill, mournful shouts of "Thank you, Jesus!" and "Hallelujah!" were heard. In the midst of all of this born-again fervor, I felt a little light and strange inside. As good as I felt, I held on a little while longer. One steamy, hot day, still during revival week, I suddenly felt moved by the Spirit. I felt I had found the Lord and was ready for the ritual of baptism.

Baptized

Baptismal submersion is the act of being completely submerged underwater. In my case, it was in a pool. Baptism was a denominational and cultural expectation. If you were Baptist, submersion meant the pure waters of holy forgiveness would wash away your sins. Only being completely buried beneath the waters could wash you clean. Then (and only then) you could come forth renewed and cleansed as white as the driven snow. To prepare, you were spiritually dressed. Your head was properly wrapped in a white towel. Your body was completely covered in a long, white, cotton baptizing gown. The deacons and mothers of the church declared you ready. Next, a bevy of preachers and church officials prayed over you, led by a long line of marching, singing church officers and members. All was done to the tune of "Take Me to the Water to Be Baptized."

Once I was taken down four or five steps into the cool water, some of my fright left me. I was not afraid of the water. I just did not want the preacher or deacon to drop me too deeply into it. I still vividly recall marching from the church, a trembling, young soul. I wondered if I would slip and slide or fall down the steps of the pool, landing sloppily in the water before they were ready for me. My long, white baptismal gown was secured at the ankles so I would remain respectable when let down into the redemptive elements below. Fortunately for the crowds standing all around on the sides of the pond, all things private were tied down well and remained in place.

As a deacon and a mother of the church led me into the impure waters, the preacher was already standing in waist-high water with outstretched arms, waiting to receive me. Reverend Harrison cried loudly, "I baptize you, my little brother, in the name of the Father, the Son, and the Holy Ghost!" He and the deacon then submerged me completely under the cool waters, out of sight for what seemed like forever. My parents, standing proudly on the front side of the pool nearest to me, later assured me that I was really in the water for only a few seconds. The preacher tried soothing my fears with generous words, "God bless your soul, son. May he remove any and all lingering traces of sin from the darkened parts of your soul."

I wondered how my soul could be darkened when I was only nine years old. My daddy never said my soul was dark.

"May God shine the fullness of his blessed light throughout your soul. May our Lord and Savior Jesus Christ continue to keep you safe in his loving arms and guide you safely through this old, sinful world. Amen."

This act signaled my ascension into spiritual sainthood. In short, I was told I had been inducted into the order of those who were expected "to be good for the rest of my living days on this earth." All of this must have taken deep root. I have tried very hard to live a Christian life.

Between the nonstop Christian teachings of our parents and the impact of becoming a formalized Christian, I cannot recall ever committing an intentionally sinful or unfair deed. I have tried hard to deal fairly with all I have met, regardless of their race or origin. Robert and I always said it made us feel much more comfortable inside when we could end each day believing we had mistreated no one. This basic principle guided us safely and richly through every day of our work and business years.

Soon after I had found Jesus, our family was ready to move from rural McDuffie into Thomson. The year was 1930, early in the Depression. By this time, I was rushing toward ten years old. I began feeling the satisfaction and peace one feels when beginning to realize the presence of a supreme being. Even though still young, my mind was racing. I felt joy, excitement, ambition, and a will to succeed. I had felt it before. This time, the fires of getting there repeatedly swept throughout my being. The will to succeed (and working to that end) completely claimed me.

When my daddy was ready to pack us up and was sure he had enough of sharecropping's wickedness, he would not be stopped. He was a deliberate man. Some say I follow his pattern of slow, studied decision making. One night, he gathered us around the big, wooden dining table in the old country house and sadly said, "I know my boss man is going to be really mad when I tell him we are moving." I could almost feel the fear and trembling in his body as he continued speaking. His face was covered with hurt and shame. "He will probably take back our car."

Some years earlier, he was able to buy a car. Because of the way the car loan was arranged, my daddy knew he would probably never be able to pay it off. The money had been borrowed from our landowner. Here he stood, having to tell his family that the white man still controlled us. Our family car, in which his children especially had taken so much pride and bragging rights in ownership, did not really belong to us. True ownership of the car that had taken us to town, church, and even Atlanta was really in the white man's hands. However, one straw truly broke the camel's back.

7

Out of the Country, into the City

When Boyd, the owner of the farm we were sharecropping, asked my daddy to bring over our mother and us to help pick his friend's cotton, that was it. My daddy quickly started packing us up to move away. No one knew how well we would do or if we could make it, but my parents said, "When we leave this farm, it don't mean we will never pick cotton again, but it sure means we won't pick this cotton again."

My daddy was right about the car. The first words from Boyd's mouth were, "Well, Henry, you know you are not through paying for the car. If you plan to move, the car stays here. You will have to give up the car." My daddy took a deep, triumphant breath and moved on.

He packed us up, his beloveds, and headed toward Thomson. He never looked back and never asked us to look back. He always wanted us to remember our connections to hard beginnings, but he pleaded with each of us to never return. My daddy just knew God had something more abundant waiting for him. He loved to recall the passage in the Scripture that said, "Religion never was designed to make our pleasure less." He added, "God intended for us to enjoy our share of the world's goods. He just intended for us colored people to work a little harder for our share." My daddy did work hard...too hard.

He moved us into an old, but bigger, house with five rooms. Later, he even added another room, which our mother furnished with a beautiful dresser that I know now looked like mahogany. She bought matching tables to go on each side of the bed. She was so happy because she had bought the furniture with money she had saved from raising and selling turkeys. The house had large, built-in closets, which were skimpy but useful. The previous tenants decided they needed closet space, so they took a considerable section of each bedroom and very solidly boxed in and shelved sections. There were no doors on the closets, just open shelves. However, those closets were much more than what we had when we hung our clothes on a nail on the back of a door and covered them with a sheet.

A massive dirt yard and big trees surrounded our new home, which we had to keep swept clean. In the fall, piles of brown, red, green, and yellow leaves covered the ground. This meant plenty of yard sweeping had to be done. We went into the woods and broke branches from the smallest tree limbs. We then broke the limbs into even lengths and fashioned them into yard brooms. Once a week, usually on Saturday mornings, my sisters and I took turns doing the yard sweeping.

The trees did not just create work. They were also a source of great fun and pleasure. Most Southern black families can remember gliding high through the air on the seat of a homemade swing strongly crafted from the makings of gathered materials. My older brothers and my daddy made swings for us younger ones. The swings were securely hung from the heaviest tree limbs.

One time, when it was time for Gussie and Annie Mae to sweep the yard, they decided to take a break and go for a swing. The girls jumped into the swing seat. One sat as the other stood. Before anyone could stop their double occupancy, they were sailing back and forth through the air, singing loudly, "Milk in the pitcher/Butter in the bowl/I can't get a sweetheart/To save my soul."

Somewhere between "I can't get a sweetheart" and "To save my soul," the swing broke. Both Gussie and Annie Mae landed on the ground. Annie Mae was lying as if she was out cold, but she was not. Gussie was resting on her laurels. Our older sister, Claudie, was standing in the yard. She began laughing so hard that she cried. Gussie got so mad that she pulled herself up and started throwing punches at Claudie. Our daddy was sitting on the porch and loudly ordered the girls, "Stop it! Stop that fighting!" Gussie did not listen. She just kept slugging away. That was the first (and last) time I ever saw my father spank anyone of us. I was nine; Gussie was thirteen.

Our father was a gentle, kindly man, but he could be very stern when times demanded it. He was not going to have his offspring fighting each other. He taught us, "You cannot ever hope to get ahead in this world, fighting or hurting each other. If you are busy fighting and acting like fools among yourselves, who will be left to defend and stand up tall when someone else attacks from the outside?" From that day forward, I never allowed our father to see me having an argument or a fight with any of my sisters or brothers.

Still on a farm, but just inside the city limits of Thomson, our new home was a temporary step toward better housing, better conditions, and better lives. Gussie said, "Poppa not only moved us into town, but he looked for a house that was much more comfortable. He bought us a beautiful living room suite. He and momma dressed up that living room with a colorful, lovely wool carpet. We were so happy that we were all squealing like little pigs. I still remember how happy we were when Daddy told us that, when we moved, we would also have a pretty room to sleep in. It was wonderful!" He had kept his promise!

A long, wide, wooden table with wooden benches on each side was in the kitchen. Two large wooden chairs sat at each end of the table. Our big, black, iron stove, used for cooking and sometimes for heating, was fired up with wood. My brothers and I often helped our daddy find, cut, stack, and bring in our wood supply. In rural areas, that was not a hard job because trees and tree limbs regularly fell. We just had to round up the wood, measure it, and cut it up to fit inside the stove. Two big, black, iron kettles held water for cooking. Two other big pots held water for bathing.

A well was near our house. It was our water source. A pail, hung from each end of a long chain, made it possible for us to draw the cool, clean water. A heavy wooden top covered the well to keep out rabbits, squirrels, snakes, and other crawling creatures. There was no indoor plumbing. Only white folks had indoor toilets. We had a big outhouse. It was rough, but our folks worked hard to keep our outhouse smelling clean.

I even found a way to feel good as I did my chores. I counted. I counted the rows as I dropped the corn for planting. I counted the buckets of water it took to quench the thirst of other families working in the fields. Filling each big pail with water, I put a dipper in the bucket and took the pail around for each worker to take a cool drink. Wells were dug deep into the ground. The water was so clear and cool that it usually tasted like ice water.

Our lives were pure country. Every day, except Sunday, our workday started early in the morning. We used a scrub board to wash our clothes. Barrels were cut in half to use for washtubs, and water had to be kept in the barrels. The water kept the wood swollen so the metal hoops around the barrels would not fall off. If the hoops dropped off, our washtubs would have fallen apart. We also took baths in our tin tubs. We washed our hands in a basin with water poured from a large pitcher that sat on a washstand in the hallway. A clean towel was kept nearby. Bath water was heated in that large kettle, which always held its place of respect on the kitchen stove. Washing our bodies was not such a challenge. Washing our clothes? That was another matter.

We had two large, black pots placed on top of stacks of bricks and fired by wood kindling. These were used to boil our clothes to expert cleanliness. The pots were filled almost to the top, and the water was brought to a boil. Slices of homemade lye soap were placed into the boiling water. When the water melted the soap, the pots were ready. Dirty clothes, which had been pre-washed or scrubbed, were placed into the boiling, soapy water. Sometimes, when we had it, we added washing powder. The clothes were then boiled and poked and beaten with the battling stick until they were deemed super clean. They were then rinsed repeatedly, wrung out by hand, and hung out to dry.

My mother tended a flock of turkeys for which she did not receive much money. She cooked for all of us, baked cakes and pies the white folks loved, and sewed. Gussie said, "We would go with Momma to pick out and buy material. She would bring the cloth home. In a few days, we girls would have lovely outfits. Momma would sometimes make shirts for the boys, too. She could look at pictures in catalogues, especially from Sears Roebuck and Montgomery Ward, and she would make clothes for us that looked exactly like the ones in the ordering books. She would make clothes for our cousins, too. Our cousins were older than we were, but they would always come to our house to help on the farm. We all worked together to bring in the crops. By the time harvesting was over, Momma would have sewn enough beautiful clothing for all of us. Oh, we all looked really pretty."

Like many other black mothers, in addition to sewing some of our clothes, she also made store-like curtains for each window in our house. Saying she wanted to bring the sunshine inside, she selected the brightest, boldest floral prints. She also took great care tending her large orchards of apples and peaches. Of course, we children often helped. Those orchards were her prizes. She seemed to know exactly when the buds and blooms would appear. Gussie said, "I just cannot see how one woman did as much as our mother did, and she never complained. She grew that big garden and prepared the family meals. Sometimes, company would come to eat. Sadly, most of the time, her creative sewing skills used up any time she would have had for resting."

"Then, she did not just sew lovely clothes for all of us girls. She made and sold those colorfully designed and patterned quilts. She gave away some. Oh, she did so much. She cooked and sold cakes and pies as well as picked cotton. It seemed Momma did everything!"

"All this because she truly worked to do her part to hasten and hurry the Paschal family's day of freedom and release from sharecropping. Lizzie Paschal was not just standing there, in those fields of drudgery, hoping for better times to just come and 'light' down on us. She had a marked purpose in mind. She was laying a bedrock, a reputation as a cotton-picking lady with class and the most honorable credentials."

Even though we had moved into town, my mother still planted and nurtured several acres of a family garden. At times and as needed, we chipped in and helped her. Her fresh vegetables and fruits received special loving care to bring them to full fruition in large numbers and blessed perfection. Our personal livestock was also raised right at home. We had Rhode Island Reds and Plymouth Rock chickens as well as turkeys, cows, and pigs. Sometimes, it was hard for us to sit before a platter of fried chicken, which contained the deep-fried remains of one of our friends.

It seemed to us that our mother must have worked twenty-four hours each day. So many times, she would get us off to bed. I later slipped out of bed and found her sitting at her dining room table, sewing and mending our clothes. At dawn the next morning, she was up, calling her family to breakfast. Even now, Gussie and I often wonder how she did all that every day with all she had to do and still work in the fields.

Many times, my daddy combined fieldwork with his job at the Knox Hotel. He left our mother and the children completely in charge of harvesting of the crops. He knew he had taught each child well. We had to show our respect for our daddy by giving true life and our very best know-how to any honest labor.

Although there was real segregation in those days, my daddy kept telling us that we needed to try to get along as well as possible with all of the whites. We tried, and our family sometimes succeeded. Whites regularly came to our house to taste or ask for some of our mother's cooking. So, they must have trusted us. Every week, our mother baked these delicious cakes and pies. The whites came in a regular stream. I do not know if they ever paid her adequately, but I never heard her complain. We never had any problems, but the whites could go to the homes of black folks and then ask for or take what they wanted. They came, whether we wanted their visits or not.

On the other hand, no blacks could go to a white home unless you worked for them. Then, your entry was through their back door. Crazy, isn't it? A black person could exit the white person's front door to sweep the front porch, wash the front windows, or water the flowers. You could even take the baby for a stroll in the front yard. However, when you arrived for domestic duty, you had to enter through the back door.

My father was well-known. Most often, the whites in the Thomson community treated him well. Some say he was well-respected. Later, when I was running my business called James' Place, I had a bit of slot machine help from the local white police and sheriff. Gussie thinks it may have been for two reasons. One reason was a possible connection with the Watson family from Thomson.

Just days after Robert died, a newspaper article refers to the Paschals by a Mr. Tom Watson Brown.[1] Brown tells dinner guests that my brother hailed from McDuffie County, the same area as old Tom Watson (Tom Watson Brown's cousin).

"There could be a family connection," Brown says. A Brown cousin once knew an old man named Paschal who walked past the Watson homestead en route to town. Tom Brown suggests a Watson ancestor might have once owned a slave named Paschal. The slave's gender was not mentioned, but, considering the times, there could definitely be a Watson-Paschal family connection. Though clandestine, like so many other slave master/slave woman connections, the bloodline may have been irrevocably manifested through those of us children of lighter complexions.

The other reason was that my daddy could fool the white folks into thinking he was subservient. They could not feel his inner rage. He controlled his inner resistance to all we were living through. He said he had to set the example. Whether he was operating that large farm, picking cotton, tending the cattle and the fowl, or making the fields and the orchards burst forth with plenty, he worked hard to be a pro with a passion and determination I do not think even he knew rested within himself. He plowed, planted, and watered the fields (often with his own hands and a flimsy, old tin bucket while praying for seasonal rains). He worked fourteen- to fifteen-hour days.

We may have been very poor in money, but we were brought up with excellent values and a love-filled family life. We believed it was our responsibility to always help take good care of each other. This does not mean we were not victims of the times. Like other black children of that time, white children

---

1. Gary M. Pomerantz, "From the Heart: Race in Atlanta," *Atlanta Journal-Constitution*, 1997.

harassed us and called us "niggers" and other dirty names. However, we tried hard to hold fast to those fundamental principles instilled in us within the loving walls of our home. "Do not ever try to repay meanness. That is the Lord's business. Vengeance is his. Let the Lord keep his promise to repay, and repay he will."

One time, everyone in our family was sick with the flu, except Gussie and my parents. Gussie said, "I just knew I was very special. I had been spared so I could take care of everybody else. About the second day, I was sweeping the kitchen floor. Suddenly, I became so ill that I could hardly stand on my feet. Our mother noticed the way I was leaning and swaying as I swept. Momma said, 'Gussie, you're sick, aren't you?' I started crying. I wanted to stay well so I could be the main one to nurse everyone else. Momma opened the bed up and told me to lie down. I was so sick. Everyone started crying when I asked Momma, 'Am I going to die?'"

All of us were saved. Our good friends, the Currys, also had a garden. They brought us a mixture of vegetables, which my mother cooked. She then made all of us sick ones drink the juice. Soon, we began feeling much better. Being cured by the juice of vegetables and herbs had a continuing place in our collection of "must keep" remedies.

By this time, my daddy had begun giving us a few of the things that a little more money could buy, though the struggle was not far from the old, familiar poor. He felt proud he could sometimes buy us two pairs of socks instead of one. He could buy us all a new outfit for Easter or Christmas, instead of us wearing the same ones repeatedly. Easter and Christmas were joyful times in our home. We sang Christmas carols, roasted marshmallows and peanuts, and made candy. Friends and family came together for big dinners and suppers. Some even came for breakfast. Being out of school at Christmastime was lots of fun, but all of us had to memorize our speeches and recitations to be delivered on the Christmas program at church. If you forgot your speech or did not speak loud enough, mighty teasing times were waiting when you got home.

We had a big, old, mahogany-veneered, upright radio with black knobs for volume and tuning. The radio sat on an old table in a corner of our living room. On Sunday afternoons, often after church and dinner, we sat around the radio. Any programs taking us into a world far beyond our living room kept our ears attentive. We listened quietly to programs from the faraway shores of New York City. I prayed I would not only live to go there, but I would have enough money to buy anything my heart desired while I was there. At that young age and for many of the years ahead, my dreams were still centered in Thomson though. All that really mattered was how I could make money in Thomson. By the time we made the move from country to town, I was ready to launch my business, selling vegetables.

From a somewhat rickety stand my daddy helped me build, I bought fresh vegetables wholesale and sold them on the streets of Thomson. My vegetable sales took place after a part of my summertime day was spent in the intown cotton fields owned by one of Thomson's white merchants. Here they were again! We had left the country, but not the cotton.

Picking cotton only made me hungrier to grow up, leave, and become more successful than he who owned the cotton fields. I wanted to feel more than the success he felt. I wanted to learn more about business than he knew. I wanted to become better dressed than he was. I wanted to eat where he ate, if I wanted to do so. I wanted a house bigger than the huge, white one in which he and his family lived.

I began saving as much money as I could from my earnings. Soon, my ten-year-old eyes were set on purchasing a used bicycle. I had worked so hard that summer that I was able to purchase my first ride, which got me a flourishing newspaper route. Now, my enterprise consisted of picking cotton, throwing papers and selling vegetables.

Cotton. Those hated masses of cotton continued to get the best of me. Cotton bolls made me tired and angry and further intensified that mean streak against picking cotton, which, I swear, must have been born inside of me. I remember thinking I would work hard, for a lifetime if I must, to become my own boss, to become an owner.

Labor as hard as I could, I could never match Robert's cotton-picking successes. He really loved to boast that he never saw a cotton boll he could not conquer, though he hated every second of having to pick. He could easily and deftly outshine the whole family as he breezed up and down those interminable cotton rows. On the other hand, I yearned endlessly for a less sweaty and more profitable route to gain.

He later said, "James, you didn't think I really loved picking all that damn cotton, did you? Man, at each end of each row and at the end of each tiring day, I saw another step toward a way out of Thomson, a way to the other side. I figured the faster I went and the more rows I picked, the quicker I could end my cotton-picking days!" As my brother always said, "We wouldn't exchange money or fame for our journey, but Lord knows it was a hell of a ride."

My Vegetable Sales

Between 1932 and 1934, my vision became clearer. When I was not throwing papers and after my old, rickety vegetable stand fell down, I quickly attached my wagon to my bicycle. I peddled that wagon around town and sold all the watermelons, corn, cantaloupes, collard greens, apples, plums, and peaches I could load onto my old, shaky wagon. I pulled, sweated, and hollered, "Fresh vegetables! Get your watermelons! Get your collards! Get your fresh-shucked corn! I have plums! I have pears! I have everything you need!"

Though shamed by having to humble myself as a street-peddling, vegetable-and-fruit man, joy, pride, and sweet anticipation lay beneath that shame. By this time, I knew success would come. I could feel it in my bones. I also felt pride in celebrating and selling my picture-perfect fruits and vegetables. Although I had to buy my vegetables from the wholesalers, I selected only the best. All of my selections were always polished, colorful, and beautiful.

Located in the plots of land surrounding our family's new home, my mother always planted a spring and summer garden which she lovingly tended and closely watched. Even her greens were seasonal and special. There were turnips, mustards, and the hardy, big, flapping green leaves of her collards lasting into fall and the winter. In fact, it was said there is nothing better tasting than a bunch of collards touched by the first frosts of winter. My mother knew which seasons were most favorable to the growth of which fruits and vegetables. She knew the correct proportions of water and fertilizer needed to ensure success. I think all things grown and touched by the loving hands of my mother loved her back. She planted her gardens for the eating pleasure of family and friends. She had an excellent eye for recognizing harvest-ready veggies.

I could always vary my products because of the abundance and the variety of produce grown in the rich soil of McDufffie County. I calculated how much I would earn and save from each load of fruits and vegetables. Even as I was selling, I was thinking, "How can I expand? How can I make more money?" It soon became obvious that my customer numbers continued growing.

All my male friends had wagons, and summers could be very profitable because all the white ladies wanted fresh fruits and vegetables to take home for their "girls," as they called their black maids and cooks, to prepare. I felt I could trust most of my five or six friends to sell for me and accurately report the sales. Targeting those for whom I had any doubts, I trained the rest of my team to watch and report any shenanigans. I had one "main man" whom I knew would honestly assist me in keeping watch over the whole operation.

My friends brought their wagons to my store, "James' Place," for loading. I carefully inventoried the contents of each wagon. We all worked, forming an assembly line and piling our wagons high with watermelons, cantaloupes, greens, plums, and other produce. These friends/employees made their daily rounds and reported sales directly to me. Even the elements seemed to want me blessed. Before I knew it, I was making enough money to pay my help and realize a growing profit.

During our happy summer selling marathons, bad or threatening weather rarely stopped my high-stepping vegetable brigades. One friend dubbed me "Boss James." After everyone reported in, I paid each fellow his fair share of the day's profits, a previously agreed upon amount. I watched gleefully as my own cache of capital grew and expanded. I knew then I was in business for the long haul. I kept working and kept my crew working as the dollars literally piled up. I was overjoyed! I was soon ready to give money to my family and lend small amounts to my siblings. We always made an agreement about how much interest each would pay me, depending on the size of the loan. The amount never exceeded five dollars.

Robert, Stretching Out His Arms

Robert loved to laugh about how he could feel Atlanta calling his name. He was thankful for the work at the sawmill, but Atlanta, some 150 miles away from McDuffie County, was calling him much louder. He said he often stayed awake during many sleepless, long winter nights, reliving how our family toiled together. On bitter cold days, we often had to work, clearing, digging, hoeing, raking, and removing trash from the fields, making ready for the next seasons of planting.

"It was during those times that I could hear Atlanta call to me, 'Git yo behin' and hans offa that white man's mules, pigs, cotton, logs, dogs, an' lan', 'n git yo sef on ovah heah.'"

And so he did. Later on, both Gilmer and Hodges followed him to Atlanta, although Gilmer returned often to Thomson to help me in the store that I had built into a thriving business. Both Gilmer and Hodges eventually moved to New York, where Gilmer remained. However, after Hodges was discharged from military service, he returned to Atlanta and worked with Robert and me at Paschal's Restaurant.

After working at the sawmill for several years, Robert left for Atlanta in 1934. We watched with tears in our eyes as he packed to move on. I can still hear our parents say, "God bless your move." Lord knows I missed my brother when he left for the city, but, in my heart, I knew I had to let him go. Our family knew Atlanta would pose absolutely no challenge for Robert. His familiar expression and battle cry was, "I love to work, and anything I do once can be done much better the next time I try." This motto served him well in his newly adopted city.

Robert was proud to talk about how he got up at 5:00 AM, worked his paper route, and then pulled his cooking shift at the white-owned Vaughn's Cafeteria, his first Atlanta job, located in downtown Atlanta. He did anything he was called to do, including sweep floors, wash dishes and windows, and cook. He also kept his eyes open. After spending three years at Vaughn's listening and learning, he heard about a better job at Jacob's Drug Store. Knowing that even a little bit more money meant more to save, Robert moved on.

He began his work at Jacob's by setting up drink machines, cleaning and preparing them for service. Later, he became the cook and soda jerk. Jacob's Drug Store was where so many native and nonnative Atlantans—from Auburn Avenue to West Hunter Street—got to know Robert. One of our friends often said, "Bob was always at Jacob's, every day and into the night. If he was not behind that counter, we asked, 'Is Bob sick today?' While the rest of us boys were partying at the Peacock or some other place, Bob Paschal was at Jacob's. We all thought he couldn't have a day off."

There are those who honestly believe Jacob's was Robert's personal testing ground for things to come. We do not think he even took much time to go to church. Some have said that Jacob's must have been the place where Robert Paschal's hopes for offering superior hospitality services began to take shape. He was a master at what he did, and Jacob's was the place where Paschal ideas were allowed to take root, blossom, and come gloriously alive.

Robert was his own best testimony. He loved to talk about how it was all that "sho nuff" hard work and getting to know some of Atlanta's right folks at Jacobs that would help to bring the two of us into our hard-earned place in time. He also tried out some of our family values at Jacob's. He was often overheard advising young workers, "Regardless of how well a job is done, it can always be done even better if one just tries hard enough…Never be satisfied with just doing a task. Always see if you can improve on what you have done...If you polish a drink counter, keep polishing until that counter does not just shine. Make it glitter...I came to Atlanta on a visit to see how things were, and I stayed. But I brought my work ethic with me."

Therefore, Robert Paschal, my beloved brother, co-owner and coproprietor of the not-yet-born Paschal business empire, was never ashamed to tell how his Atlanta career and journey toward the top of success began as a busboy in a neighborhood drugstore/restaurant.

Robert worked his way up. He observed, questioned, and listened. He took every chance he was given to learn and make his bosses look good. He was soon promoted to chef. Robert knew he had found his rightful place but only, as he said, "for a few moments in time." He knew he would never realize his dream by just being a chef. He wanted to be the owner, the head, and boss. He also knew I was still working and learning how to build a business. He said he could feel me closing in on him, hot on his heels, with that taste for providing services to people and making money for us.

Jacob's owned several pharmacies. At first, Robert's main responsibility was setting up the entire soda fountain operation in each drugstore and then running from store to store. Though very tiring, he did all the work himself while he supervised and trained newly hired help until they learned the ropes. His trainees had to watch him and then do as he did until each could show the ability to manage the fountains as efficiently as Robert demanded. Every one of his supervisees knew, in order to pass Robert's white glove test and fountain inspection, their management skills had to be superb. You had to polish it up, decorate it up, fill it up, dress it up, supply it up, and show you could serve it up—all to perfection. There were no excuses or anything half-done. Once, I talked to him about buying out the Jacob's chain. We knew we would be successful. If Jacob's could do it, we could do it even bigger. That idea met an early death. We had to get real because we were not yet ready.

The entire time, Robert dreamed, planned, and regularly put away a little money, and I was doing the same. We knew that saving to invest in our own business plan was key to making things happen. It had to be because we were both working hard toward our partnership with our other siblings contributing that much-needed spark of encouragement and, often, help.

Meanwhile, before they sought better lives in New York City, our sisters remained in Thomson and helped me swing the pendulum of success further in favor of Robert and myself. I will never forget how they worked so hard to show their love and faith in God's will for us. Gussie (my older sister), Annie

Mae (the middle sister), and Claudie (the youngest) helped propel my various deals and me toward Atlanta.

I wanted to gain the wisdom needed to help my family, others, and myself who were struggling. I could see so many who could not seem to escape or fight their way out of degrading poverty, whether real or only in their minds. That is, I have met thousands of our people who appear to have been locked, in their minds, in the cotton fields of sharecropping. Many who have never known the realities of such a life seem to have acquired a taste for the "my ankles are shackled and bound, and I cannot take not even one step out" mentality. By themselves, they do not seem to have what it takes, as Robert said, "to make a run for it." Some folks just need a little push. Sometimes, just a little help will get them going toward a better life.

As a youngster, I wanted to help people spring forward, and I believed this world did not have to be mean. The world can become whatever you are willing to fight hard for and work hard for. I always knew I would never settle for "just so." I had begun to believe, as my parents did, that it was God's intent that all people be blessed, if only they would work hard enough. Therefore, Robert and I worked on and continued sewing together and strengthening the fabric of our dreams while waiting for me to join him in Atlanta.

8

Promises to Keep

Between the ages of ten and thirteen, I began feeling I had so many promises to keep. Our daddy had kept the most important promise of moving us closer to heaven by moving us into town. After living in outer McDuffie County, Thomson really did feel like heaven. It wasn't perfect, but it was so much better. Plus, by 1935, the year after Robert left for Atlanta, not only had I set up a thriving vegetable business and kept my paper route, but I had also built and set up several shoeshine stands along Thomson's Main Street and on the sidewalk outside the town's one black barber shop. I had begun saving enough money to take my next step into expansion.

The Keystone Corporation was noted across America for seeking people to sell their beauty products. On my written inquiry, they said yes to me becoming one of their weekend salespersons. My family always encouraged me. When needed, they helped operate my growing number of businesses, so getting help with my Keystone venture was not a problem.

My older sister, Annie Mae, and I agreed she would become my Keystone beauty products stock and salesperson for a small salary. Annie Mae kept my inventory, and she targeted, marketed, and helped me sell to Thomson's small population of black schoolteachers whom she knew wanted to keep looking pretty. We also went after the town's church ladies. Our major market was the perfumes, lipsticks, face powder, cold cream, lotion, and other popular cosmetics. Black people have always taken great pride in our ability to dress up, look good, and smell good. However, my collection of Keystone items had something for every home. Even some whites also knew about the famous Keystone ointments. My work and investments began expanding so rapidly

70

that I employed my younger brother, Hodges, within a few months. He focused his time on the shoeshine stands. Gussie said, "By age eleven, James, you were gone! Momma, Poppa, and all of us were so proud of you. We were so glad you were our brother. All we could do was look in surprise and shock and give you handclaps and hugs! We all knew early on that your head for business was towers and mountains above the rest of us! You just never stopped working hard. You always wanted more. It was a joy to watch you set your sails in the direction of success!"

Soon after we moved into Thomson, my father became ill. Arthritis had taken him over so badly that he had to sit in a chair at night in order to fall asleep. A white acquaintance of his heard about his condition. The man went into the woods, gathered some wild herbs, and used them to prepare a medicine for my daddy to drink. The mixture worked so well that he could go to bed at night and sleep. The white man said, "Henry, you and your family are such good workers that we need you to get well. The medicine I gave you was the same I gave to my father when he had arthritis. The medicine was passed on down to us from my granddaddy."

I was a teenager, but I remember thinking, "That man does not really care about my father. He just wants his 'working nigger' back on the job, anybody's job." Many times, I have wished I could have known just what the herb mixture contained. However, I was too angry to care at the time.

Our family still picked cotton for some of the intown farmers. My daddy still struggled up and down rows of cotton. His lumpy, pained hands haltingly grabbed the resisting cotton bolls. We saw his health beginning to fail fast. His average-sized body was beginning to bend, break, and crumble. Sometimes, he hurt so badly that he wrung his hands in pain. Many times, we had to tie his shoes for him. Still, he was our wellspring for shelter, clothing, food, and supplying all the family comforts possible.

My father's love for our mother and his brood remained boundless, but neither his back nor his fingers supported his will to be self-sufficient. We often heard him cry to God for relief. Yet, he kept working, determined to keep alive within all of us the belief of a better day coming. When we seemed to be stuck in the outskirts of McDuffie County, his constant prayer was, "Lord, let me live long enough to bring my family out of this land of bondage."

The move into town seemed to breathe a new fervor, a new energy, into him. Despite his failing health, this man of faith, this self-described "true soldier of the cross, follower of the Lamb," continued. In addition to working the fields, he also worked as a waiter at Thomson's grand, white-only Knox Hotel.

Before daylight and through mid morning, he picked pounds of cotton. He then went home, cleaned himself up, changed into his best work clothes, and hurried over in time to prepare to ring the lunch bell, announce lunch, and start waiting tables.

Because he was not always feeling well, he often took me to work with him. I soon became his regular helper. At first, I helped by washing dishes and ringing the lunch bell. My daddy looked me in the eyes and said, "James, I know you do not want to do this kind of work. But, it is honest work, and it will help you move to higher grounds." I kept that sermon forever in my brain. "Honest work will help you move to higher ground." Sure enough, the Knox experience really taught me how to take a more solid grip and just hold on. I washed the hell out of those dishes, and I pealed that bell so it should have been heard into the next county.

Monday through Friday, after school and after our assignments had been carefully organized for easy completion, I went into action. First, I shed my anger and transformed myself into a calm, positive, observing, and thinking soul. Our parents said, "Anger is a first cousin of ignorance, and they breed from making love to each other. Don't you ever be found guilty. If you do, you will be helping others inflict your own wounds." After this little communion with self, my best-looking work outfit came off the hanger from the nail on the back of the bedroom door.

I set out my white shirt with its starched, perfectly ironed collar and my creased trousers. I ironed my own cotton shirts and pants, wanting desperately to learn perfect ironing. Then, hopping on my bicycle and quickly stopping by my other operations, I went to the Knox Hotel.

I also served diligently to help my daddy pull his shift as waiter. We often worked until well into the dark of night, taking orders, serving, and cleaning up. Whites gave us an order and then behaved as if they were looking right through us, even though we were serving them. So often, we were not even worthy of a "hello." However, we also watched their every move. The ugly attitudes of some of the white men who looked at us with such hate and venom helped steel my backbone to stand tall and stay determined to lead the fight for our God-given rights.

During the Civil Rights years, when the throngs gathered at Paschal's, I told them to refuse any and all wishes to become evil. In our fights for justice, we must remind ourselves to stand tall and remain prayerful. Above all, think about your grandmothers, grandfathers, and all those before them who died so we might live and be better equipped to join the continuing battle for freedom.

Sometimes, my daddy and I laughed heartily about and reflected sadly on how hollow their thinking must have been. There were times though when I swear I could see a spark of human kindness in the eyes of a few. Not one was willing to bear their friends' ridicule though. They would have been called "nigger lovers" or worse. To lessen the weight, my dad might say, "Did you see old Mr. So-and-So? He would not let anyone else get a word in. He hogged the conversation, and he 'hogged' the food down, too."

My daddy's advice always served me well. Robert once said, "Old Henry Paschal was one smart old prophet. He said white folks could often be cunning and sometimes downright mean. You just have to know when and how to win them over when it's in your best interest to do so."

Holding onto Visions

Robert and I stood tall, watched white folks, studied their good ways, worked hard, and held onto a matchless work ethic and a deeper black pride. Our heads were never bloodied, never bowed. With the Lord on our side, we began successfully crossing over the rivers. Our vision merged with our mission to become the Paschal passionate, simple goal: "Work hard. Do not even think about how long it will take. Just keep working. Keep focused, get your grip, and hold on. Your work will reward you."

Many years later, Mrs. Alice Washington, one of Atlanta's historically vested black families, told us:

> You and Robert remind me so much of what my grandmother always told me. When you feel you are slipping in life, if you feel your mission in life is about to become foggy, or if you know you are about to slip, spit in your hands, get a tighter grip, and hold on for dear life. You two brothers, I am sure, encountered many very early mornings and late, late nights when giving up may have seemed such an easy thing to do. Instead, you must have joined hands together, did a lot of 'double spits,' got not just a tighter grip, but a steel-like tighter grip, and held on tenaciously. God! Didn't you hold on!

We kept holding on until we found the payoff rules and results. Attitude, dress, intelligence, hard work, the will to learn, standing tall, respecting others, holding onto hope, faith, love, and courage became a vital part of our lives. Learning how to protect and hold onto our hard-earned money later also proved to be among our most valuable assets. Oh, I have spent well. So did Robert, more often as needed, rather than as wanted. For example, I have long since purchased and taken care of my first previously owned bike.

That bike was a need more than a luxury, and it played a major role in transfusing visions of possibilities far beyond Thomson and the Knox Hotel into my mind. I went on my rounds every day, working hard to perfect and manage my enterprise. Except for the summer months, my routine became an after-school passion. While I did not know what I was truly doing, I soon learned I was indeed tightening my grip and repeatedly—time after time—just fiercely holding on.

Learning and understanding how business was best done became my passion. I dedicated myself to learning all I could. I studied harder in school. I learned from the moneyed whites. My anger and fierce determination combined to bring about this vow: "For the rest of my life, if need be, I would work hard, sweat, plan, listen, observe, and commit myself to becoming the undisputed man at the top." Without ceasing, I have strived in every way possible to keep every promise I ever made.

Regardless of how clean, neatly dressed, articulate, and courteous I had been trained to be, I could only ring the Knox Hotel lunch bell and announce, "Lunch is served." If I was hungry, I had to eat in the kitchen, out of the sight of the lunching whites. However, that was all right because it was there that I began taking a lasting turn toward destinies fulfilled.

At the Knox Hotel, I worked to perfect every task. I tried to be so profoundly effective, so absolutely complete in every job I was directed to perform, that there would be no room for questions. I tried to ensure the right people would notice me, and my labors were rewarded.

One day, Mrs. Kate Pace, the white lady whose family owned the Knox Hotel, called me over. "James," she said, "I have been observing you very closely. You have learned well. You are very smart. Everyone who knows the Paschal family calls you the 'smart one.' One of these days, you will own your own hotel. I want to encourage you to begin thinking about owning your own hotel." Mrs. Kate Pace was one of those good white folks. I kept her words hidden in my heart. I would make those words serve me well.

Her words stuck as though they were a part of me, and I never forgot her prediction. I was soon performing my duties so well that, as arthritis consumed more of my father's body, I became his alter ego. I learned to do everything he could do at the Knox and more. I began setting tables, taking orders, and telling the patrons what was favored on the menu. My daddy was so proud of me. He knew I was not just working a job. By now, I was working a plan. When he became too weighted down with arthritis, I took over his duties while still keeping my shoeshine stands filled up, fired up, and forever ready. When I began shining shoes at the white barbershop across the street from the hotel, I truly felt like I was on my way.

I was young, but I made money, which I shared to help others. I paid my helpers. I saved and sparingly spent money. I guarded every penny. From watching and listening to the big white boys, I learned it took money to walk in their shoes. I did not want to just walk in their shoes. I wanted to march to a drumbeat that would take me miles beyond where their footsteps had taken them. It was not easy. It was very hard going to school every day, doing my paper route, and then going to the hotel after school. At night, after my father and I returned home, I still had to get my lesson. Early the next morning, I was off to school and starting my daily work routine all over again.

To me, it was important to look, feel, and act the part. Every big, business-looking white man I observed was always dressed to perfection. I promised myself I would always do the same. To this day, I care every day about how I look when I step out of my home. The men at the Knox always wore very impressive business jackets. I also noticed their usually white, starched-to-perfection shirts, sharply creased pants, suits, ties, and highly polished shoes. These men seemed to have been the driving forces in Thomson and all of McDuffie County. They were the moneymakers, the business owners, even the big farmers. I suspected they had descended from a lineage of slave owners. If learning their ways (except for the chicanery and other dastardly deeds) would deliver me to the ultimate station in life, I would be their willing student, twenty-four hours a day.

Monday through Friday, after school and homework as well as after I was well assured that all of my other deals were in perfect accord with my aims, I wrapped myself in my homemade CEO appearance and hastened to the Knox. I watched and listened, even eavesdropped. I began hearing words and phrases, such as investing, marketing avenues, closing deals, and so on. I was learning another, completely unknown, amazing way of life.

After several years of successful work in lesser assignments, I was promoted to the regular job of bellman. As guests checked in, they rang a bell for the bellman, who took the luggage to their rooms. Even though my dad was ill, he continued to wait tables and give me lessons. In order for him to continue in his proud position of being my daddy, I helped him believe he was still doing his job. Finally, when he became too ill to work a regular shift, I moved up during the summer months when school was out. When he could return to part-time duty, I set up the dining room, rang the lunch bell, and sometimes washed dishes. At lunchtime, I took that king of a ringer and announced "Lunch is ready" to the town's elite, mostly merchants, who gathered on the porch at noon. Many times, I laughed to myself thinking, "If you old geezers think I will still be ringing your old lunch bell ten or fifteen years from now, you are all about as crazy as you look."

Not Getting Blown Upside Down, Nor Sideways

These were the worst possible times to be planting the seeds of dreams. However, Robert and I could never allow ourselves to wallow in what a friend of ours later called reluctant pessimism. Instead, we stretched our minds and our bodies to their farthest limits, set our aims very high, and fought hard. We knew early on that ordinary things would never please us.

Over the years, we neither found nor did seek any hours out of the twenty-four for wasting precious time. Our father was noted for reminding his brood, "Life on this earth is very short. God promises us only seventy short summers. Use your time here well, and make it pay off for you." As the weeks and months passed, God's promise to allow me seventy years on this earth was kept in front of my every move. Doing something worthwhile stayed on my mind during every moment I was not sleeping and filled my dreams when I was. For me, fulfillment meant accepting personal responsibility for making the best use of my limited time, abilities, and relationships. I would not waste any time with involvement in worthless things or causes. I promised God that, if he would bless and smile upon my work, I would work very hard, never knowingly cheat anyone, never knowingly be dishonest, or take advantage of anyone. God has abundantly kept his promises to me. I continue to pray daily and seek to keep my promises to God.

Holding onto my visions of a world outside of Thomson could be called a "rags to riches" saga. Instead, I prefer to call my life "a life of promises prayerfully kept." I was still young, but my visions and dreams were already set. The possibilities of all of them would only expand. It was almost as if I had to keep making space in my mind for all the blessings that were sure to become mine. With every accomplishment, I began feeling a deepening sense of inner peace. Yet, I always felt an overpowering urgency to move with haste onto the next beckoning chapter in my life. It was as if God kept moving me along, pushing me to continue seeking my place and purpose in the world. My visions and dreams became richer, more vivid, and more real.

By the time I had reached junior high school, my talents on the basketball court were rapidly emerging. Some folks even said my abilities were noteworthy and hinted at the possibility of stardom. However, my personal priorities did not include charging up and down basketball courts. Anyway, athletic chances for service, fame, and fortune were not yet open to us at that time, though I admit I still love the game.

My businesses were already paying off. After I had graduated from McDuffie County Training School in June 1941, I put myself on a self-designed fast track to entrepreneurship. My parents kept saying; "Where you go in life has absolutely nothing to do with where you start out. Only you can determine where you go and how high you reach in life." In my heart, I knew I was not destined to live out the rest of the days of my life in McDuffie County. The Knox Hotel had made me know, with God's help, I would do everything in my power to become an unstoppable locomotive on the rail of success.

9

No Conflict of Mission

I was just ten years old when I first began taking very serious steps forward toward my destiny. Little did I know there was so much more for me to learn. In 1935, I was still a growing, but courageous and hardworking, young teenager. I was already thinking manly thoughts of growing rich. With my goat experience still fresh in my memory, I felt ready to take a flying leap into fulfilling my dreams.

There was never a conflict of mission. I always knew just where I wanted to go, and I wanted to take others with me. Every day, I repeated, "Learn. Keep learning. Work. Keep working. Save. Keep saving. Believe you can, and you will. Add in some praying, stir in a deep belief in the Almighty, and you are off and running toward the heights of achievement."

I ached inside with hope and want. I wanted my rightful opportunity to share in what white men had greedily grabbed from the rest of us. Plus, I wanted to show every one of them that I could work and I could own. I wanted to show them, in God's world of plenty, no one—male, female, white, black, red, yellow, or brown—has to step on the back of another human being to gather as much as one can to enjoy and share in this world's riches. I just wanted that chance.

By that unshaven age of thirteen, I could hardly believe what I had accomplished. I had become boss over several moneymaking ventures and was picking cotton for the owner of a large farm just outside of town. I had set up two shoeshine stands. One was inside a black-owned barbershop in the "colored section" of town, and one was in its counterpart across town at a white-owned barbershop. I operated the stand at the white barbershop downtown on Main Street, just across from the Knox Hotel.

Placing myself there in the sight and midst of most of the town's white businessmen, I wanted to be there—to see, hear, and learn as much as I could from them. Plus, I wanted them to see me, see I was coming after a piece of their pie. Robert had already bid good-bye to sharecropping, and I was aching to follow him. While the mission remained very clear, I had more growing up and learning to do. Later, this period would figure very importantly in the whole Paschal scheme of things. I let nothing turn me around. All extras, including girls, would have to wait. I was no different from any other teenager. I just had a different mission in life.

Staying the Course

Gilmer and Hodges managed my shoeshine business at the black barbershop. Now, I was free to work my paper route. I rode my bike into and through white enclaves, munching my lunch as I threw papers so I would not miss any observing and listening time at the Knox Hotel. Between noon and 2:00 PM, all the power brokers gathered for lunch at the Knox. After stuffing their bellies, they sat for a shoeshine and a spell of midday banter. Often, each boasted about his latest business success. Listening with undivided attention, I was never intrusive. I just turned attentive ears in their direction. I always dressed the part so I would never be seen as objectionable. As soon as I could get home, I added to my notes what I had learned that day.

As my father had taught me, I kept respectful connections among Thomson's white business owners. I let every one of them know I was always available to shine their shoes, throw their papers, clean their yards, or even pick their cotton. It would not be forever, only for a season. I was known for working all summer long, Saturdays, and after school on weekdays, if I did not have basketball practice. For the plan I had in mind, I knew I needed these white men of substance until I could spring myself from their clutches.

On my bike, I covered Thomson like a Dixie frost. I was everywhere, working and smiling. Always respectful and dignified, I never left a useful stone unturned. Some people have said I am courteous to a fault. Attorney Donald L. Hollowell, my longtime friend, often said, "James, I cannot conjure up in my mind any picture of you even having a wrinkle in your pants or a frown on your face."

Later, these early connections to the real world of profit-making paid off. I continued working and praying. I can tell you truthfully that young boys and girls can pray. My sisters told me how they had their own little prayer services, lifting my name up to the Lord and asking for my success. I already knew our parents were praying for me.

While I was still thirteen, even as all my little Thomson enterprises continued flourishing and growing, I was blessed to buy my first big business. Gussie loves to call this period in my life, "James' miracle interlude." Gussie said:

> My brother was something else! He learned quickly how to make money the same way white folks learned how to make money. Let me tell you, James also quickly learned how to deal with people, white or black. Our parents had taught us about treating people right. But we always wondered how in the world he kept it all going so beautifully. In addition to his paper route and his shoeshine stands, he also cleaned yards and picked cotton. In the fall, he picked up pecans. At one point, James got involved with the owners of Thomson's theatres. The next thing we knew, he was getting paid for distributing flyers for the movie theatres. On weekends, he was selling Keystone cosmetics and other products. One time, my brother even helped a white woman sell candy door-to-door. I thought all along his goal was to raise enough money to finance a bigger business. When James' great moment came, he was ready.

James' Place

I started my first business trial by renting a small store. This untidy little candy store sat right across the street from my high school, the McDuffie County Training School, the county's only high school for blacks. The store was failing. The owner was not selling products and items that would attract the students or the grown folks. I literally begged her to let me take it over. "Boy," she said, "you don't look like you know nothing about running no store, but I am gonna let you try it." Inside, I was jumping up and down because I was so full of joy. My goal was to work to raise enough money to buy or build a bigger business. First, I had to make this store a success, and I did. The year was 1937. I was almost sixteen years old, but I was not going to fail.

My family joined me in my joy and my work. Everyone supported me by working to help with all that needed to be done to get my store open and keep it going. My daddy was busy working two jobs, so he could only help in the store when he could carve out short periods away from his own work. However, the pride in his eyes and his encouraging words were enough to keep me going.

We worked for hours and days getting things ready for our grand opening. It had to be just right! Each day, our family cleaned, scrubbed, arranged, and stocked the store. I had saved enough money to supply all the stock we would need. I had talked with my fellow students and knew what they would buy. I also had my mind on what the grown folks wanted. By the time we put our stock in place, our store was ready.

By now, everyone in Thomson had gotten to know or had heard about me. Soon, all of the school kids were coming in to buy from me as well as many of the grown folks. I sold candy, school supplies, soda, and cookies. I purposely sold everything the previous owner did not think of selling. Each morning, before leaving for school, I hurried over and opened my store for business.

I wanted my customers to know I was not only the owner, but I truly cared about serving them. That kind of operation meant I had to rise and shine early, every morning. My parents, Gussie, and I were the first people up in our house. No one was late for whatever he or she had to do. I just had to add my own flavor to each and every day. Gussie says my eyes swept wide and then narrowed over every single board, shelf, nail, and stocked item of the entire structure. She says no small cluster of dirt or dust, smallest piece of stray trash, or item out of its rightful place on a single shelf could rest in peace during my examinations. I could let nothing rob me of starting a perfect day.

My mother and Gussie managed my store while I attended school. Even though my school day was very demanding, often because it included basketball practice, I took the short time needed to run across the street to see how the day had gone. The principal was also my basketball coach and an understanding man. If I had to occasionally take care of store business, causing me to be a few minutes late to practice, he told me he knew how hard I was working. He also said he was proud of me and I needed to get some rest.

Frequently, on some days, I went to school, checked on my store, practiced basketball, did a bit of yard work, returned to my store to help with the work, and then closed up shop for the day. Sometimes, I delivered Keystone products that were new or had just arrived. My bicycle was my means of transportation, and I soon began learning the art of trading in. My string of businesses was not all close together. Traveling among them caused so much wear and tear on my bikes that I had to trade them in every year. I literally worked my rides to death.

If I wanted to be successful at what I was doing, I knew I had to perform all my tasks daily, often into the evening hours. Sleeping late and dragging around was not an option, and I always had to be on time. Throughout all of this, I remained a good student. Everything was going as planned…for a while.

My rented store flourished, prospered, and grew far beyond anyone's expectations, including the previous owner's. Students and grown folks were coming in droves. They were buying and enjoying being at the store. If the items they asked for were not in stock, they knew I would hurry to purchase them. I had become a smashing success. James' Place ran like a well-oiled dream machine, the highlight of the community. I was riding high, and it was just too good to last.

The original owner, who was renting me the place, suddenly came to me. She said she no longer wanted to rent the property. "We need to take our store back," she said. She was envious and serious. She would not have thought once about throwing my stuff and me on the streets. So, for a time, I was forced to give it up.

I had built up the store, shelf by shelf and product by product. While the jealous lady was reclaiming the business, I was proudly adding up what I had learned and how much money I had made. My plans were clear, sturdy, and determined. I would not be rerouted from my goal. I simply refreshed my plan. My work around town and my familiarity with many of the town's key people paid off. I asked Thomson's only Black funeral director for his opinion, counsel, and help. I convinced him to build me another store. I wanted one that would be bigger and better than the one before. Although the building he agreed to offer was an ordinary, relatively small, nondescript, wooden structure, I was filled with joyful thanksgiving and glee. I planned to bathe that place in love and hard work, willing to making it a shining example of a variety store. My new little James' Place became an almost instant success.

In the ways of a small town, word about my new business spread quickly. Even though it was located on the outskirts of town, I did not have to worry about customers. James' Place soon became a lively, warm oasis of fun, music, measured folly, food, and other needs for the body. It was a popular meeting place for teenagers and a shopping center for adults. I built my place into a combination grocery store, meat market, and amusement parlor. I then set aside part of it as a dance hall with a jukebox, also known as a Rock-Ola. Fed by nickels and dimes, the jukebox played large records that played all the latest boogie-woogie and jitterbugs. To the disbelief of everyone, including my family, I also had amusement machines, better known as slot machines.

The Paschal system of chance and possible reward was given—permitted—a quiet, thriving culture of its own. The slot machines at James' Place moved full steam ahead, secure. I quickly expanded our base of friends and customers. In the beginning, I was generating many more friends than dollars. That did not bother me. Within weeks, I was making money.

James' Place continued to grow and prosper. Even during what was usually called the slow summer months, business progressed at a fast rate. This was when I brought loads of fruits and vegetables to the store, called my friends, and put them to work. As supply and demand dictated, I sent my crew around town as salespersons. We covered all the sections of Thomson, white and black. Again, they loaded their wagons and sold watermelons, cantaloupes, pears, blackberries, plums, collard greens, string beans, okra, tomatoes, cucumbers, and a variety of other garden goodies.

To keep a close eye on my inventory, I set up my own system of checks and balances. I told one friend to be sure to keep watchful eyes on the other, especially before and after wagons were loaded and goods were sold. If I could tell one was trustworthy, he was in charge of counting, loading, and checking sales and inventory. Each friend was secretly primed to look out for any sneaky tricks. I trained and paid them well. I never lost inventory.

As for the safe operation of my slot machines, I often think about that now. I believe the town sheriff and other lawmen kind of looked the other way because I was a Paschal. As I grew older, time and other events confirmed what we grew up believing. Those lawmen quietly pulled me into their own code of ethics, protecting each other's bent for dancing around the law when making money was the issue. I was not going to complain. The fact I was nurtured and raised by my parents and all Paschal children were well-known and well-respected helped my entrance into that circle. Then, there was also always the rumor that great-granddaddy Paschal was a descendent of a rich, old, Thomson landholder and slave owner named Paschal. So, James' Place thrived and brought services to many of Thomson's people of color.

After James' Place started growing and expanding at such a rapid rate, I began making loans to schoolteachers who sometimes had a hard time making ends meet from one month to the next. Especially during the summer months, their little public school paychecks would often not be enough to keep them going until they went back to work. At that time, black teachers were paid less than white teachers, even though many blacks often had the same (or greater) levels of training. Some of those teachers were never able to repay me.

I had a teacher once who, simply because she did not like me, threatened to give me failing grades "until I drop dead," to quote the teacher. However, a day arrived when I had to allow credit at James' Place for this same teacher. She had come upon hard times and needed to buy food for her family, on credit. I imagined hearing my mother's voice: "Always repay evil with good." So I did. I have followed this principle throughout my entire life, and it has paid off more than a thousandfold.

Claimed by the United States Army

Whatever the reasons were for the town's white lawmen to leave me alone to build my growing enterprise, I was grateful and very happy. I was making more money than I could have ever imagined possible. However, after four glorious years of profiteering, fate intervened. The United States Army summoned me for military service. I was eighteen years old. Military service meant that my burning dreams of linking up with Robert in Atlanta had to be put on hold for a time. I had to sell James' Place.

In 1941, I became the unwilling property of the United States Army. I served well with dedication until I was injured going through the wicked obstacle course. I ran, crawled, pushed, pulled, and strained. I was determined to be the best on my assigned team. I was a little too determined. I fell from the highest climbing wall and crushed my ankle. My unit was preparing to be dispatched, but the injury was so severe that I was honorably discharged. Being in the Army taught me a lot more about strict discipline, order, and the need to always get the proper training to get any job done in a superior fashion.

Our beloved mother passed away while I was in the Army. To this day, I remain deeply pained that she never got to really share in and truly enjoy the plenty that Robert and I had dreamed of providing for her. She deserved so much. She and our father had been cut off much too early. But they always told us, "If we are taken on home by God before all your dreams come true, just keep on working and praying. It will happen. God will will it so."

Finally, after my discharge from the Army, I could go to Atlanta to hook up with Robert and hopefully help save some money so we could get started in business. Finding good paying work for colored people, or Negroes, as we were called then, was a little tough. However, a major obstacle was the reality of the time. War was with us. Even if I had found that needed job, no restaurant equipment was being built. All materials for heavy building was being devoted to defense. Everywhere I went looking for the things we needed to set up our business, the answer was the same. All of what you are looking to buy is frozen. There are no such items for sale to civilians. The materials are for military use.

From our Thomson days, Robert and I knew we would go into the restaurant business. We wanted to work for ourselves and build our own high road to success. We had carefully laid out our plans to open a business, and we had pinched, saved, and held onto every dollar we could. It was not a lot, but it was enough to get ourselves started. I thought we were ready. It was not yet to be.

10

On to Other Things

Deeply disappointed, I left Atlanta in late 1943 and decided to go look for work and perhaps study in Cleveland, Ohio. Why Cleveland? I guess the name just sounded good. Robert was still working at Jacob's in Atlanta. He said, "You go on. Our time will come. I will stay here and wait for you." I remained in Cleveland for about a year and a half and attended Cleveland Technical School at night. I took every business course offered. I wanted to learn all I could about business.

When I got to Cleveland, I could only find work in an iron foundry, the Cleveland division of United States Aluminum, and it was rougher than I could have possibly thought. I stayed, bodily tired, mentally frayed, and just broken down. I worked in the cold Cleveland winters, the heat of the summers, and scary closeness to steel smelting pots. I was a handyman to the boss, the real working men, and everyone else. I had to fill up and push a loaded wheelbarrow, often uphill, to the other workers. When they needed something loaded (iron, steel, cement, or dirt), I was their dragger. So I pulled, dragged, lifted, and pushed. If some other mess needed cleaning up, I was their man. I worked hard, but I stayed really mad.

I got tired of the drudgery, sweat, and sheer exhaustion of doing the same menial work. I was also tired of being just a helper to the more seasoned workers who were making twice as much money as I was. When my boss *promoted* me by giving me a larger wheelbarrow, I parked it, walked right into his office, and said to him, a man of considerable size, "I would like to have some work that will pay more than what I am being paid." He peered at me over his heavy, black-rimmed eyeglasses and began laughing.

"Boy," he said, sneering a little, "what do you know about making money? Is there more to this? Did one of those other boys push you up to come in here? Boy, you are frozen to this job."

I looked straight into his eyes and replied, "Well, as soon as I thaw out, I'm leaving."

His face said, "Leave anytime you want, but you ain't gettin' no more pay." I quit the foundry. With my head held high and fire in my soul, I felt good and happily moved on.

After that, for nearly two years from 1945 to late 1946, I worked as a Pullman porter, a job I got through a man who was a friend to Robert. This man knew I was just out of the Army and wanted to go into the restaurant business. He worked out of the New York office of the Brotherhood of Pullman Car Porters and often visited the district office based in Atlanta. Good jobs were very hard to find anyway. If you were a man or a woman of color looking for a special kind of job, it was even harder. It did not matter if you had honorably served your country. We knew, if I could get into Pullman porter work while waiting for restaurant equipment to become available, I would be even better prepared in terms of money and skills when my needed materials were back on the market.

Being a Pullman porter was supposedly one of the better kinds of prestige service jobs, especially for black men. If you were hired on, you were thought to be smart, polished, and even well-to-do. You traveled all over the country. Robert and his friend knew that going into the hospitality service business was still my burning passion. They also knew the fire would never go out or I would not think of taking a step backward or sideways until Robert and I had achieved our goal. As a Pullman porter, not only could I learn a lot about how to fulfill that lifelong dream, I could almost certainly meet the right folks, see the right places, do the right things, and actually learn more about the business.

Were they right! Robert's friend helped me get hired, I believe, due to his place and activities in the union, and I will remain forever grateful. The job of Pullman porter was always different and exciting, and it always required a lot of energy. I learned more than I could have ever imagined about the hospitality business, and I was blessed to travel throughout this nation. The work could challenge you to use every best behavior your parents ever taught you. However, you soon found out, if you did your best work, you would be successful.

I was always the one to address needs, problems, and potential problems, and I was always full of questions. Robert was always more subdued. I was never afraid to introduce myself to the highest-ranking officials or bosses. I introduced myself to anyone I felt might have some useful knowledge tucked away that would help me get ahead in my chosen business. Of course, they were most often the white moguls, but I usually found most to be very willing to share. I worked hard to make some of them my friends.

With Robert always in my thoughts, I worked hard to learn everything I could about planning, management, decorum, selecting staff, and focus on the highest quality of service. I learned how and what to purchase to make customers want to seek out a special place of service. I wanted the Paschal brothers' business to shine. Ultimately, I learned how to build an atmosphere of comfort, courtesy, caring, loyalty, trust, and profit. I was taught well.

Pullman cars were actually private cars, separated from the regular railcars. Each Pullman car had a drawing room, a kind of living room. Each car was composed of twenty-four private compartments in which the passenger berth seats were converted into beds for sleeping. In the morning, the thickly padded berth seats were rearranged for daytime sitting. The porter's job included letting those passenger seats down nightly and making them into comfortable beds. In the morning, it was our duty to return all seats to comfortable sitting positions.

Pullman cars were felt to be the domain of the rich and famous. In the morning, as soon as passengers headed to the dining car, the porters went into action. We cleaned, polished, and put everything back in perfect order. We were always addressed by our first names or "boy." We were always in demand to bring something or to do something. We were always expected to provide the best of service in making passengers comfortable.

Every Pullman porter was required to give first-class service to the passengers, and there was a good market for riders. For example, if there was a football game between Georgia Tech and the University of Georgia, passengers traveled from Atlanta to Athens. The Pullman became a wheeled hotel. Each porter had to ensure every bed was properly made and the dining car tables were set with the finest white table linens, stemware, and china. Compartments were regularly serviced with food, drink, or whatever else the occupants needed or wanted. Pullman porters were required to serve, and they were trained how to meet every service request available to passengers who rode in the Pullman cars. In fact, the public knew that passengers in the Pullman cars were the exceptional riders. Every Pullman car had "Pullman" emblazoned on both sides of each car.

The life of a Pullman porter was not an easy sojourn at all. Regardless of how long it was, when the train pulled into the Pullman yard at the end of a run, you had to find your own way out of the yard into the city or town. Many times at the end of our trips, the trains we were working on would be cut off from the engines and left in darkened freight yards. The workers often had to walk, sometimes a far distance, and find our own way out of the strangeness of the yards and into the town. At times, we even had to dodge oncoming trains. There was no hot bath waiting for us or food. We had to make our own way.

The Pullman runs were from cities as large as New York City to the smallest town in Mississippi. Imagine yourself, a young, well-dressed, tired black man emerging into the light of a small town in Mississippi declaring you were lost and looking for a place to sleep. Between 1943 and 1945, this was not the best condition in which to be, but I knew when I needed to say a polite "Yes, ma'am" or "Yes, sir." It never hurt me, and there were times when it may have helped.

During that same time, so many people needed some kind of help. I decided I wanted to help someone in some way every day. Around nearly every train station at which my Pullman car stopped (or not too far off), I found people who needed some kind of help I could provide. Some people needed directions or something to eat. Some needed help to make a telephone call. Others needed a letter mailed or just a helping hand when boarding the train.

The life and pay of a Pullman porter, though good, was not enough. Although my daily thoughts rested on that ribbon of highway that ran from Thomson into Atlanta, I took in every bit of knowledge I could swallow. I stayed as close as possible to the men who managed the operations and those who planned, organized, and ran the Pullman porter end of rail travels.

As I traveled far away from my deeply segregated, native South, I was introduced to many people and many ideas. I stayed in hotel after hotel and gained more experience, which helped me solidify my dream of owning a restaurant and hotel. I held in deep thanksgiving all that I had learned and was ready to use from riding the rails. I had not just ridden. I had watched every detail of how things were done in the Pullman service. I watched the cooks, waiters, and managers. I watched inside and outside of the trains. Every time we stopped in a city, even briefly, I tried making it to the largest hotel, even when coloreds could not sit in the main dining room. Sometimes, I talked to the workers and asked them questions about their work. I wanted to know how they were treated and how they had been trained for their work. I wanted to learn everything, positive and negative.

I did not become a Pullman porter with any desire to stay with it for the rest of my life. I went in with a mission, so my departure was not only timely, but planned. The industry got to a point where not as many porters were needed. In modern terms, they were downsizing. I wanted to put into use and place, in my own life and in that of my brother and family, what I had learned as a direct result of my Pullman porter years.

While Atlanta was not as big as it is today, compared with the Thomson I knew, in those days, going to Atlanta was like going to New York City. Better things were waiting there for me. I was on my way to hook up with Robert, who saw himself becoming the grand chef and I the grand CEO. When we could talk together or write to each other, we found we were still on the same main line. Our thoughts still fitted like designer gloves.

Hard work and hard times could not destroy the images that Robert and I continued to keep fresh in our minds. They would survive on the richness and power of their own substance. I still believe that things done right will take you over the top, especially when that includes good deeds for family and others. We knew that opportunities were waiting for us. However, if we had even thought of letting our chances for success go to waste, we knew we might never get a second chance. Our very survival and prosperity hung solidly in the balance of us being able to show it did not matter how poor we were or had been. We would face the charges we knew we had to keep. Our daddy, the deacon, often led the congregation of Mt. Carmel Baptist Church in the raising and singing of the old, Baptist hymn, "A Charge to Keep I Have." We always kept the power of its words in our hearts. I could see and feel all the details of a triumphant calling on the horizon, and that call was coming from Atlanta. It was as if I could hear Atlanta telling me the time was ripening. I was truly ready to fall fresh from the tree of little fruit into the garden of abundance and plenty.

First, during my travels through Pennsylvania, I met my beloved wife-to-be, Phyllis.

A Rose from the Gardens of Homewood

Meeting and marrying Phyllis remains at the top of my list among the best, most sustaining, and most wonderful things that have happened in my life. Phyllis was born Phyllis Johnson on March 21, 1928, in the little town of Homewood, a suburban enclave just outside Pittsburgh. There were only two children: Phyllis and her sister, Marian.

When Phyllis was a child, the steel mills were going full speed, twenty-four hours each day. Every day, when she opened her eyes, she could smell the acrid smoke and feel the sting of the sticky, black soot as it lazily attached itself to unsuspecting surfaces. Steel mill grit and grime did not make a distinction in persons, clothing, cars, homes, or anything lying flat or standing upright. Those infectious clouds did not even care where your folks worked. Phyllis said everything and everybody was covered with dirt and soot.

She grew up in a neighborhood where most of the families were of Italian descent. From where she lived, Phyllis could breathe in the provocative smells of the freshly baked, hot, Italian breads daily. Phyllis' mother bought the breads, and the family could even take out the rich, meaty, Italian spaghetti from the neighborhood restaurant. However, the family could not sit inside and have the meal they had just purchased. The Johnson family could attend the one, small movie theater in Homewood's shopping center. However, it was arranged so blacks and whites sat in different sections. There would be no cross-cultural or cross-racial communications taking place at all. Blacks could buy ice cream at the ice cream store, but they had to eat their purchases outside.

Phyllis said, "I guess we just accepted our segregated lifestyle. There were no laws to help. We just went on with our lives, secretly hoping for a better day. We walked to school. There were no buses for black children. Everybody seemed to have lived within walking distance of our school. Of course, you went to school. No excuses. Snow, rain, ice, and freezing winds, nothing stopped us. Snowstorms did not even matter."

Phyllis' mother, Mrs. Edith Johnson, whom everyone called Mrs. E., worked full-time in the custodial department of the Pittsburgh school system. Though a single, working mother, she placed attendance at school first in the lives of her own two daughters. She often talked to other mothers about keeping their children in school, and she was sometimes successful. A beautiful, stately woman, Mrs. E. had divorced the children's father when they were quite young. Being a lone parent did not—would not—stop her from making every possible effort to spread light and enjoyment of life for Phyllis and Marian. She pampered her girls, but she also guided them toward living lives of dignity, respect, love, and honor.

Even as she fell ill and until her death, Mrs. E. always reminded her daughters, "Regardless of whatever happens to me or your father, always remember that you two will always have each other." Today, I believe Mrs. E's wishes for her daughters are vibrantly alive. Phyllis and Marian are very similar and claim a special strain of sisterhood. They share an obvious, immeasurable love. Both will unashamedly speak openly about the lasting legacy of their mother's tender influence. They will also tell you that their mother had a strong source of support.

Mrs. E. often worked beyond normal working hours, so Phyllis and Marian spent much of their early lives with their beloved grandmother, Rosa Wilson and, to quote my wife, "an old-maid aunt, Lucy, who was lovingly called Aunt Sis." Grandmother Rose did not work outside the home, so she often cared for Phyllis and Marian until Mrs. E. came home from work. Although Aunt Sis did domestic work, she was a true study of class and social grace. There was also their grandfather, Daddy Bill. Phyllis and Marian dearly loved Daddy Bill with a special kind of respect and dedication. These kin "took no mess." They all believed in raising children right and in the fear of the Lord. When kindly, but firm, Daddy Bill was in charge, no one had to want for attention. As they grew up, everyone in and around Homewood and Pittsburgh came to know Phyllis and Marian as "those sweet Johnson sisters."

Grandmother Rosie and Aunt Sis had been reared in Forsyth, Georgia, about sixty miles south of Atlanta. At this time, my beloved Phil was almost a college-ready teenager. In the summer of 1946, Grandmother Rosie began feeling a sudden, unquenchable desire to come South to visit her relatives. Phyllis came with her. There was also a cousin, Johnnie, who lived in Atlanta. Grandmother and granddaughter could not come all the way into the South and not pay due homage to Cousin Johnnie and, of course, Atlanta. Phyllis and I have asked ourselves so many times, "Could there have been some godly purpose directing this inevitable drama?"

Cousin Johnnie told Phyllis that she wanted her to meet a young man named James Paschal. She agreed, and I went over to Cousin Johnnie's, where the first "hellos" were exchanged between the Southern young man and the shy, polished, soft-spoken, Northeastern young woman. With that first meeting, we each seemed to know that our love was meant to be.

Phyllis said, "In a few days of our meeting, knowing I would soon have to return home, I wanted time to just stand still. James was such a gentleman. I asked myself, 'Is he real? Can he be my true knight in shining armor?' All through my childhood, I had quietly and very privately envisioned my dream man. And here he was, in the living, loving, oh-so-gentlemanly flesh! And he seemed interested.

"He immediately asked Cousin Johnnie if he could take me to the movies. My heart fluttered. The evening's charm and dazzle was shattered when James revealed he would also be leaving town, almost as immediately as I was.

Would my images of a budding romance and a possible lasting love story be shattered? When I returned home from the movies, I went straight to bed and cried my eyes out. All I could think about was that I may never see him again. Although I knew he was leaving to complete his plans for returning to Atlanta, I was unsure of what my future held. I was a senior, getting ready to graduate from high school. I knew it was expected that I would go to college. But where was yet to be decided.

"Although James had tried to assure me that we would keep in touch, I was simply too overcome with fear and sadness to let his promise sink in. In my head, all I could hear was the deafening, painful question, 'Am I going to lose this once-in-a-lifetime blessing?' I fought hard to control my sorrow. I had to believe this blessing would be mine. Though filled to the brim, with all this imagined uncertainty, I had to believe that, what is for you, nothing or no one can take away. I kept telling myself that things will work out.

"I felt as though magically touched by this privileged encounter with this man. He was surely the most wonderful specimen of a male I had ever been blessed to behold. In fact, James is so genuinely loving and gentlemanly that, when we were first married and he wanted to get my attention, he would call me Mrs. Paschal instead of Phyllis or Phil. I soon learned that all he had said and promised proved to be true, far beyond my deepest hopes. In a few days, Grandmother Rosie and I returned home to Homewood. All I could think about was, 'Well, if I never see him again, James Paschal had certainly left me with some loving, unforgettable memories.' But I am eternally grateful to God that James Paschal did not forget."

In a few days, I reached across the miles and telephoned Phil, but she was not at home. Later, she told me that her heart dropped when she learned I had kept my word and called. She said she kept thinking, "Will he care enough to call again?" She had underestimated my determination and resolve. I had already made the same decision about Phil that she had made about me. My calls continued and at very regular intervals. We both made the promise to work hard to keep our growing hunger for each other's closeness and company vibrantly alive and warm. Phyllis promised to seek the counsel and support of her family as well as rely on her faith and reasoning. She had some hard decisions to make.

My future wife graduated from high school. I rounded out my plans and returned to Atlanta to join Robert. Time was fast approaching when Phil would need to decide just where she would attend college. Later, she con-fessed she had already begun wrestling with the thought of how she could possibly work out things to come South to study. She had always thought she wanted to become a registered nurse, but Grandmother Rosie became ill. Considering Phyllis' squeamish response to the responsibilities and duties of nursing, she was convinced that another profession would best fit her.

In the meantime, I was working hard to keep our blossoming connections going. I could hardly contain my excitement when I learned she was thinking, "Why not Morris Brown College in Atlanta?" Her grandfather offered to help, and Phyllis was accepted into Morris Brown College. In 1984, thirty-seven years later, when Morris Brown awarded my cherished honorary doctor of laws degree to me, I wanted to tell them that I should have rewarded them for their role in helping me find the love of my life.

So it was that. In the fall of 1946, with Daddy Bill's blessings and assistance, Phyllis went to Morris Brown. Later, she teased me and told me she had to admit my strength and romantic pull really drew her to the South. When she arrived with her giant-sized trunk and all the other lady things in tow, she encountered her first setback of college life. Her two roommates had preceded her, and they had already staked out their respective spaces in the living quarters. Phil was left with the leavings, which were less than adequate.

Though she spent many pleasant, enjoyable days on the campus of Morris Brown College, the residences were uncomfortably crowded at that time. It was a quiet stroke of luck when Grandmother Rose's sister-in-law invited Phyllis to come live with her and her husband. Phil happily accepted. The move afforded us more regular visits and the opportunity to develop a more personal, intimate relationship.

When we needed breaks (she from her studies and I from my entrepreneurial pursuits), we were inseparable. We had so much fun together. We saw all the good movies, went to football games, dined out, and visited our small but growing circle of close-knit friends. Phil and I laughed easily together. The more time we spent together, the more we came to know that we were truly perfect for each other. Within a few months, we both knew that ours was a genuine romance. My twenty-fifth birthday was right around the corner. Our business outlook was favorable, and I was in love. I was ready to take a giant step toward permanence, ready to seek a wife.

Early in January 1947, I took matters into my own hands. The fact that Phil was still in college could not be a deterrent. I wrote directly to her mother. Just as many old-fashioned Southern men have done, I asked for Phil's hand in marriage. Mrs. Johnson's reply was quick and positive. We became engaged on Phil's birthday, March 21, 1947. I told her that, as my wife, she would never have to work and she would be supremely provided for. God has helped me keep that promise. She left Morris Brown and Atlanta and went home, returning to Atlanta a few weeks before our wedding to complete final tasks.

We became husband and wife on June 8, 1947. All was beautiful! Both families had decided on a simple, intimate ceremony. Our two families were united in the parsonage of Liberty Baptist Church, the church of membership of Robert's wife, Florine. Quite early on, Phil and Florine had become close friends. So it seemed only natural that we wanted Florine's pastor, the Reverend B. L. Davis, to perform our marriage rites. Through the years, our two families remained as one. Neither of us can ever remember exchanging a cross or angry word between our families. Phil and Florine were more like sisters, and the same held true in her relationship with Robert. In fact, in later years, as our prosperity became more secure and full, Phil and Florine loved to team up on Robert and me. Chiding us as "those two black Santas to everybody," they said, "Not much will be left for us when you two Paschal brothers finish giving." They knew our families always came first.

There have been times when, on reflection, Phil and I had to stop and give serious thought to the true extent of our blessings. She, a small town Pennsylvania girl, and I, son of a small town Georgia sharecropper, never want to forget the truth about the directions our charmed lives have taken. There have been times late at night that we have found ourselves lying awake, asking ourselves, "Why are we so blessed? Is this all a dream?"

11

Atlanta

Good things were beginning to happen for people of color in America in 1947, even though sports had taken the lead. Jackie Robinson had joined the Brooklyn Dodgers as the first black player in Major League Baseball. Talk about better days ahead had taken on new fervor in the land. Robert and I opened our first little sandwich shop in this year. It was also the same year I entered into holy matrimony with my beloved wife, Phyllis. It was one year before Atlanta hired its first black police officers. By now, I was feeling right grand!

Robert had been in Atlanta for thirteen years. His first visit to Atlanta was in 1924 when he was only fifteen years old. The possibilities he saw deeply touched his heart. He prayed for answers to do what was right. After his official move to Atlanta in 1934, he only returned to Thomson for visits. Atlanta had become his home. But, Robert often said how it had hurt him to leave home, yet he knew, if he stayed on in Thomson, not only could he have been unable to build the kind of life we both dreamed of, only God could have protected him from losing sight of our dreams. He also knew, if he stayed, only God could have saved him from getting into it with some old, mean, racist, cracker of a white man.

I often found myself thanking God. Robert decided we could better help our family and ourselves by leaving Thomson. We had been taught that just walking away is always more honorable than engaging in violence. Walking away is having your life. If you have your life, you have hope and possibilities. If either of us had ever lost our temper and become violent, the white man's jail or, worse, a hanging tree was awaiting our black behinds.

By the time I made it to Atlanta, Robert had been working hard for other people. He had also bought a bike and taken on a paper route, delivering papers to 520 homes between 2:00 and 6:00 AM so he could make extra money. Many times, he slept little. Robert and I had saved some money. He had already been looking around for a place where we could cast our first venue, and we wanted a restaurant. We knew we needed to offer something good, something people wanted, and something very special.

A True Beginning: Building on Principle

Every time Robert could find a little time, he got to know Atlanta. He almost went over Auburn Avenue with a fine-toothed comb before taking in West Hunter Street and the Atlanta University Center. He talked to anyone. He wanted to get to know everyone and everything he could about black life and politics in Atlanta, such as they were (or were not) at the time.

Matters for black people in Atlanta were not much different than they were in Thomson when Robert first moved to the city. Just as whites in Thomson had seen us as less than human, so did whites in Atlanta. Black life and white life ran on separate tracks. By the time I arrived, we could smell the winds of change blowing hard toward Atlanta. Robert had done his homework well. We were planning our restaurant, planning how we could build a clientele for something very special. When we opened that first little shop, we were not yet prepared to offer a specialty or even to begin thinking of one. At first, we only served cold cut sandwiches and soft drinks.

One day, Robert told me that he had seen a cook use a secret weapon in a recipe to prepare fried fish. The customers loved it! He just knew, by making a small change in that recipe for chicken, including a few extra-special spices and letting the birds marinate, he could serve fried chicken so good that, according to him, "That chicken leg would do a royal bow and happily beg to be eaten."

Fried chicken sandwiches became our specialty, and the results were great! It was beyond anyone's wildest expectations. We thought people, particularly the students of the Atlanta University Center, just wanted some place to go out to for a while, especially on weekends. We learned better. Soon, customers, young and old, were lining up for our cold cut sandwiches and sodas. When we could add our specialty dish, they began lining up for fried chicken sandwiches. The lines grew longer and longer.

We could have never foreseen or expected the true breadth and richness of our dreams that were born in poverty and were now coming to life. We could have not foreseen what we would be blessed to do and build with a lowly fried chicken. We soon learned this principle: "The human spirit is a most powerful force when you are armed with God's blessing of faith, trust, and a deep belief in yourself." Paschal's was founded on this principle, and it is the basis of our survival and progression for more than fifty years.

Paschal prosperity did not just happen. There were many hills and valleys along the way. The economic recessions of the 1940s and 1950s nearly sank some businesses, but not ours. Robert and I respected our own and the territories of other businesses. The little money we struggled to save amounted to $2,000 between us. We looked each other in the eyes and had to admit that we were still short. Because we had agreed I would handle the business end of growing our plans, I knew we needed to look for additional capital, even though we planned to start small.

I began the search for money. The first stop was the black-owned Citizens Trust Bank. I thought they would welcome me gladly, but they refused our loan. Before they would grant us a loan, they wanted us to prove that "we were about something." I guess that made sense to them at that time. But we were about something—something grand, beautiful, and lasting! Only Robert and I knew how we had struggled to save the little money we had.

In the Paschal way, I pushed back my shoulders, held my head high, and briskly marched down the street to the white-owned Trust Company of Georgia. There, we were able to make a loan for $3,000. As our highway to prosperity began stretching brightly and solidly ahead of us, our black brothers of wealth became some of our loudest cheerleaders and biggest lenders. Years later, I was invited to join the board of directors of the very financial institution that had initially looked the other way.

When Trust Company said yes to our request, we knew the Paschal brothers were on their way. However, as the years progressed, we found that all would not be easy. The road was particularly rocky when we tried securing loans, hiring honest workers, and securing supplies from white businesses that were not used to dealing with a black-owned business. More than once, friends said, "Don't you ever just want to curse the hell out of a few people?" Yes. Even now, I regularly revisit those times when our parents gathered us around the dinner table and reminded each of us, "We will not always be with you. Remember, you can go on to be whatever you want to be if you work hard, stay honest, trust God, love each other, and treat your fellow man as you wish to be treated." We developed our own Paschal cre[ ] that guidance.

The Paschal Creed

- Develop, treasure, protect, and believe in a binding brotherly and sisterly love built on respect, trust, loyalty, confidence, and a common vision.

- Believe in and live by our parents' teachings.

- Believe we could see our dreams become real.

- Believe, if we tried to do the right things, God would show us grace, mercy, guidance, and love.

- Work hard, as if we believed there would be only one chance to reach each of our goals.

- Believe that reaching one's goal with excellence would make the next goal easier to reach.

- Work hard, pray a lot, and save for each next step toward reaching each goal.

- Place service and quality before profit. Live by these values, and the profit will come.

- Be fair, and treat everybody right.

- Never knowingly mistreat, hurt, or cheat anyone.

- Commit to sharing and helping others on the way to helping our families and ourselves.

- Show hatred for no one.

- Create and build success, one day at a time.

- Offer all who worked for us encouragement to improve themselves.

ɹnow deep thanks and appreciation to all who would seek out and patronize our businesses.

We may have started out small, but we lived by our creed. From the depths of our hearts, we prayed to keep our cool and work our way around the bumps and curves in the road. First, getting needed capital was not always easy. Finding, hiring, and training help, especially in the beginning, often posed a problem. Good people who are happy in their jobs are not quick to leave them and bring themselves, their talents and skills, and, sometimes, their families into a completely new situation.

We did not even own a stove in our first little place of business. Robert cooked the food in his home, keeping it warm on an old-fashioned coal bucket. Because neither of us could afford a car then, we relied on taxis to get the food to the restaurant. Besides Robert and me, there were only three other employees. Despite our many other responsibilities, he and I made and served the sandwiches. We were also the dishwashers and janitors. Robert often said, "You know, I think we must have had the first shuttle service and the first drive-in." When the forty seats at the eight tables inside our first little restaurant were filled, people were happy to be handed a fried chicken sandwich through the walk-up window.

As our business grew and news spread that we offered fair treatment and opportunities for training and good pay, males and females began seeking us out for jobs. In fact, one of our best workers ever, Jim Maddox, a man who became a city councilman in Atlanta, simply walked into our restaurant, went into the kitchen, picked up a towel, and announced to Robert, "Mr. Paschal, I need a job." Robert sent Maddox to my office and the future councilman's Paschal tenure began that day. Many others also came, worked successfully, and soared to greater heights. Clarence T. "CT" Martin was another staff member who became a city councilman in Atlanta. Clarence's father was our friend. He worked for us, delivering chicken sandwiches during Paschal's small-scale catering days. When we opened La Carrousel Lounge in 1960, CT was promoted to be its manager. We sent him to school for training in hotel management. From our very small beginnings, our reach soon began extending very far and wide. In 1995, Councilman Martin proudly introduced and led passage of the City of Atlanta ordinance renaming Atlanta's popular Jeptha Street to Paschal Boulevard.

Robert and I tried helping all who came our way, especially those who wanted to learn and could show us that they understood and could practice the

Paschal work ethic. Many of our dedicated supporters also became some of our dearest friends. One family lived in public housing and had lost their father. For years, they had become regular, weekly customers. Every Saturday afternoon, the father brought in his wife and nine-year-old son for the family's weekly fried chicken sandwich. Near the end of that same year, the father died. Christmas was nearing, and the young boy wanted some skates and a bike. About a month before Christmas, we found the kid sitting in front of the restaurant, crying. He said his mother was not going to be able to buy him that bike. Was that mother mad when she discovered what the child had done! She was extremely angry! However, Robert and I told her that we would buy the boy's bicycle—with some obligations. The mother was so happy that she hugged her child and wept uncontrollably.

We told the young boy to come back the next day after school to discuss his bike and his Paschal's job. Sheer happiness shone in his eyes. Robert and I decided to offer him Saturday work until he paid off the cost of his bike. He grew up working for us. He left Atlanta when he was older and became very successful. I had forgotten the episode until he came by to offer his deep appreciation, nearly 39 years later. So many others had given so much of themselves, helping us as much or more than we could have ever helped them.

At first, we were making little profit. However, our friends and customers truly believed that we could—and would—grow. Soon, we had to begin planning our first expansion. More and more people filled those first forty seats. Robert's fried chicken had caught on, consistently garnering praise and larger crowds. We were happy and thankful to God to see the need growing for a larger, more comfortable facility.

Laying the Foundation, Brick by Brick

Paschal's was one of a very few black-owned service businesses in Atlanta at that time. We had been very careful to offer a very good product, one that many people would want and enjoy. Moreover, we had located our restaurant on the fast-growing West Hunter Street. Most importantly, we had kept a promise to ourselves. We held onto our desire to do something big, always with a smile and respectful of others. In addition, we always offered the best service and the best quality possible. We would always be fair, honest, and truthful with ourselves and all we served.

Like the rest of the nation below the Mason-Dixon Line then, Atlanta was not integrated. At the time of our new venture, black folks in Atlanta who sought comfortable cultural identity, food, fun, services, and sophisticated leisure came mostly to Auburn Avenue and West Hunter Street. Like Auburn Avenue, West Hunter was becoming a bustling strip of black-focused activities. Getting saved or filled with fun, whatever your choice, was readily available to you. The area encompassing West Hunter from Northside Drive to just west of Ashby Street, all the way beyond the university collective and over to Lee Street, was alive with action and looking good to us in our dream-making.

We wanted our place to be one that could—and would—speak eloquently to the service needs of our total community. We would offer the best to families and the religious, social, educational, political, tourist, and general populations of the city. We would not turn away anyone, regardless of ethnicity. At many points in time, they came happily through Paschal's doors. Quickly, we became a vital part of Atlanta's bold emergence into the rapidly expanding and history-making cultures and politics of the twentieth century.

Changes were becoming visible, especially along those blocks of West Hunter, which were bordered by E. A. Ware Elementary School and Morris Brown College. One block west of Morris Brown stood the Herndon Home, home of Norris Herndon, founder of Atlanta Life Insurance Company. Many visitors who came to Atlanta to visit Atlanta's attractions made Paschal's a part of their tour. Church memberships soon began finding out, if they needed food and relaxation, Paschal's was available. They were most welcome. Congregations quickly became some of our most loyal, dedicated customers. We often hosted their banquets, receptions, and dinners. Besides Morris Brown College, all the other vibrant, growing schools were in the Atlanta University Center. There were Clark, Spelman, and Morehouse Colleges as well as the graduate school, Atlanta University. Later, the Interdenominational Theological Center joined these schools.

In 1947, my brother and I sought to become welcomed business neighbors and make our little restaurant an exciting partner to the other already established black-owned businesses. Emerging along a considerable part of West Hunter Street at that time were Wilson Realty Company, Inc., Fred Morris Jewelers, Superior Barber Shop, Robie Real Estate, Jones and Leonard Laundry, Deluxe One Hour Cleaners, and Q. V. Williamson's Realty.

The advancing 1950s and 1960s saw other successful black business pioneers respond to the needs of a growing Atlanta, including Lottie Watkins Enterprises, Lucy Jackson's Busy Bee Café, Bronner Brothers Beauty Supply

Company, Frazier's Café, Sellers Brothers Funeral Home, and Don Clendenon's Supper Club. Our hard work and long hours, often fifteen hours per day, were beginning to pay off. Soon, our successes had earned us the right to become known, at first intimately among our neighbors and then nationally, as the "Paschal brothers." We grew to love it.

A West Hunter Street feature was its closeness to the Atlanta University (AU) Center. AU Center students, parents, professors, and even the presidents and staff joined the out-of-town throngs and others in the Atlanta community who began making West Hunter Street the second hallowed quarter for mingling and testifying. Soon, Paschal's became the eating and meeting place. As we progressed and expanded, the AU Center college community became our friends and customers, and they brought their out-of-town guests. We were commended for our quality of service, comfort, cultural leadership, and customer safety. Little known to us at the time, Dr. Ralph David Abernathy later referred to Paschal's as "The Place." During the Civil Rights Movement, he described West Hunter as "probably the most important street in black America." We had not planned it that way. It just happened. Robert and I simply wanted to help support the Movement. As the fight for justice and civil rights grew, our own history moved us into taking a firm stand and commitment to action.

Into this spreading wildfire to win justice and due rights or die trying came a stalwart soldier for justice and freedom, Attorney Donald Lee Hollowell, who opened his law offices on West Hunter Street in the early 1960s.[1] The times were turbulent, and black lives were being threatened and viciously taken. Many blacks were killed trying to earn their freedom. Hollowell came with a sense of knowing, deep convictions, and the will to give of himself and his broad range of legal and social talents. It was as if he could deeply feel the urgent need for strong, daring representation in the growing West Hunter civil liberties matrix. Immediately, he built a team of attorneys who were fearless and knowledgeable about what lay ahead. They came prepared for the frightening, bloody, and often deadly future that was awaiting those who dared join the battle for human dignity. After a few years on West Hunter, Hollowell partnered with Horace Ward, who later became one of the nation's prominent and highly respected judges.

---

1.   Don Hollowell died on December 27, 2004. He was eighty-seven.

In 1960, Hollowell and Ward were summoned to take the lead in earning Atlanta students Charlayne Hunter and Hamilton Holmes, their rightful places as students at the University of Georgia, Georgia's flagship institution of higher education. During that same period, so many other lawyers served in Hollowell's firm and won many battles. Soon, all were found at the top of the list of who's who in the fight to gain freedom and justice for people of color, including Vernon Jordan and Howard Moore. Moore became a nationally recognized attorney. Jordan headed the National Urban League for several years. Later, he became a close friend and confidant to President Bill Clinton. He ultimately gained fame and fortune as a highly respected Washington DC insider and attorney as well as New York financier. Years later, President Bill Clinton and Vice President Al Gore "stopped by Paschal's" more than once.

Those were the mean times in Atlanta and around our nation. Those were the times when black people were barred from entering any of Atlanta's downtown hotels, except through back doors designated for servants. Until the Civil Rights Movement of the 1950s and 1960s, black people had no legal protection to make travel and the needed comforts open to us. In many places, we could not use the restroom, even at service stations where we had just purchased gas. West Hunter Street became our precious testing ground.

It was the era of the Montgomery bus boycott and the Greensboro sit-ins. Growing and increasingly restless, civil rights groups began gathering at Paschal's. All along West Hunter Street, young people were already beginning to behave as if they wanted to be right in the thick of things. AU Center students, many Paschal's regulars, were eager to place themselves into the forthcoming battles. Songs of the Civil Rights Movement, clapping hands, and shouts of "Be with us, Lord" and "We are your children!" could be heard wafting loudly and spiritedly up and down West Hunter Street and all across the nearby AU Center.

It was into this group of wonderful, dedicated, well-wishing group of men and women (and during this historical era) that Robert and I joined the West Hunter Street business partnerships. My brother and I were happily in the midst. Here, we reached milestone after milestone in the forward, progressive movement of Atlanta, the Movement, and the growing influence of Atlanta's minority businesses. Progress was not always easy, but we were feeling we had plenty to be thankful for. Robert's fried chicken had the crowds pouring in. At times, there was standing room only.

12

A New Life

The brown paper bag that held the day's receipts kept getting heavier. Phil carried our sack of money home in her purse each night. Robert and I were beginning to see the blessings from our years of hard struggles. We also knew we had to gratefully, happily expand. Seated, waiting to be seated, or picking up an order at the window, the crowds kept growing.

Robert and I sank everything we had saved into building an improved home for his fried chicken. We worked harder, often helping the builders complete the next chapter of our dreams. We carried buckets of nails to the carpenters. We carried buckets of water to the mortar mixers. We watched together, sometimes with heads bowed in prayerful thanksgiving, as the growing shapes and spaces began emerging.

A larger place meant we would be able to offer dining space to an additional forty people. Praise God, we would have a kitchen with a stove! We could now really serve freshly seasoned, hot, fried chicken right from the frying pan. Paschal's fried chicken sandwiches began taking on a life of their own. Demand grew, and college students began making regular visits. We were fast becoming the most favored place for Sunday afternoon dates.

Hardly a year passed when we felt the need to grow again. Growth was part of our vision. Growth meant we could hire young people who wanted jobs. They were not permanent jobs, but it was work to help them better themselves. Of course, we would hire full-time, staying personnel, but we had to bring in college students who really needed jobs to help them through school. But, we knew this next step would not be easy.

Fulfilling our dreams of building and expanding an even bigger, better, and more comfortable Paschal's Enterprise would take far more capital than our initial $2,500 investment. In the 1930s and 1940s, black folks saving that amount of cash money for anything was like finding the pot of gold at the end of the rainbow. Hoping to borrow money from white lenders was even more of a fleeting dream.

Just trying to get needed loans caused us many sleepless nights. We truly had to study all of the possibilities. Without any thought of failure, Robert and I knew we could do it. Our parents always said, "People like to see you sweat. They may sometimes want you to humble yourself. If that is what it takes, be strong, and press ahead. You will come out on top with God's help every time." Soon, we began having enough money to save for further growth. We were also making lasting friendships and leaving black footprints in the sands of our children's future.

In 1959, we opened Paschal's Restaurant at 837 West Hunter Street, now Martin Luther King Drive, across the street from our first location. Our very first expansion afforded us an opportunity to double our seating space and offer our customers a more relaxing, comfortable place for dining. We had a modern grill and a beautiful dining room. Our reputation for serving good food had spread throughout the community and beyond. Almost immediately, the new restaurant began feeling pinched. Many of the first wave of growing customers were AU Center students. Paschal's became the place where the young men brought their dates for a Sunday afternoon "sweet hour" of courting. Others brought visiting family members. They were always very respectful and well behaved, as if they wanted to make their families very proud of them. Those young people helped to make Paschal's what it ultimately became.

And We Continued Growing

Robert and I now had to get ready to meet the urgent demand for another expansion. We were relatively young men then. I was in my forties; Robert was in his fifties. We both believed that time to fulfill our many dreams was still on our side.

The demand for our chicken sandwiches was growing beyond our wildest dreams. One time, Robert told someone, "When we decided to make fried chicken our specialty, do you know how many chickens I bought the first day? Two. Just two fryers." He had to send out for more birds. We laughed about how we went from buying two chickens a day to twenty then thirty. After we moved, our daily need for chickens shot up to 70 and then 80. Suddenly, other unbelievable events were happening.

One day, we received an order for 5,000 chicken sandwiches for an event at Atlanta's Old Lakewood Park. Five thousand chicken sandwiches? We thought someone was playing a joke. We could not believe it! Once the order was confirmed and we had recovered, we called our staff into action. Once they had also recovered, we shouted for joy and got to work. We fried and fried and fried. We got those sandwiches done, wrapped, and covered so they would stay warm until they arrived at Lakewood. Then, no special heat-saving equipment or wrappings were available, such as now. We loaded the crispy fried birds onto a truck and warned the driver to not break any speed laws, but we told him to get those sandwiches delivered as quickly as possible. The people in attendance were told where the food had been prepared and that it had just been delivered. People called us to say that we had won the hearts and taste buds of all. We had won still more Paschal's customers.

Apparently, they were right because people continued coming. We continued trying to please each customer and serve the freshest, best fried chicken sandwiches anyone had ever tasted. We had special contracts with ice and refrigerator companies. We monitored our food supply strictly for freshness and purity. We let nothing short of quality go forward. God continued smiling on us, and people continued coming and buying. Larger numbers of customers began showing up for lunch, telling us Paschal's was becoming their second home.

More customers began lingering for quite a while after lunch, talking and exchanging thoughts about just about everything, especially the Civil Rights Movement, which was rapidly gaining momentum. We could not possibly know then how those gatherings would grow, expand, and then burst forth into more than fifty years of mighty ideas and actions. Out of those Paschal gatherings would come real political activities and celebrations of many civil rights' milestones. Recently, a friend said:

> One of the things that made you, Robert, and Paschal's so special to all of us was that, even after we had come in, been sitting down, and finally ordered and bought the sandwich and coffee and after we would take just about forever to eat what we had paid for, you all never ran us off. You just let us sit, talk, and build those dreams for a better day. Another thing, after we had talked and talked sitting down inside, we knew it was all right with

you and Robert if we wanted to go outside your restaurant and stand
around and still talk and talk.

Our old friend was right. Those were the days when nearly everyone knew
each other. Paschal's was becoming a friendly, safe meeting place, inside and
outside. About this time, our lunchtime customers began asking almost daily,
"When are you going to start serving us dinner?"

The media began taking note of our stability and promising future. Radio
programs began highlighting "Paschal's food and service." The *Atlanta Daily
World*, Atlanta's oldest black press, was among the first of the media to publi-
cize our early efforts and success. Later, Paschal's was widely noted on the airways and in print, including *The Atlanta Voice, Atlanta Inquirer, Black
Enterprise Magazine, Ebony, Jet, The Atlanta Journal, The Atlanta Tribune, People,* a local publication, and church and club newsletters.

News anchor and radio talk show host, Hal Lamar, whose distinctive voice
was heard on the airways for many years in Atlanta, wrote an article about
Paschal's in 1994. Later, he said, "Mr. James, you and Mr. Robert knew we all
loved you two, and we loved Paschal's, no matter what we said about the
place."

"Breakfast at Paschal's (Personal Reflections)" by Hal Lamar

What is this place which seems to have us in its clutches? Paschal's.

I've broken bread at that place since I was a kid. I had my first date there,
circa 1960, following an elementary school prom. We dined on the fried
chicken that made them famous, early June peas, and salad amid soft lights
that two twelve-year-olds could scarcely appreciate.

Over the years, much of my money and I have parted company at Paschal's.
The name is synonymous to Atlanta. Three years in military service and a
broadcast/print career could not free me from the clutches of the eatery started
by James and Robert Paschal back in the year of our Lord 1947.

In a military mess hall in Vietnam, thousands of miles from Martin Luther
King Jr. Drive (then called Hunter Street), a fellow GI sitting across from me
remarked the fried chicken being served up that evening was pale in comparison to the "chicken I ate at Paschal's when I visited Atlanta one summer."

As a reporter, I learned a long time ago that Paschal's is the place for
scoops. It's an oasis. On any given hour of the day, there is no telling who
might have their feet parked under one of Paschal's tables.

If I need to track down a politician playing duck and dodge, the chances are pretty good I'll find him or her at Paschal's (eventually). For entertainment, Paschal's is tantamount to a Brown Derby in LA or Toots Shoore's in the Big Apple. The late Robert F. Kennedy set up an office in one of the meeting rooms during Dr. Martin Luther King Jr.'s funeral in 1968. King was a frequent diner who frequently dialogued with regulars and visitors in the restaurant's famed front room. Such lively conversations among the knows and don't knows continue even to this day. It is said that starlet Jayne Mansfield once frequented the restaurant. Jesse Jackson dines there when in town, and politicos like Julian Bond, John Lewis, Hosea Williams, and Maynard Jackson launched careers there one day over chicken salad.

Over the last eight years, Concerned Black Clergy has met there every Monday morning. They would attract a lot of newsmakers. I seldom leave Paschal's wanting for a good story or exclusive twist to a current one.

In forty-seven years, the Paschal Brothers restaurant, the La Carrousel Lounge, and hotel, added in the early and late 1960s, respectively, form a lot of word-of-mouth advertising. It's as much an attraction or thing to do in Atlanta as taking in a Braves game, riding the MARTA rail, visiting the King Center, or touring Underground Atlanta.

For regulars like me, it means daily sojourn for the morning meal and conversation with Jake the mechanic, Al the preacher, Henry the lifelong politician, Johnson the dry cleaner, and other assorted characters. We'll size up the new mayor; rip up the old mayor; hug Miss Sherman, Paschal's famous receptionist; tease the waitress about getting a husband, boyfriend, or a bad attitude; or gripe about the bacon that's old, the sausage that's too hot, the hotcakes that got cold too quick, or the coffee that might have been fresh two hours ago.

But after about two hours of that and occupying a booth that we should have long since given up, we reach deep, tip our servers generously, and bid each other the best day of our lives.

In twenty-four hours, we'll see one another again.

Such is life, which would not be complete without breakfast at Paschal's.[1]

When Hal showed up the next day, we thanked him and offered a few editorial jabs. Hal was a fine young man who had gained a reputation for speak-

---

1.   Hal Lamar, "Breakfast at Paschal's (Personal Reflections)" *Atlanta Inquirer*, 1994.

ing his mind. He was not alone in his thinking that we were happily holding him and so many others in our clutches. In a recent chance meeting with my friend, William T. Robie, of West Hunter Street Real Estate, Robie made me laugh aloud when he declared, "James, do you remember how so many of us began having breakfast, lunch, and, soon, dinner at Paschal's that we became known as the Paschal Gang? Oh, yes, we formed the Breakfast at Paschal's Club. Man, I must have spent at least $300 a week at Paschal's!"

We both had to laugh at that figure, though it may not have been too far off.

Encouraged by the enthusiasm of the growing crowds of regular customers, we felt we had to try serving an evening meal. Because we were already experiencing a space pinch, we could not comfortably serve more customers in our present location. We went in search of a new location, and God soon blessed our search.

Behind the restaurant was a small house, which we rented and converted into a dining space. Moreover, the house had a kitchen. Wonderful! We could now offer our specialty, cooked and served fresh out of the pan, right on the premises. One customer said, "We were darn glad more of us could sit down. But others still started to stand around, waiting for you to hurry up, eat your fried chicken, and give up your seat."

That was true. More people had started to find us. By this time, our clientele had also taken a dramatic, controversial turn. Growing numbers of whites who were brave enough to stand up to the times had also begun stopping by Paschal's. They knew they were welcome to come and enjoy good food and excellent service, even though blacks were not allowed to patronize their eating places, neither downtown nor anyplace else in Atlanta.

Regardless of how much money you had in your pockets, during the decades preceding the 1960s, Southern whites behaved as if your dollars were some color other than "money green." Atlanta was no exception. Increasing numbers of whites in and around Atlanta and across this nation soon learned, not only were they welcome to come in and enjoy Paschal's good food, they could also comfortably join the growing, deepening discussions around the political, cultural, and social issues of the day. Many times, those strong enough to brave the resentment and wrath of friends and, often, family said they felt a kind of healthy liberation at Paschal's. Some said they had long carried with them a deep inner sadness about how badly so many whites had treated black people, but they were helpless to act. At last, they felt a joyous relief to be able to get to know people and talk freely.

Bringing Curtis Home

Phyllis and I had been married for about ten years. We wanted children, but we had remained childless. We had only thought about adoption, but events began happening so smoothly and so quickly that we could not believe it. We had close friends who were familiar with the operations of Atlanta's Division of Family and Children Services (DEFACS). The more information we received, the more excited we became. DEFACS official Mrs. Becky O'Neil offered us the kind of professional guidance and consultation that made us feel we were about to be on our way to receiving our firstborn. One day, it happened…the telephone call! We already knew we had successfully passed scrutiny and had been approved. The call meant our baby was almost ready for us. We would visit to determine our fit. Did we want the baby, and did he want us?

On a pleasant fall afternoon in 1959, Phyllis and I hurried over to the agency's appointed place. From the moment we entered the room, our eyes became locked on this angelic-looking, round-faced baby boy. He had big brown eyes, a head full of curly black locks, and a killer smile. Almost instantly, we knew the baby was strong and healthy, and he made sure that we were fully aware that he was all boy. He forcibly moved his body across the room in his stroller by the push/pull of his plump, six-month-old legs. As he glided across the floor, he was grinning. At times, he laughed aloud and clapped his hands. Phyllis and I were certain this little boy would become our special blessing.

Following our initial visit, Phyllis and I had many conversations that were full of questions. Did we really want to take on such an awesome responsibility, particularly at a time when our business ventures were so demanding? Could we be the kind of parents that we knew a young child needed? I would be literally buried in the business. Would it be fair to Phil to make her the prime parent? Were we ready to become the best parents possible to this rip-roaring, robust, beautiful baby?

We could not get this lovely child out of our thoughts. He stayed with us, day and night, and was our constant topic of conversation. We told ourselves we needed this child and he needed us. While it was obvious the real day-to-day caretaking responsibilities would rest primarily on Phil's shoulders, we saw no need to approach our blessing with fear and trembling. She knew (we both knew) I would do everything in my power to be the best father I could possibly be. Our outlook was very bright and very positive. Feeling proud and confident, we moved swiftly ahead through final consultations with family, our minister, and agency officials. The nearer we moved toward finalizing our great dream and decision, the more elated and thankful we became.

A couple of days before Christmas, we brought our beautiful baby boy home. We placed him into a big, circular, wicker basket that we had dressed with blue pillows, blankets, burping towels, and blue ribbons. Relatives, friends, and neighbors poured into our home. One visiting couple literally thought the baby in the wicker basket was a doll. As word spread around our immediate community that he had arrived, the crowds grew larger. We welcomed them all and even listened attentively to all of the advisors on how best to do this and that when caring for a new baby. When my wife called her mother to share our blessing, Mrs. E. began crying, just like the baby we were telling her about. Phil still laughs aloud when talking about that moment. On the eventful naming day, the new arrival to Fountain Drive was named Curtis Alston Paschal. Everybody loved Curtis.

Our little boy angel was showered with everything wonderful. Phyllis invested all of her talents, time, love, hard work, wit, and motherly instincts into providing the very best care for Curtis. As a deeply proud father, I worked to be the best the world has ever known. Very soon, our entire family thought, as they say, the sun rose and set in Curtis Alston Paschal. For me, Curtis was the son I had always yearned for, the son I would pray hard to create an irrevocable father-son bond. While I knew that many of my days were already spoken for, I would forge regular time for my son. I would work unceasingly and untiringly to make each evening, each night before bedtime, and any waking hours I could find to build love, trust, loyalty, and substance into our lives.

By this time, we had already moved from West Hunter Street where we had lived for nine years to Fountain Drive in southwest Atlanta. We knew it would take some time to work with the surveyors, architects, and builders. The Fountain Drive community was a very close-knit neighborhood of so-called black, bourgeois JUNs, or "Just Us Neighbors." As often as we could, Phil and I participated in all the different neighborhood functions, meetings, cleanup campaigns, parties, special celebrations, or everything. With hands held together, we took little Curtis right along.

Mrs. Margaret Davis Bowens was president of our community club. She would go up and down Fountain Drive like a pied piper, making sure the lawns were cut and all the trash was kept out of sight. There was no such thing as not cooperating. If there were certain dates for Christmas decorations to be placed in the community, your decorations were up! If the theme was bells, you hung your bells! Because I worked late, there were times when I was putting up Christmas decorations at night. I think we need some more Mrs. Davis in some of our neighborhoods today.

13

More to Come

Robert and I were able to take a grand step toward completely realizing our big dreams in 1959. Potent growth was rapidly taking shape in the heart of Atlanta's West Side, especially along West Hunter Street. We spent sleepless nights and many days sacrificing, saving, praying, working, and hoping. Our long hours and hard work were really paying off...big. It was wonderful for us to be on our way, to becoming a part of an advancing city. The entire Paschal family and our friends rejoiced. 1947 to 1959 had been tremendously successful. On our own, we had started our first, almost streetside, lunch counter. Through very hard work, we had given life to our first little expansion. Now, we were in serious search of an even broader avenue.

The restaurant had been operating for more than ten years, and our customer numbers had continued growing. Again, we had to look toward expanding. We did not have a choice. Growth was getting uncontrollable. First, if we wanted to reach for the moon, we needed to know two things. Had we had made enough of an impression with our business know-how? Had we built enough trust in the business community among those who could truly help us? We had saved some money, but it was not enough to buy the needed land and build a really fine, more expansive place of business.

We were still working fourteen and fifteen hours a day. At the end of the day, we still had to work late many late nights. We had to think, "How much money would we need? How big could we afford for the place to be? How much would the land cost? How much would our building actually cost? What about design, equipment, overall design, and construction costs?" There were so many questions to be thought through and answers to determine.

Finally, we thought we were ready to approach lenders, architects, and potential builders. We wanted to build a restaurant directly across the street from where we were. We needed to be able to seat many more customers, at least 120. Land across the street was available for purchase. We only needed the money.

We sought the services of Joseph Hardy and Associates first, and our ideas began coming to life. We had also been noticing and doing business with several prominent, growing Atlanta financial corporations. We did not know it then, but they had been watching us as well. Robert and I could never have guessed what partnerships were in the making. We sought out officials of Atlanta Life Insurance Company, Citizens Trust Bank,[1] and, later, Mutual Federal Savings and Loan, all black-owned financial institutions. All would play vital roles in our march toward becoming a more expansive, exciting Paschal's.

We qualified for an improvement loan, which totaled $115,000. This meant we could move to purchase the land we had our sights on, which was selling for $30,000. Atlanta Life Insurance Company was to become our first financial partner. Next, the construction of our restaurant would cost $85,000. Citizen's Trust Company, Atlanta's black bank, financed this loan.

When Atlanta Life Insurance Company agreed to finance us, our loan was believed to be the biggest all-black financial transaction in American history. Mr. W. H. Smith, vice president and chief investment officer of Atlanta Life Insurance Company, was in our corner. Mr. Smith was a very modest, "let us get on with the business at hand" man. A native of Chattanooga, Tennessee, and a graduate of Atlanta University and the Harvard School of Business, he was said to have been one of the most knowledgeable men in America in finance and investments, black or white. By the time we enlarged Paschal's to include our motor hotel, Atlanta Life had lent us more than one million dollars. Citizens Trust Bank also became a vital resource in our continued growth and expansion.

In 1959, at that moment, our time had come. When word got out that Paschal's was ready to build a place across the street from our tight quarters, we were literally flooded with positive and happy reactions. Atlanta's West Side

---

1. Beginning in the 1980s, James Paschal served a fifteen-year term on the bank's board of directors.

was growing. Businesses were prospering because they were meeting the increasing demands for service. Atlanta was beginning to spread its wings.

The 1950s had already begun shaping our thoughts. The turbulent, often frightening decade of the 1960s, was just around the corner. More people were congregating at our restaurant, and there was talk about Paschal's becoming the headquarters for holding discussions, collecting information, and making plans for getting involved in the Movement. We had long since become the favorite neighborhood hangout. The fact that customers began staying around to hold meetings seemed like a natural evolution of things.

In May 1954, the United States Supreme Court had ruled in Brown vs. Board of Education that the doctrine of "separate but equal" was unconstitutional. Interest in what was happening across the country was growing like wildfire at the AU Center. It only made sense that, because of Paschal's proximity to the AU campus, talk about what should, would, could, and must be done soon would become daily topics at our restaurant. Crowds grew bigger, and talk grew more intense. Robert and I marveled at how quickly our plans to expand began taking shape and linking with the times.

We had carefully and meticulously followed each and every detail as progress continued on the building of our new place. We were committed to giving our patrons the best and finest surroundings. Our builders had followed every step to make the dining room beautiful and inviting. The soothing music we piped in for continuous play featured many of America's favorite artists, past and present.

The dining room was divided into three separate parts, which meant we could comfortably accommodate three social, political, or cultural gatherings, undisturbed, at the same time. We took great care to make the place beautiful. Everything had been carefully scrutinized and selected, including wall colorings to the selection of draperies, tables, and chairs. Naturally, we had not overlooked our kitchen. We wanted it to be spacious, modern, and equipped with a modern grill. Music would be piped in so our kitchen employees could enjoy the same comfort and atmosphere as our patrons.

By Christmas 1959, we moved into our new quarters. Without fanfare or formal announcement, we were ready to serve as many as 120 customers. It was a joyous day. Later, in early 1960, we would hold a magnificent opening ceremony.

As soon as our doors opened, throngs of Atlantans and out-of-town visitors welcomed our first official day of business. As business grew, we hired and trained twelve full-time employees. These first twelve ladies received the best training available at that time.

Waitresses at Paschal Brothers in "School"

Waitresses at the new Paschal Brothers Restaurant are learning to put their best foot forward through the distributive education course in customer food service.

This ten-hour course is taught by Mrs. Lula Whatley, coordinator (of) food service training, distributive education, Atlanta and Fulton County. Carver Vocational School was the training location. The course includes such important topics as grooming, standards of cleanliness, personality, posture, special techniques in customer service, and all those things that deal with the essential qualifications, procedures, and techniques that make for courteous, efficient, customer service. Films, illustrative materials, demonstrations, and discussions are included in the training.

A unit certificate is given upon the completion of each ten-hour course, and a specialized diploma is awarded by the Atlanta Board of Education of Distributive Education after completion of 100 hours.

There are four required courses. To complete the remaining sixty hours, selections may be made from [a course] list.[2]

That first day, everyone stayed so busy that they could hardly take rest breaks. By closing time, we knew we would have to hire and train additional help. Robert and I were so tired that we could hardly stand. But we kept on working.

Paschal's was the first black restaurant in Atlanta to hire white waitresses, but we also hired college students from the AU Center first as our additional help. We were often giving them their very first work/study opportunity. We even sat with students to help them organize various work shifts so their work hours would fit their class hours and study schedules. Some students would work while others studied. We encouraged them to alternate, that is, work for two hours and study for one. We never wanted to be guilty of standing in the way of students not graduating because of their work hours.

Parents have often said to us that we made it possible for their child, or children, to finish college. We had even become father figures to their chil-

---

2. "Waitresses at Paschal Brothers in 'School'," *Atlanta Daily World*, 26 January 1960.

dren. Many times, Robert and I counseled students on what showing good, respectful behaviors would mean to them later in life. We told parents we felt obligated to help and their children had made it possible for us to meet our growing need for additional employees without having to go outside of our community to find them. It was wonderful to work with young people who wanted to bring their talents and skills to our growing business. We believed it was our duty to make our contribution in ways that would help increase the numbers of our boys and girls who wanted to become educated citizens, who would become prepared, in much larger ways, to contribute to building a better society.

One Atlanta newspaper wrote that people were "surging forth in swollen numbers, and thousands were soon shuffling through the portals" of our restaurant. Others wrote that people were coming in such numbers that even our newly installed dining room with wider, more roomy floor space would soon be too small to serve them. By the spring of 1960, we had trained and hired thirty-six employees. In all the years of our business, we were never accused of mistreating or underpaying a single employee.

Our new space had already become cramped. From the beginning, it seemed our blessings had flowed forth in such abundance that we always needed more space. We began receiving requests to accommodate local and visiting athletic teams, fraternity and sorority conclaves, delegations to church conferences, and private parties. So many requests had to go unfulfilled, and that fact worried us. Not only did we feel sorrowful and inadequate, but we were losing opportunities to render additional services and increase our profits. However, we were not going to lower our standards. We would never be found guilty of cramming our beloved customers into inadequate spaces. Then, Robert and I were approached with yet another pressing need.

La Carrousel Is Born

Our regular customers and growing numbers of new ones told us they wanted a cocktail before dinner. So, we took another bold step in 1960. We decided we would build a cocktail lounge. Thus, the idea of a nightclub was born. We had already demonstrated to our lenders that we were good credit risks. By December 1960, we were ready to open La Carrousel. The lounge was an immediate success and quickly became synonymous with all of Paschal's. Of course, music must come with a nightclub.

Robert and I were not strangers to music. There were the church choirs, and we had grown up in a home where music, though mostly religious, was a part of our daily lives. There were the gatherings for singing at our home on Sundays after church. We also listened to music on the old, tattered wooden radio that sat on the table in our living room. Then, there was our mother's constant humming of the old, familiar hymns. Early on, we learned to love music. We loved the fact that it truly brings folks together. For centuries, people all over the world have communicated through music.

Music and entertainment quickly became one of the major integrating factors of the times, in Atlanta and across the country. Attendance at La Carrousel took on a life of its own. We began having a larger proportion of white customers than any other black-owned business in Atlanta. The lounge brought together people of all races and classes, often with standing room only capacity. Patrons, black and white, linked arms to swing and sway lovingly to the best in good music. Some of these same people were to become some of the country's key movers and shakers in the Civil Rights Movement. People of different backgrounds and even educational levels converged on La Carrousel where they found common ground for social and civil rights activism.

Increased white clientele provided us another opportunity to give thanks, and we were very thankful. However, we had never thought of ourselves, nor operated as, a "colored only" business. We had always had some white business, even when our small restaurant was across the street, and we never had any trouble. Before we even made our first move, whites often stood outside on the sidewalk and joined in lively, friendly conversation with blacks. My brother and I often said the only law we knew we had ever broken was serving white folks. We never could turn away anyone who came seeking our food and service.

Even though our annually renewed food service permit had "for colored people only" clearly stamped on it, we served all customers. It took a long time for the special "colored only" part of our permit to be removed, allowing Paschal's to operate fully within the law. Later, when we were legally able to seat white patrons, they already knew Paschal's would welcome them. There would have been no interference, certainly not from my brother and me, nor apparently from Atlanta's white police. Paschal's was called as the only black-white safe haven for social mixing in Atlanta. Our proximity to the AU Center also played a major role in the popularity of the lounge, and whites who loved modern jazz had no other place in Atlanta to find it. Soon, their already large numbers mushroomed.

One reason we drew growing numbers of jazz lovers was our name talent. We were able to bring in the best, including Dizzy Gillespie, Ahmad Jamal, Hugh Masakela, Nina Simone, Aretha Franklin, Lou Rawls, Jimmy Smith, Paul Mitchell, Cannonball Adderly, the Billy Mitchell Trio, Horace Silver, the Ramsey Lewis Trio, Roy Hamilton, Wynton Kelly and his Trio, the Murdock Jazz Quintet, and all others who would make Paschal's of Atlanta the jazz gathering of the South. Joe Williams and Harry Belafonte also stopped by. Ramsey Lewis became known as the first Paschal regular. When he was in town, he played no other club. La Carrousel became known as Atlanta's Jazz Mecca. Other musicians who became regulars at Paschal's included Jean Carnes and the great Curtis Mayfield.

People often asked us how we decided to emphasize jazz. During the planning stages, we had decided that, like the restaurant, La Carrousel needed to have a specialty. When we completed the lounge, the nation was in the middle of a folk, jazz, and rock-and-roll era. We decided on jazz and then recruited the very best artists available.

However, we did not forget those kids who were on their way up and some who were truly struggling. We showcased all who came to us and needed a break, long before they became famous. Sam Eckstein, our public relations man at the time, enjoyed talking about new, young talent, like Ramsey Lewis. He said, "Ramsey called the Paschal brothers his Atlanta daddies and Paschal's his Atlanta home." La Carrousel became a haven for both the jazz greats and their following. As its reputation grew, so did the number of celebrities.

With a seating capacity of 125, La Carrousel became so popular that movie stars, sports figures, and other artists in town for appearances frequently stopped by. Some stopped by to see and meet the Paschal brothers, just see Paschal's, or taste Robert's now-famous fried chicken. Boxing champ Muhammad Ali was an occasional visitor. Until we sold the site to Clark Atlanta University in 1995, he stopped by whenever he was in the city.

Former Chicago Bears football star Gayle Sayers always stopped by. One night, Sayers and his teammate, running back Brian Piccolo, spent several fun-filled hours at La Carrousel. Piccolo's early death from cancer was later the subject of a television movie. To me, he seemed to feel right at home during his visits. Jayne Mansfield was also among our most prominent guests.

We had received a report that she had arrived by taxi. Miss Mansfield was staying at a downtown hotel. When she demanded to stop by Paschal's, the car owned by her public relations man would not start. Exercising her widely known reputation for aggressive independence, she said to him, "Get a taxi.

We are going to Paschal's." Miss Mansfield was gracious beyond belief. She even wanted to see Robert doing his thing with those chickens. By this time, La Carrousel was enjoying a fast-growing reputation for being one of the leading nightclubs for "Le Jazz Extraordinaire." Miss Mansfield stayed on and enjoyed La Carrousel until nearly closing time at 2:00 AM.

Even in later years, into the late 1970s, La Carrousel was holding its own and still called "Atlanta's home of modern jazz, long known throughout the United States for featuring well-known entertainers in the jazz field."[3] Sometimes, I wish I had kept a list of all the celebrities who honored us with their presence. We always tried making every one of them feel they and we were glad they had visited Atlanta.

This feeling of welcome home for everyone quickly became visible and alive in the person of Mrs. Ora Belle Sherman, hostess at Paschal's since the opening of La Carrousel. Always dressed and made up to perfection, she was a true jewel. Everyone who came to Paschal's grew to know and love "Miss Sherman." In her sweet, soft-spoken, and almost intimate approach to all, Mrs. Sherman helped to seal the Paschal effect. She remembered everyone, and everyone remembered her. She loved to recall how twenty-seven ambassadors to the United Nations had been advised to stop by Paschal's while in Atlanta and Ralph Bunche was in that number. Mrs. Sherman says she was "blessed to meet thirty-three of the world's richest men," who had convened upstairs one evening before coming downstairs to enjoy jazz at La Carrousel. She said she "gushed and almost fainted" the first time Dizzy Gillespie hugged her.

She called everyone baby or sweetheart and could often be heard happily proclaiming, "Oh-h-h, everybody just loves to come to Paschal's." She never let us forget about the time the segregationist Governor Marvin Griffin visited Paschal's. It was said, when he was seen leaving and was asked by one of his colleagues what business he had at Paschal's, an integrated place, he supposedly replied he was on a "fact-finding mission." Mrs. Sherman gushed, "Yeah! I'll bet he was. He knows this is where all the right people gather. He is looking for votes. But, I think, in the wrong place." Mrs. Sherman worked for us for nearly forty years, from early 1959 to 1995. She remembered the names of all the celebrities who had stopped by. She continued working at Paschal's for Clark Atlanta University, until the college closed the restaurant in 2002.

---

3.   "Around Atlanta Visitor/Newcomer Guide" (March 1977).

Not only did La Carrousel play a social role, it played a political role as well. Many times, after the end of demanding planning sessions around civil rights issues, patrons moved from a conference room or hotel room to the lounge. Often, the sessions resumed. La Carrousel's fame and reputation soon became an independent, but symbiotic, arm of Paschal's.

> Paschal's La Carrousel, reputed to be the most beautiful lounge of its type in the Southeast, is a decorator's dream. It is a symphony of tasteful color from the entrance to its outer walls. Since opening, La Carrousel has steadily gained popularity locally as the meeting place of friends, civil rights activists, politicians, and would-be politicians. In addition, the La Carrousel Lounge has attracted a large number of out-of-towners (including all of the top name entertainers), many of Atlanta's foreign visitors, and scholars from America's leading universities and those abroad. Thus, the lounge has come to have a distinct "cosmopolitan" or "international atmosphere." Truly, it is a place where both East and West have met. No color line is drawn, and no racial distinction is made. The Paschal Brothers have spared no effort or expense in making the service of the La Carrousel the finest available. The waiters and waitresses who attend you are neatly and tastefully attired and well-trained. La Carrousel enables persons of modest income to enjoy the best Atlanta has to offer.[4]

---

4. *Atlanta Inquirer*, June 1961.

14

Trying Times

I remember the later lives of so many college students. They were really just growing up when I first met them. Several became fervent civil rights activists and famous politicians, including Martin Luther King Jr., Julian Bond, John Lewis, and Maynard Jackson. Both Julian Bond and John Lewis, as young activists, also worked with the Student Nonviolent Coordinating Committee, headquartered just down the block from Paschal's.

When I first met Martin Luther King Jr., he was a student at Morehouse College and a guest in our restaurant. I was very impressed with the way he behaved. Though some of his schoolmates described him as "one who sometimes moved rather slowly and appeared to be somewhat easygoing," I noticed he was more deliberate than slow. Even then, his fellow students listened to him. There was something about the way he expressed himself, the way he thought, the things he said, and the way he said them. Sometimes, it was deliberate. Sometimes, it was with fire in his voice. He could hold his listeners' attention. What he said always seemed to stick with you. The civil rights activities of that time had begun growing in number and fervor, and they only added to Martin's growing popularity and following. Robert and I could see something special in him early in his college life. I remember one conversation I had with Daddy King, Martin's father, the Reverend Martin Luther King Sr.

Daddy King's pride in all of his children always came shining through whenever we had time to talk. This particular day, as he enjoyed his regular fried chicken and potato salad lunch, I shared my personal pleasure in seeing the growing and visionary leadership with him, which Martin Jr. was giving to the emerging life and fervor of the Civil Rights Movement. A man of God

and a proud man of great stature, Daddy King was never one to show any sign
of doubt or fear. If he was worried about Martin's safety, he held back, especially during the early days of the Movement. He was proud of Martin and
confident his work would bear tremendous, lasting fruit. He said, "I ask God,
every day, to just watch over him."

When Martin was assassinated on April 4, 1968, Daddy King's faith in
God and his own personal strength also shone through. "I must try to be
strong," he said. "The devil is testing me and all of us, and my family needs
me. The people need me." Nevertheless, deep, desperate hurt stayed fixed on
his face, in his eyes. He would feel Martin's loss and then that of his other son,
AD, in 1969. He would later feel the loss of his beloved wife, Alberta. Her life
was snuffed out on a Sunday morning in June 1974 while she was seated at the
piano in Ebenezer Church. Daddy King always thanked us for "Paschal's place
in all of this. We, all of us, are in your debt, forever." He never listened to my
objections that we were only doing our part. As we spoke about the last time
Robert and I had seen Martin alive, I had to fight back my tears.

Martin Luther King Jr. truly dreamed of the world he pleaded for in his "I
Have a Dream" speech delivered during the 1963 March on Washington. The
last time the team gathered for one of many strategy sessions at Paschal's,
King was calling for all people—blacks, whites, Hispanics, Asian Americans,
low-income people, Native Americans, country people, and city people—to
share in his dream. Martin believed, if you were truly American, you should be
a friend, believer, partner, helpmate, supporter, and defender of every other
American. He hoped America would reach a state where race would not matter. Many times, he and his partners in the battle were caught up in the very
center of the struggle.

Robert and I were pledged and committed to offer Paschal's as a place of
comfort and sanctuary. So, as the student gatherings began increasing in size,
Robert and I had already made some key decisions. We just wanted to share
our blessings. We had no idea how historic and important our decisions would
become.

By 1960, our restaurant and the La Carrousel Lounge had already become
the favorite unofficial gathering and meeting place of the neighborhood. Folks
from in town, out of town, and even from other countries had started swelling
our numbers.

By design, Robert and I made every effort to continue to ensure all who
came in good faith would see Paschal's as a place for building and nourishing
dreams for a better America. We knew, if their minds would dream in peace

and with faith, their bellies needed food to help them keep those dreams alive, sensible, and possible. Before long, Paschal's had become the unofficial headquarters of the Civil Rights Movement in Atlanta. Robert and I felt it was right to do whatever we could, to give what we could to support our people and help make the country a better place for all Americans. God had brought us so far and delivered us so completely from our lowly beginnings. We never even questioned if or how we would help. In fact, we felt very deeply that our blessings—our thousands of customers and our ability to serve the community—mandated a calling, an obligation, which we absolutely believed we could not ignore.

Paschal's just seemed to be the natural place for convening representatives of those students. Many were among our first customers. During the student sit-ins, demonstrators began seeing Paschal's as their home base. Student demonstrators gathered at Paschal's. They sang the ever-growing familiar songs of the Movement. They sang old, familiar hymns. They prayed. Hosea Williams, Ralph David Abernathy, Andy Young, Julian Bond, and other civil rights leaders taught, reviewed, and told "how to maintain our dignity, how to protect your bodies from deadly harm, and how to march and sit-in." They headed to the fields of battle. After engaging in the selected action, they returned "home" to Paschal's to eat, review, assess the actions taken, and, often, sleep. Years later, Jondelle Johnson, the longtime executive director of the Atlanta branch of the National Association for the Advancement of Colored People (NAACP), said, "Much of the course of civil rights history was orchestrated right there at Paschal's because the Paschal brothers promoted an atmosphere where we could talk and work things out. We knew we could meet and plan in complete and secured privacy. A lot of people would not have wanted you sitting somewhere after you drank your coffee and ate your sandwich. But the Paschal brothers did not bother you. Their hospitality and warmth, as much as their cooking, was a key factor as the center of social activity."

The Honorable Carolyn Long Banks, a former member of the Atlanta City Council, made a statement about this particular period of time that was a part of the program at "An Evening Honoring Robert and James Paschal":

> We, the students of the 1960s student movement, will be ever grateful to the Paschals. They gave us food for our bellies, sustenance for our spiritual souls, and bail for our bonds.

Mrs. Banks, a former Clark College student, had been very active in the student sit-ins. She was among the many students that Robert and I bailed out of jail, brought to our restaurant, and fed. Sometimes, there were so many that we had to seat them in shifts, but that was just fine with us because Paschal's had become the place where students and demonstrators could look to as a refuge. Mrs. Banks' sister, Mrs. Wylma Long Blanding, a retired Atlanta Public Schools principal, was a Paschal's employee while she attended Clark College.

We kept the restaurant opened all night when those young people sat in at the white folks' lunch counters and were refused service. Julian Bond, Lonnie King, and Ben Brown were there. Many civil rights veterans planned strategy and shared ideas, often right at the table where they were dining. The Selma march had its beginning at Paschal's and its ending on Bloody Sunday, March 7, 1965, on the Edmund Pettus Bridge. Paschal's was also the place where frightened, anxious parents knew they could come to pick up their children after they had been released from jail. People asked us, "Aren't you afraid the police will raid your place, or the Ku Klux Klan will start marching?" Yes, we were. Throughout the 1960s, as the battle heated up, we felt a sense of unease many times. There were several touchy situations and many nasty, threatening telephone calls. Oh, they said all kinds of ugly things. However, they were never brave enough to show their faces. We felt that some of the threats were connected with the fact that sixty-five to seventy percent of our clientele was white, even though our business license was stamped "colored only." Paschal's turned away no one.

Prying Open Immovable Doors

During the frightening 1960s and 1970s, we did not know what would happen. We just knew we had to help. Planning meetings always started with a prayer and the singing of a "freedom" song. Robert and I joined in, although neither of us had a voice for singing. We just wanted to be a part of helping to break the chains binding us all. As they left to literally place their bodies on the line in the battle for all of our civil rights, we told them, "As long as you keep marching, sitting in, and banging on doors, we promise you, when you come in good faith, Paschal's will always receive you in good faith. You have our prayers and our support."

Many of those young black people who marched and demonstrated, who were beaten and spat upon, who were knocked down by high-pressure water hoses and attacked by snarling, vicious dogs, who were jailed and sat in, unwanted, at lunch counters and other public places, made good. They became ambassadors, educators, mayors, councilpersons, legislators, congresspersons, businesspersons, and heads of organizations.

Members of our own staff were often among marchers and demonstrators. Robert and I had fulfilled our promise to provide jobs for as many college students as we could afford. It was only right that we bail out of jail as many as our money would allow. In addition to food (and before we built the hotel), the demonstrators knew Paschal's would also be a safe place at which to rest. Many times, the bailed-out marchers sat bent over chairs. Their heads rested on a table, or their tired bodies dropped in heaps on the carpeted floor in various corners of the restaurant. Each soldier who made it back safely to Paschal's received a hero's welcome, free chicken sandwiches and soft drinks. We considered the sharing of our wealth a blessing from God.

As Martin Luther King Jr. began seeing the growing unrest and hearing the swelling tides of hatred that were becoming rampant in the late 1950s and early 1960s, he had to respond to the passionate cries for his leadership. He came directly to us and asked if he could bring his team members and guests to Paschal's to eat, meet, rest, plan, and strategize. How could we refuse? We had the resources and the place. We believed we had been called to be a part of the Movement.

Many of these groups were just organizing. Some were organized at Paschal's or found their way there for meetings or conferences or to feast on Robert's fried chicken. Some called Paschal's either their first or second home, including the Southern Christian Leadership Conference (SCLC), the Student Nonviolent Coordinating Committee (SNCC), and the Congress of Racial Equality (CORE). CORE's representatives had come to Atlanta and Paschal's in connection with the Freedom Rides. In addition, the students of the Atlanta student sit-ins came.

Many of these groups had little or no money. Robert and I had decided we could help by organizing or sponsoring a luncheon or dinner or providing a hotel room or meeting room. Those who could pay did so. Our books still hold some of the debts of those who could not pay. For all who were authentic and truly in need, we never said no.

In early 1962, we set aside a meeting room for Martin and his team to lay fundamental groundwork and plan. Some of the work for the 1963 March on

Washington took place at Paschal's. After that march, hundreds of people converged on Atlanta. So many of them gathered at Paschal's. The same was true when the 1964 Civil Rights Act was passed.

Daddy King, Ambassador Andrew Young, Hosea Williams, Dr. Ralph David Abernathy, Congressman John Lewis, Julian Bond, the Reverend Fred Shuttlesworth, the Reverend Joseph Lowery, Attorney Vernon Jordan, and Attorney Donald Lee Hollowell were some of Martin's key team members and strategists. So many stalwart leaders came to Paschal's from across the country to be involved in Martin's work, including Reverend James Bevel, Reverend C. T. Vivian, and Attorney Thurgood Marshall. On Sundays, many would bring their families to lunch or dinner. Paschal's was blessed to be the site of planning and strategizing for so many significant events of the Movement. Strategy for the 1965 March from Selma to Montgomery had been developed in a designated meeting room at Paschal's, as was the 1968 Poor People's Campaign.

As expected, there were a number of threatening calls and ugly acts. One night, some Ku Klux Klan nightriders were seen driving slowly by on Hunter Street. Martin, Robert, and I later laughed. With that large crowd of coloreds and whites on our premises, they probably thought, "Drive on. Too many niggers and 'nigger-lovin' white folks there tonight." Well, we knew, any night they chose to drive or stop by Paschal's, they would see lots of coloreds and whites, trying to work together for a better world. We thought it was sad. They could not see or dream of a world where all of our lives would greatly improve if all people in the world lived in love and respect for each other.

Building More Worthy Spaces

La Carrousel had operated successfully for nearly five years. The lounge had shown profit margins far beyond our dreams. However, customers were clamoring for more space. Could we deliver? We truly believed, as God had shepherded us this far, he certainly would not leave us now. We knew we had to move forward, but we needed more money than we could possibly have gathered together on our own.

All around us, we could see how our hard work and perseverance had already paid off at La Carrousel. The lounge had brought us so much joy, satisfaction, and profit. So, we moved ahead with plans to add a hotel.

When Atlanta Life agreed to provide major financing and Citizens Trust Bank agreed to become a corresponding financial partner, all of Atlanta said we had pulled off a historical coup. Atlanta Life became our permanent financier. Citizens Trust Company Bank provided the financing for construction. Phew! We were off and running. This funding was "believed to be the biggest Negro-financed transaction ever."[1] Our loan was definitely the largest, single commercial loan in the history of both Atlanta Life Insurance Company and Citizens Trust. Robert and I felt proud, but very humble and blessed by God.

We often traced our steps and progress. Each year had given us a blessed chapter and story. Sometimes, we would even draw a crude picture of a stepladder in front of us to help us see, once again, how the Lord had brought us so far. We would repeat this scene many times. We were sometimes tired and weary, but were always thankful, humble, and gleefully happy.

Every time Mr. Norris B. Herndon, president of Atlanta Life Insurance Company, stopped by Paschal's, he said, "The two of you just keep on building and serving. When you are about doing something, as you two brothers are, I am with you, every step of the way. You two are on your way to great prosperity." Robert and I held his words in our hearts as inspiration. To us, his life and that of his father's were patterns worthy of following.

On Tuesday, August 3, 1965, our proud families joined with staff, city officials, and well-wishers in formal groundbreaking ceremonies for our new Paschal's Motor Hotel. The entire time, our goal had been to build a combination restaurant/lounge and, ultimately, a luxurious hotel. We wanted to be able to take care of all of our customers' needs—food, drink, fun, and sleep—around the clock, in the same roomy, luxurious place.

We almost had to hold back the tears (our families and friends as well) as Ivan Allen Jr., Atlanta's mayor, linked hands with Robert and me on the shovel's handle. As we lifted high the first silver-plated shovel full of soil from the earth, the beats of my heart quickened. To make it all truly official, the three of us twice unearthed a scoop of dirt from our three-acre tract of land. Mayor Allen said our "historic shovel would be put on display with twenty-nine other shovels, symbolic of more than $29 million worth of new construction" then underway in the city. Allen, who often either sent or brought distinguished visitors to Atlanta to Paschal's, promised his continuing support. He religiously kept his promise.

---

1. *Atlanta Inquirer*, Vol. 7, No. 5, 4 February 1967.

The Atlanta press, black and white, carried the news of our most daring business venture. Many people referred to this new groundbreaking as another milestone in the progress of Atlanta and its Negro businesses. Construction plans called for a seventy-two-room, five-story motel with a pool. We set our opening date for less than two years away.

Mayor Allen publicly praised us for stepping out into what he called "no small venture." He said he was proud and that we should be proud. We were taking another brave, bold step in providing housing and entertainment for those who will enjoy this "place of rest and relaxation in a growing city." Allen further praised the kind of "Negro leadership" that had aided and abetted the development of our planned business. He had already quietly proven that he was truly ready to see Atlanta move ahead toward progress in race relations.

In 1963, Mayor Allen took a great personal and political risk when he testified in favor of President Kennedy's Public Accommodations Bill, part of the 1964 Civil Rights Act. When Martin Luther King Jr. was assassinated in Memphis, Allen rushed to the King home to comfort Martin's widow, Coretta Scott King. It was a rainy night in Atlanta. Holding an umbrella to shield her from the rain, the mayor gently guided Mrs. King into the Atlanta airport. Few, if any, ever questioned the depth of his sincerity again in helping to make Atlanta truly the "city too busy to hate."

Blacks who were involved or just watching Georgia politics shouted with joy when Allen defeated the well-known "Battle-axe" Lester Maddox to become mayor of Atlanta in 1961. Maddox had chased black people away from his restaurant, The Pickrick, by swinging axe handles, daring black people to enter. On the day Dr. King's funeral was held in Atlanta, Maddox, then governor, raised the state's flag back to full-staff, which had been lowered to half-staff in King's honor. We later learned Maddox had surrounded himself with his sympathizers and Georgia state troopers when he performed this act.

We planned for our building to remain exactly where it was. We were located near the AU Center, and we were in close proximity to the fast-growing, developing middle- and upper-income section of southwest Atlanta. West Hunter, Mitchell, and Jeptha Streets would border our complex. We would also be very close to downtown, growing West Side businesses, and other professional and recreational facilities.

We promised to make everything ultramodern. The rooms would vary in size and have balconies. There would be connecting suites with portable bars and a swimming pool with sundecks. We would feature a spacious banquet room decorated in beautiful colors, which could accommodate up to 350 people. The dining room would have disappearing partitions for those desiring privacy. Robert and I wanted the entire facility to be suitable for any business, cultural, religious, or recreational interests and needs, present or future.

As we moved toward erecting our grandest dream, I asked myself, "What would the very best white-only hotel look like?" I wanted to offer our people all of the beauty, luxury, and services we could afford. We would train our people and require every single Paschal staffer always be on his or her very best behavior in every department, in every job. We wanted every person associated with and working for Paschal's to be every bit a proud part of our dream, as proud as the Paschal brothers.

We worked hard and very carefully with our architectural design firm, Millkey and Associates, and our construction contractors, Eller and Heyward. Little did we know (nor could we have ever guessed), the building of the hotel would make Paschal's synonymous with and a model for the place to see and be seen and heard in Atlanta. Paschal's had truly become the place where politicians and the famous gathered, blacks and whites developed lasting friendships, and you could get help if you needed it. Lovers have told us that Paschal's was where they had found each other.

Construction began in 1965, and the 120-room hotel was completed in 1967. So much public fanfare heralded this major development that Robert and I could hardly hold our peace.

$1,000,000 Paschal Motor Hotel Opens Ribbon-Cutting Ceremonies, Tuesday, February 7
Mayor Allen to Officially Open Doors at 5:30 PM

…the fantabulous Paschal Brothers Motor Hotel, 830 Hunter Street, S.W.

This magnificent structure, modern in every detail, houses 120 luxuriously carpeted, individually climate-controlled, exquisitely furnished guest rooms. The rooms, from the $75 a day three-room executive suite to the very reasonably priced single, hold the distinction of being larger than any other hotel or motel rooms in the city of comparable price.

Each room is lit by beautiful designer lamps that sit either on marble-topped desks (executive and studio suites) or wood-grained desks and tables (double and single rooms). Each contains a full-sized bath with bathtub and shower.

To meet the listening and viewing needs of guests, each room is equipped with a combination radio/television, which, when combined with the bedside telephone, puts civilization never more than an arm's length away.

With the construction of this magnificent, much-needed multistory building for the accommodation of travelers, the Paschal brothers have emphatically stated their confidence in the future growth of this area of Atlanta and the growth of the total city.

The construction of this magnificent facility and all of the long years of toil that contributed to raising it signals, as much as or more than any other single project in Atlanta, the continuing successful efforts of members of America's largest racial minority to enter into the mainstream of this country's economic life.[2]

The article described every detail of the new hotel, indicating how we had spared "no pain" to assure all of our guests would be as comfortable and their stay as pleasant, as was humanly and technologically possible. The lobby, according to the newspaper article, was "an area so constructed as to permit the simultaneous accommodation of groups numbering from ten to five hundred." We took great care to ensure we could happily offer ample space to conventions, club affairs, families, churches, and others for meetings, food service, and relaxation.

By March 1967, Robert and I had officially welcomed our first hotel manager, Purvis Easley. Mr. Easley was from Williamsburg, South Carolina, a former chief warrant officer of the United States Army, and a graduate of Morehouse College with a degree in history. Easley immediately set about guiding the training and hiring of additional help, bringing a measure of personal excitement and dedication to his position with him.

Purvis, Robert, and I were happy to talk freely about our plans for the weeks and months ahead. We had complete confidence in the future of our new hotel. The city of Atlanta was growing, and our deeply positive feelings about its future did not need to be kept secret. It was time to speak loudly and clearly. The Paschal brothers had come with a clearly focused vision of where we wanted to go. Moreover, with us, we wanted to take along all who were willing and ready to share in what Robert and I believed had proven to be an unbeatable investment.

---

2. *Atlanta Daily World*, 5 February 1967.

Freedom's Chapters Continued

The Civil Rights Movement had pushed and battled its way into full momentum and was rumbling into the South with unstoppable fervor. Times were heating up. More people were coming to Atlanta. You could see the fires of determination and the desire for justice in the eyes of so many. We could not wait for perfect to come to us. We were ready to plan, create, develop, deliver, manage, and hold on to anything and all things, great or small, which could be called even possible perfection. Thanks be to God, Robert and I were blessed to be in the center ring.

Our doors would be open, our facilities would be swinging, and our staff would be trained to be as receptive and supportive as possible. Increasing staff size was also a must, but that did not mean Robert and I would—or could rest—on our laurels, even if we had wanted to.

Humbly, we had already begun watching the plaques and awards roll in. However, collecting awards was never our reason for being. By the time Robert left us in 1997, we had been blessed to have enough honors and awards to fill rooms bestowed upon us. All of the visible, tangible milestones of success simply meant we would work even harder than we had worked when we served our first menu of sandwiches and sodas in Atlanta more than fifty years ago. Things were changing, and we had to stay right in step with that change.

A larger share of the hotel business began coming our way. The Paschal brothers were a visible force in tourism and hospitality in Atlanta, Georgia, and around the country. Black folks wanted to enjoy luxurious surroundings in comfort and relaxation. Paschal's was where they were wanted and welcomed. Most white folks who checked in (and there were some) seemed to really have wanted to enjoy those same surroundings. Also, we saw that many of those whites who came to Paschal's wanted to stay where they could build new relationships and benefit from varied kinds of social, political, and cultural interactions with black folks.

We predicted, as soon as we became fully operational, we would have about 115 people in our employ, with a weekly payroll of more than $8,500. It was so fulfilling. In 1967, we were providing jobs, adding to Atlanta's growth, and investing in the changing of America.

> Atlanta and the nation are far richer today than they would have been if James and Robert Paschal had decided to favor Thomson, Georgia, rather

than Atlanta with their presence, creativity, brilliance, and dedication to service.[3]

When we completed the building of the hotel, we were in a grand position to offer additional services and support to the Civil Rights Movement. By this time, I suppose I can say we had become veterans. I can truthfully say there were times when our nerves were frayed, when we were just plain scared. We received calls from white men who objected loudly and with threats when I hired our first white waitress. One call stands out in my mind. It was late at night, just before we were preparing to close La Carrousel and the restaurant. The caller said, "Can't you find enough nigger waitresses to serve over there?" That waitress was Miss Susan Beatty from Ohio. She worked out well and fit right in. She was dependable and a loyal worker for more than ten years.

At times, we felt we were fighting two battles. We were waging a fight against hatred and racism on one front. On another, we were fighting to remain focused. We served a God who was giving us the muster and everything else we needed to stay in the brutal battle. We had to fight on. But not all of our fright was generated by white men.

Robert and I were determined to keep our entire complex operating on a very high level. Quite a few times, we nearly had to butt heads with some not-so-understanding men. There were the bugs, or men who felt, if my brother and I were rolling out welcome mats for everyone else, they had just as much right to be given room at the inn. Honestly, they saw Paschal's as a location for writing their numbers. In their thinking, we had the people, and they could come into our place and offer the people a service. Back in those days, playing the numbers was really big business. Some of the numbers men got upset with us. Some even tried to force themselves a place at Paschal's. Several times, I simply had to ask them to leave. I then threatened to call the police. We soon began receiving rather scary telephone calls, but we stood our ground.

Then there were the Black Muslims. They saw themselves as providing a service that met a spiritual, historical need of the growing crowds, especially blacks who continued to gather at our hotel, lounge, restaurant, or just outside on the street around Paschal's. While the work of the Muslims may certainly have had a huge role to play for those who wanted to follow their teachings,

---

3. *Atlanta Daily World*, 5 February 1967.

Paschal's civil rights efforts were specifically focused. Our aim was to join in with those persons directly involved in the Movement headed by Martin Luther King Jr. and his team.

Paschal's philosophy and work was with those who saw—and still see—the integration of American society with all of its diversity as America's saving grace. One Saturday morning, H. Rap Brown was with the group. They came right into our restaurant. Without permission, they began taking pictures of me talking with several white people. They resented the idea that we were serving white people. It was almost like being in a bottle! One time, the Black Muslims, led by a young man who said his name was Frank, crashed a meeting of the Atlanta Medical Association. I had to handle the situation calmly as I nudged the uninvited guests to leave the premises.

Paschal's was not about helping SNCC, the Black Muslims, or any other organization to advance their agendas. We were solely dedicated to advancing those topics and actions that sought to bring together all of the world's people in peace. So, Robert and I remained resolute and stayed our course. We wanted a facility in which everyone who wanted to come could feel free, safe, and comfortable. We wanted to be open to the introduction of a mix of ideas and possible resolutions.

Not long afterward, we were able to begin housing, feeding, and offering stylish recreation for our guests. Many began calling our place "Paschal's Precinct" and "Atlanta's Safest Black and White Gathering Place." The marchers continued coming as well, sometimes by the busloads. If they did not have any money, we never turned them away. If the SCLC, Martin, Andy, Hosea, Ralph, or John Lewis said those who came were okay, we welcomed them. Robert and I could only say, again, as we had done many times before, "Thank you, Lord."

Some have felt that our highly successful venture had been maintained due to our determination to build and hold onto our integrated patronage. White clientele at the hotel and restaurant remained more than thirty-five percent. White patronage at the La Carrousel kept averaging sixty-five percent. It was as if we were operating in unfamiliar places in the world, but we had come to feel quite comfortable there.

"Paschal's hotel and restaurant have become nationally known. For anyone visiting Atlanta, a stop at Paschal's is a *must*. The 120-room hotel is said to be among the finest in the nation and certainly among the top hotels owned and operated by blacks anywhere in the world."[4]

Recently, Reverend Timothy McDonald, who had served for some time as program chairman of Concerned Black Clergy, said after one of their breakfast meetings, "Mr. James, you know Paschal's was the official, 'Unofficial City Hall of Atlanta' for twenty-five years." We both laughed, but it felt true. So many of the leaders of the day as well as the protesters, freedom riders, and picketers of all races were with us.

The 1965 Selma to Montgomery march, at which so many brave people were beaten bloody by Alabama state troopers on the Edmund Pettus Bridge, started on their way from Paschal's. "A lot of our key decisions were made over fried chicken at the restaurant, and that decision to march was one of them," said Congressman John Lewis. "We drove right from Paschal's to Selma." In fact, the last time Lewis saw Martin alive was at Paschal's. During this same period, when Martin and his team came to Paschal's, he always kept that easygoing, almost prayerful attitude I had seen in him the first time he came into Paschal's as a Morehouse student. I believe it was late March 1968 when he presided over a Poor People's Campaign meeting in our Matador Room with black, white, and Hispanic leaders. That was the last time Robert and I saw Martin alive.

The night of Dr. King's death, hundreds of people quickly converged on Paschal's. Among the throngs were several local ministers who were trying very hard to quell the rising unrest among the growing crowd. Word kept coming back that fires were being set. Ambulances were racing through the streets of Atlanta. An American flag, draped across the front of Paschal's, was snatched down and thrown into the street. Hundreds of people were inside. Hundreds more were pushing against the doors, trying to get in. For everyone's safety, we decided we had to close our doors.

Attorney General Robert Kennedy set up his headquarters at Paschal's, as did United Nations Official, Dr. Ralph Bunche. Stokely Carmichael and H. Rap Brown were also in the house. Those were trying times.

---

4.   *Atlanta Daily World*, 1968.

15

Adventures

Robert often laughed and asked, "Is this big enough for you?" He was talking about how, back in the old, dreary Thomson days, we talked about wanting to live long enough to "do something big." We did. It took years of hard work, prayer, and sacrifice, but we did.

At Hartsfield International Airport, when Maynard Holbrook Jackson was mayor of Atlanta, my brother and I became truly introduced to and initiated into the inner domain of corporate business. In 1969, I had been elected to the board of directors of the Atlanta chapter of the Georgia Restaurant Association. However, nearly ten years later, when Maynard was mayor, Robert and I experienced a crucial breakthrough into the real world of black-white finances. We were fortunate to get to know Maynard long before he was elected vice mayor and then mayor.

Maynard had recently been reelected to a second term. This particular morning, he called me at my office. I could feel the fervor in his booming voice immediately after I answered.

"Mr. James, how are you today? May I stop by for a few minutes? I need to have an urgent conference with you!"

By this time, the world knew Mayor Jackson was literally turning the business world upside down with his mandates for black-white joint venturing and fair play for blacks with all who sought contracts at Atlanta's airport. Under Mayor Jackson, sharing in the City of Atlanta contracts took on added color—literally. He insisted blacks be treated fairly while seeking contracts with the city, especially at the airport. Of course, I said yes to him stopping by.

It seemed like only a few minutes had passed before his giant frame and warm, smiling face graced my office. He got right to the point.

"I just felt the need today to connect up briefly, in a brotherly way, with another who is truly in touch with the growing harmony, progress, and dedication that is becoming Atlanta. Thanks to you and your brother for all you are doing."

Our personal relationships with Maynard seemed to deepen throughout the entire period he was in office. He often brought out-of-town visitors to Atlanta directly to Paschal's, saying, "I wanted these folks to have a Paschal welcome to Atlanta! What better way to introduce them to Atlanta and the South?"

More recently, Maynard hosted groups at the new Paschal's Restaurant on Northside Drive. He was a leading member of the generation of leaders who created a better world for all of us through sheer talent, determination, and vision. A man of impeccable character and integrity, Maynard's death has left a void that can never be filled. He always reached out to address any issues and remove any obstacles that may have stood in the way of moving Atlanta toward becoming the world's next great city. He loved Atlanta with an unspeakable passion.

Early on, Maynard knew I was one of the original members of the Atlanta Action Forum, which addressed some of the major issues and emerging needs and moved Atlanta successfully through that trying period of interracial discomfort. Other members included John Portman; Tom Cousins; Paul Austin, president of Coca-Cola; Dave Garrett, president of Delta Airlines; Jesse Hill of Atlanta Life; John Cox; Bill Stern, president of Trust Company of Georgia; and Bill Calloway, president of Calloway Enterprises. I believe Herman Russell was also a member of the original group. If not, he was an early member.

Through the Forum, I learned Dobbs House was looking for a reputable black businessman to form a joint venture with. Dobbs House was then the major provider of food services to the Atlanta airport. Bill Brooks was its district president, and he called one day, wanting to know if he could bring Bob Bryant, president of the company, by Paschal's to meet with me. I asked myself, "Am I dreaming? Could these business moguls really be searching out the Paschal brothers?" Yes, they were! Others joined in our unbridled excitement. Almost daily, Ira Jackson, John Cox, and Jesse Hill gathered around my brother and me, urging us to study, analyze, and sign on to perhaps the biggest joint venture movement in Atlanta. When Robert and I met with our distinguished guest, our session was immediately cordial, mutually respectful, and positive.

John Cox jumped right into the middle of things. Knowing that I already knew Dave Garrett, he suggested I apprise Dave of our interest in the whole concept of joint venture, which I did. Garrett expressed his pleasure and said he would immediately call Bill Brooks and Bob Bryant. I later learned that Dave gave me a glowing recommendation as an excellent candidate for joint venture. At that time, only concrete and mud stood where "Maynard's Airport" would take shape.

Dobbs-Paschal Midfield Corporation was born in 1978, after many of what seemed like nonstop sessions to explore, assess, review, plan, analyze, and blueprint every possible detail. However, our work had only just begun.

Dobbs-Paschal Midfield Corporation bid for and won the city contract for inside food and beverage concessions at the airport. I was executive vice president of this joint venture, making me the first black to hold such a high-level position. The corporation then leased space to other food and beverage concessionaires in the passenger terminal, including our Paschal's Concessions, Inc., which continues to serve Hartsfield-Jackson International Airport.

From 1980 to 1995, Dobbs-Paschal was the airport's principal concessionaire. This meant that our joint venture leased space to all subconcessionaires in the passenger terminal, including our own Paschal's Concessions, Inc. After the contracts were signed, Maynard gave one of his famous talks to all principal parties. He clearly stated that he expected us to "work together, to get along, as if you are blood brothers." And we did.

Under the Honorable Mayor Andrew J. Young, Dobbs-Paschal Midfield Corporation continued prospering and growing. Our joint venture remained solid from 1980 to 1995. We demonstrated what it really means to make a business commitment and then honor your commitment beyond the call of duty. Under that successful bid, Dobbs-Paschal had not just entered into a contract. We had promised the city of Atlanta the fulfillment of our contract for $240 million with a fifteen-year timeline. Not only did we fulfill our contractual agreement, we met the terms ahead of time.

It was a blessed experience. We all learned so much. We learned we each had knowledge and experience to share with each other. As partners, we were in on the planning for construction specifications as well as selecting space designs, equipment, furnishings, and beverage and food needs for all food service locations, newsstands, and gift shops for the entire airport. Both Dobbs and Paschal's were right there during all of the constructing, interfacing, and building out with all other contractors in the airport. I informed Robert daily, received his input, and answered his questions. He sometimes joined me in our business meetings, but he always said, "James, you handle the business end. I'll stick with the other ends of the business." When we delivered on our $240 million promise, we all knew we had made lasting history. We soon became the model for other joint ventures. It was wonderful!

After our team, which included Robert, had finalized all of our contractual requirements with the city, Dobbs-Paschal systematically worked together to establish and personalize our operational designs. Because we were responsible for everything airport-related to the designated and agreed upon concessions services, we formulated our own operational model, deciding on a three-tiered approach. My son, Curtis, knows the food and beverage business and is technologically adept as well. At the beginning of our airport ventures, Curtis worked directly with the businesses to put together our entire technology auditing system. He was eventually our comptroller and manager of the accounting department. Curtis also trained many on our management staff. Some of those people are still in positions within Paschal businesses. Curtis' efforts were key to the smooth operations of the technology and auditing segments of the three tiers of the Dobbs-Paschal Midfield Corporation.

First, we had already organized the official Dobbs-Paschal Midfield Corporation to be the overall management structure. Thus, the corporation was the parent organization, which leased concessions locations to other applicants. The Midfield Corporation systematically screened, analyzed, and approved or disapproved all applicants for concessions space. Second, the corporation then leased various space needs to Dobbs House and Paschal's. Thus, while Dobbs and Paschal's carried on business together under an umbrella arrangement, we also managed all of the other corporation's businesses. At the same time, we operated independently of each other. Unbelievably, we simultaneously thrived as close business colleagues and independent businesses. There was a Dobbs House function, and there was a Paschal's Concessions operation.

During this period, Paschal's became directly involved with the Squibb Company, which owned Dobbs House. In a few years, the Squibb Company sold Dobbs House to Chicago's Carson Pirie Scott, who eventually sold Dobbs to the Greyhound Corporation. During these numerous transactions and mergers, I became a willing, humble, and excited learner. I was so deeply pleased to have many, varied opportunities for growth and gaining experience, understanding, and insight into the fundamental elements of corporate entities.

During this time, Bob (Robert T.) Bryant, vice chairman of Carson Pirie Scott, and I became close friends. Even though Bob retired and now lives in Florida, we still keep in touch. He and his wife graciously attended "An Evening Honoring Robert and James Paschal," and Bob participated in the program. He has remained so supportive of all our joint venture undertakings, from the first day of our alliance until 1995 when our Dobbs House and Paschal's contractual operations expired. In the meantime, our joint ventures were still growing and taking on new, healthy dimensions.

Because of my experiences and growth through the Dobbs House-Paschal collaborative, I was expertly prepared to provide leadership and guidance to the next Paschal business venture. Under a somewhat different organizational model, we formed a joint venture with Concessions International. Herman Russell and I later formed a business team. For the last eleven years Herman and I have continued our strong airport business relationships, but very few of the people who started out with us remain involved at the airport.

The early venture was not always "peaches and cream." Many times, whites appeared disturbed that Robert and I were in charge. One particular incident always remains with me. I had been purchasing large volumes of frying lard (vegetable oil was not popular at the time) from one of the major supply companies. (I am talking big drums of lard.) The white deliveryman always insisted on asking for "Red" when making his deliveries, either to our West Hunter Street location or airport. He must have felt my light complexion gave him license to call me "Red" instead of Mr. Paschal or even James. I suppose it gave him some sense of real superiority. He knew he had to present the order papers to me for payment, but I guess it took too much insight for him to realize that I was helping to pay his salary.

I would appear, and he would mockingly say, "How ya doin' today, Red?" I was not going to allow any deliveryman to see any sign of anger, displeasure, or rage because of his calculated disrespect. I also knew our huge orders represented a large part of his employer's business. After the second incident, I wanted to be sure his blatant disrespect was indeed intended, and it was.

I waited until he cleared the area before I called the company's owner on the telephone. He answered, "How are you today, Mister Paschal. What can I do for you?"

I told him about his deliveryman's disrespectful behavior and said, "If you do not have another person who is capable of delivering our order in a respectful manner, then do not deliver another damn can of lard to any of the Paschal businesses." The poor man nearly had a stroke on the telephone. I never saw that deliveryman again. The next one who appeared was a perfect gentleman.

I continue to believe the ongoing success of all the Paschal business enterprises have depended very heavily upon one basic principle. Early on, Robert and I promised to always manage our anger, frustrations, disappointments, grief, and rage and handle deceit and mistreatment with a cool, studied, prayerful, humane (but direct) attack. We were never loud, boisterous, or violent. Our intelligent approach has worked with profitable outcomes for more than fifty years. Today, Paschal's Restaurants, LLC; Paschal's Concessions, Inc.; and Concessions/Paschals, J. V., keep moving along at a rather remarkable pace.

In 2001, a series of tablets, prominently displayed in the Atlanta airport, proclaim a portion of the Paschal history to the world. I am often recognized, even sought after, to share more of that history. Recently, a fiftyish man, running down the length of a long causeway between flights, rushed up to me and breathlessly gushed, "Mr. Paschal, may I please have your autograph? I want my children and grandchildren to know about you and your brother." Slightly embarrassed, I took a pen and signed my name.

It is often very hard for me to believe (it is even more difficult for me to accept) that Robert and I have lived any more heroic lives than, perhaps, many others who may have treaded similar pathways. There were so many people whose life experiences, if known, would match our own. We would sit and reflect on the rough, rugged roads we had traveled together. Admittedly, Robert's travels often were more rugged and painful than my own. "Could they really be talking about us?" Without bragging, Robert loved to whisper to the multitudes that always seemed to turn an ear his way.

"Yep," he said, "I was the one who was always stuck in the kitchen. But then, that was because I was the only one who really knew how to cook really good."

16

Home

My wife and I as well as our entire family feel privileged to be showered by God's continuous blessings. We have been able to share generously in God's love and share that love with so many others. As a family, we have remained strong in our devotion to each other, our families, and the thousands of others whose lives that, according to so many, we have been blessed to enrich.

On June 3, 2005, Phyllis and I celebrated fifty-eight years of a blessed love story. Love, faith, trust, hard work, and dreams fulfilled have solidly held our lives together. Phyllis said, "James has always made me feel pampered with distinction. In our life together, I have never had to wait to exhale. I have always felt like a loved wife who has been luxuriously kept, even when we were taking our daily proceeds home in a little brown paper bag from our first little West Hunter Street sandwich shop. James always made me feel like a million dollars, even though there was not much in those early days. We were just as happy because we had our love and our family."

Phyllis admits she has relished her role of "CEO at home" and has worked hard to do a good job. Despite a few rough patches, our blessed experiences as a wedded team will forever remain uniquely our own.

We designed our rather spacious home, which has been described as rising majestically, like a capital A, or, kind of resting as if waiting to soar. We think our home holds a distinctive position in Atlanta's fashionable Cascade Heights behind a slightly rolling lawn. I like to say that any who may enter will feel they are in a domicile transformed into a Garden of Eden. The length and breadth of our sanctuary tells you what home is to Phil, what she values, and what she enjoys. My wife has a pressing need to be surrounded by beauty and a certain order.

If you enter through any door, you are delivered into an overflowing garden of flowers. Flower arrangements are everywhere—on every table, in every corner, in every possible nook and cranny, and any corner spaces to be found on our white-carpeted floor. I believe a vital part of my wife's idea of herself as one of God's blessed, grateful creations is to be expressed through surrounding herself with beautiful floral replications, which she has sought in every color conceived by man or nature. On every kitchen counter and on both sides of our corridor-shaped kitchen, one has to almost guide the body respectfully through a pathway of colorful blossoms.

Knowledge of herself as a child of God shines through in my beloved wife's daily behaviors, including her spiritual connections, her gratefulness for a life of blessings, and her dedicated commitment as wife and mother. Her face literally lights up when she talks about her beloved, deceased mother. Phil declares proudly that Mrs. E. never felt or acted her age. One Christmas, Mrs. E. was visiting us. We had bought our son, Curtis, a skateboard. Well, Mrs. E. decided she would try it out. She got on that thing, fell flat, and broke her wrist. We had to spend an entire day at Grady Memorial Hospital.

Phil has not led an ordinary life behind the closed comforts of our orderly Cascade Heights home. Because of her untiring efforts, our home always reflected a kind of elegant order. When Robert dropped by, he always kidded her, asking in his gentle, but humorous, fashion, "Well, Mrs. Paschal, which door should I enter today? Carpet rakin' all done?"

She fired back, "Maybe not. You just wait right there until I see which is the best way for you to go!"

My wife was always busily engaged at home in her never-ending war with dirt. Her carpet-raking rituals were often targets of humor, and I started it all. In earlier times, after my wife had carefully finished her cleaning, lest I be the great spoiler of her perfection, she followed me step-by-step and reraked the carpet back into buffed, fluffy perfection. Not a tuft could be leaning or squatting. For her, home had to be as near to perfection as possible, and she made certain, as best she could by her own hands, that it was.

My wife cooked, cleaned, and did the laundry. After working hard to improve her culinary gifts, she lovingly prepared a meal for her family. To this day, regardless of what we may be able to afford, she still does it all. However, in recent years, when we have needed it, we have appreciated the supportive, committed assistance of her sister, Marian.

Phyllis is a woman of medium height and is not usually skinny. Her bright personality remains etched in the glow of her smooth, very light-tan face, which is always framed by her full, well-coiffed, black and graying hair. To me, she appears almost beatific. Unless you know she owns a mischievous, wry sense of humor, you could easily be deceived. She may appear to be always very socially correct, but, when appropriate, my sweet, loving wife is hilariously funny.

Phyllis has marched only to those few privately held societal and religious interests of her own choosing. As long as she was physically able, she fulfilled every expectation. I remember one of Phil's most cherished affiliations, the altar guild of First Congregational Church United Church of Christ. Members were scheduled to host on an alternating basis. When it was my wife's time to entertain, she was enthusiastically and energetically ready. At first, she hosted at home. Later, after our hotel accommodations were in top order, she hosted at Paschal's. Phil would spare nothing. She always required perfection in service and left no stone unturned in making sure all had a great time. Her choice of service and her participation in various activities were personal, solid, and rather low-key. Her upbringing may well have contributed to her philosophy of service where truly needed.

Thus, we have gone straightforward and full steam ahead into maintaining a life rich in measured abundance. There were issues to be addressed. At one point, my wife had to deal with her own uncertainty about what she really wanted to do. I always knew I did not want my wife to work. I wanted to take the duties and responsibilities of a man who would provide for his family without any questions asked. That was what Robert and I had promised ourselves. We both knew people might wonder, "Why aren't those two wives helping out in the business?" For more than fifty-five years, ours has been a blessed side-by-side partnership. Phyllis has been my much-needed household executive.

Because of my working hours, I depended on Phil to really take care of our home. Like my own, her job was also full-time. When we first married, we lived a walking distance from the business in a friend's small house on the corner of White House Drive and West Hunter. At first, Phil had to adjust to being at home alone in the evenings. She was not accustomed to the loneliness, so she spent a lot of time in the Ashby Street Theater. I think she saw every movie shown. She then walked to the restaurant, helped count the intake receipts for the day, and put the money in a brown bag and into her purse. We then went home, walking down Hunter Street. No one would bother you in those days. There was no need to be fearful.

We enjoyed living directly across from Washington High School. At the time, Washington and David T. Howard high schools were the only high schools for blacks in Atlanta. That was the first time Phyllis had ever seen all-black groups of students walking home from school. Several of my cousins sometimes stopped to say hello. They enjoyed teasing Phil about her cooking, asking, "What are you experimenting with today?"

My new wife did not know an awful lot about cooking. Her mother usually did the cooking in the Johnson household, so Phyllis practiced a lot on my stomach. One time, Phil spent almost an entire day cooking a chicken. Believing it was ready to serve, we cut into it. It was red inside. We had to send up to Paschal's to get some meat for dinner. But, she kept at it until she became quite a culinary artist—with no input from either Robert or me.

After Phil came to Atlanta, her beloved sister, Marian, followed and enrolled in the Grady Hospital School of Nursing. Marian went on to serve as a lieutenant nurse in the United States Air Force. She served most of her tenure in California. After separation from the military, Marian returned to Atlanta to live with us. She became my sister, not my sister-in-law. To this very day, she and I relate to each other as sister and brother. For the rest of our lives, I know Marian will be there, helping my wife try to boss me around. When I am ill, Marian helps Phil take care of me. When they think I am working too hard, they fuss at me. It does not help, but they try.

Marian lived with us for several years while working in Atlanta. However, her plans to return home to Pennsylvania remained foremost in her mind. She did return and purchase a home for herself, their stepfather, and Mrs. E. Sadly, Mrs. E. became very ill. When she passed away, Marian came back to Atlanta, bringing her and Phil's stepfather with her. It was such a time of mourning and sadness. We all felt an unimagined depth of loss over the passing of Mrs. E. Sadness visited us again when their stepfather passed.

The Abundant Life

A vital part of a life of abundance is the commitment to going first class. Whether it involves day-to-day living, church, play, food, service, shopping, or just a leisurely bit of intermittent imbibing, I am sworn to going first class. I like repeating the words I heard from one preacher's sermon entitled, "The

Abundant Life!" As he approached the end of his sermon, he looked upward, stretched both arms high, and thunderously declared:

> Brothers and sisters, religion never was designed to make our pleasures less! The Good Lord gave us a brain to know, understand, and select from all that has been created around us! Using our senses, training, and good thinking about life to enjoy our blessings in moderation pleases God! Our sensible enjoyment of a beautiful life causes God to smile! God would not have decked out this world in all its beauty and wealth if we were only to stand back and just look!

My wife likes to say I am obsessed with first class. She says:

> If James Paschal controls it, it is going to be first class, all the way. Even when we had little money, he held to his motto, 'We will go first class or stay home!' Even when he and Robert were struggling, praying, and fighting off the problems of getting money to build their dreams, keep things going forward, and fight against racism, he maintained his determination. Everything had to be first class! No riding in tourist class for us.
> My husband always wanted us to take vacations—always first class. He said, when he was a child, he remembers how he would cry when he would see white folks packing their families into cars or station wagons and leaving for vacations. He promised himself, when he became a husband, he would always take his family on yearly vacations.
> He always takes us to the most beautiful, exquisite places. He just loves being around the oceans at the loveliest resorts. Our very first faraway vacation was to Nassau, Bahamas. We lived at the Sheraton, and one of our most beautiful dining experiences was at the Sheraton's Wharf Restaurant. Unlike Atlanta at that time, New York was not totally segregated. New York invited you to come, so we traveled there regularly. If you could pay the price, you could sit or sleep in comfort, wherever you wished. We were much younger then, but it was lovely. We took in plays, movies, and shows, on and off Broadway. On several occasions, we enjoyed trips to Bermuda and the Princess Hotel in South Hampton. We have also been to Acapulco.
> There were times when I felt like I did not want to leave some of the exotic places we visited. I knew we would be returning to business as usual, and I wanted to continue being served, hand and feet. Then, I would come to myself and remember who was making it possible for us to enjoy those lands of magic and plenty. That would snap me back into reality and return me to my senses. I just needed to come back home and slide back into my "House CEO" duties.
> My beloved, James Paschal, had to return to earning the kind of living that claimed his daily dreams. He had to return to his calling of serving people,

making a life for them, and sharing his growing accumulations of plenty with the needy. I was very much aware that, for the most part, doing things in that order was primary for James.

Our family travels held much joyful meaning for us. Living with the daily sacrifices of me having to be the main, open player in a rapidly expanding business added more value to our getaway times. My wife made some tremendous sacrifices during those years when Robert and I could hardly steal time away from the business to take even a short breath and some much-needed time just being at home for a while. Before we even considered marriage, Phil indicated her willingness to take me on, even though I was completely wrapped up in growing a business. She said:

> I knew very well, before we married, that James was the other half of an inseparable brother union. I missed him daily. The dinners alone, late evenings, and, sometimes, late-night arrivals home were a challenge. This was especially true when he had to be away on many of the holidays, including Christmas.
> There were the Sundays when, while attending church alone, I said many silent prayers for strength for tolerance. There were my birthdays when he could not be there and when Curtis came along. The loneliness was painfully real. But, I knew for sure that his love and yearning for home life and intimate times together, though deep, had to be deferred. In my mind, there never was (to this day, there has never been) one iota of a hint of any reason to doubt the depths and sincerity of his love and concern. When he could be there with us, it was purely comforting and beautiful.

The fact that I had a wife who truly understood the requirements of building a business, including the demands of laying the foundations necessary to attract a patronizing public, was priceless. I found her more than willing to be a loving helpmate. I was also bearing the cross of often having to place family life in a holding pattern. Phil went about making and keeping home pleasant, beautiful, and secure. During all of those years, when Robert and I were working almost around-the-clock to strive toward Paschal's ultimate success, Phil was there. Whenever I stepped through the doorway of our home, I always encountered solace, peace, mirth, and unconditional love. For more than fifty-seven years, strong, loving, tolerant, understanding Phil has stood our tests of time.

Growing Up Paschal

My wife became the almost day-by-day everything. From the earliest days of Curtis' life, we wanted to provide our son, from preschool onward, with an education that would prepare him to be whatever he wanted to be in the world. We enrolled Curtis in the Spelman College Nursery. Phil rarely, if ever, missed a PTA meeting. Whenever possible, I was right by her side in attendance. She held offices in the PTA and took Curtis to Sunday school. She worked hard as a Sunday school teacher. We wanted nothing left to be desired in building and maintaining a strong base of parental support for Curtis. Phyllis recently said she can still see herself chauffeuring him back and forth to school, school events, meetings, church, Sunday school, and a variety of activities, thoroughly enjoying the role of Mom. Throughout his early childhood, through adolescence, and into manhood, we tried being there for our son.

Curtis is now married, but he does not have any children. Phyllis and I would have loved for him to follow me into the business world and, more specifically, into my chosen profession of hospitality and service. However, we have to let our children choose for themselves. They do have their own ideas. Curtis enjoys working in computer technology. He is also a licensed pilot. Because my philosophy of life is to just love life, I absolutely must remain open-minded and receptive to the choices he has made.

Her Great Gifts

Whether it was the coldest winter day, a sunny springtime afternoon, the hottest day of summer, or a colorful leaf-spattered day in late fall, my wife somehow always knew how to arrange, create, and recreate an atmosphere of pure happiness at home. Many times, when we celebrated birthdays, holidays, and anniversaries, neither deferred calendar dates nor the time on the clock mattered. Most of the time, we never really knew when we would be able to celebrate because we didn't know when I would be able to be released from work. Phil convinced herself that she could make things work. We found fun in her ability to work her strategies. She would find ways to rearrange any dinner, including Sunday dinner, birthday dinners, and even Thanksgiving and Christmas dinners. I never understood how she managed to cook and keep everything warm and edible while waiting for my arrival. Not once do I remember going home, regardless of what time, and a hot meal was not waiting to be served with the greatest pleasure.

Phyllis simply had a special gift of knowing how and when to delay every celebratory activity until I reached home. I often asked, "Did somebody at Paschal's call you to tell you when I would be home?" She smiled, as if to say, "No, buddy, I am just learning you." To this day, I am amazed. No presents were opened, no hot tea was sipped, no bells were rung, and no dinner was touched before I came home. When I walked through the door, if it was late on Christmas or Easter evening, it might as well have been morning. The festivities were on. At Christmastime, the tree would have been decorated. The lights, tinsel, and evergreens were hung. Husband and Daddy were home, so merrymaking could begin.

Occasionally, Phil had me send someone to our home to help with the heavy stuff. Mostly though, she did it all herself, "not as a sacrifice, but as a necessity," she would say. She did it to build, show, and nurture an atmosphere in our home, which was founded on the strength of sincere love and caring. She knew my daily presence at Paschal's was a major force in growing a business of excellence. Moreover, Robert depended heavily on my input to make basic decisions. I simply had to be there. I can never thank her adequately. Having a loving, dedicated wife at home provided the comfort I needed to grab the business world around its midriff and hold on.

All my wife did to keep our lives running smoothly at home was based upon the fact that we both did not doubt each other's loyalty. I truly sought, wanted, and valued my wife's input and opinions. She was—and still is—my wife and partner. Thus, our challenges through nearly fifty-eight years together (and there have been some that were thunderous in their rendering) have been minimal in their impact. We continued looking forward to our travels or late-night dinners. Then, there were also those cherished times together of loving embraces and reassuring expressions of eternal love. We have been divinely blessed. Phyllis said, "James has been and is truly a remarkable human being! There have been times when I thought I wanted him to get mad, just go crazy, and give a piece of his mind to some of those people who had not been fair by him. He would always say, 'Phil, you just cannot do that and succeed in this world.' I would know he was right, but I am not naturally always able to remain as cool as he is. James' goodness, and that of his brother, truly comes from deep within, deep inside of them. They seemed to have made each other complete. My husband has taught me so much."

My wife's assessment of my nature was in line with what Robert and I had always been taught and with what we both tried to live. The late Dr. Benjamin Elijah Mays, president of Morehouse College, frequently related to his Men of Morehouse students and alumni:

> Whenever you start to get really mad about something, think! It may be your goals, your objectives, or all of your endowed penchants for embracing your possibilities for success. When you start to get mad, look at Robert and James Paschal.
>
> The Paschal men are two who have been touched by every reason, if there were ever any reasons, to be raging, angry men of color. These men own all the reasons! Look at these tall-standing, prosperous, and triumphant men! You will not—cannot—find one rational-thinking human being who will say one mean thing about the Paschal brothers! These are men who have accepted God's blessings and used those blessings wisely. They are not just helping themselves. James and Robert Paschal are helping others, including some of you in this audience.
>
> These two brothers are spreading joy, happiness, blessings, and many opportunities for success abroad. These men did not take on their world's work by quitting when times got rough. When racism, jealousy, hatred, or denial could have worn them down, they boldly stood up to the tests of time and turbulence. They have fought gallantly with the full, total embodiment and personification of class and dignity, and they have become dominant, towering figures of triumph in our times.

17

Castleberry Hill

Monday, March 11, 2002, 11:00 AM

A new Paschal's restaurant, Paschal's at Castleberry Hill, opened nearly fifty-five years to the day in 1947 when Robert and I opened our first Atlanta eatery. We had struggled, worked, prayed, scrimped, and saved. We had marched out from picking cotton, shining shoes, being busboys, and driving lumber trucks back home in Thomson and McDuffie County. We had used our own money and had borrowed other people's money. Some people called our first restaurant the "chicken shack on West Hunter Street," where fried chicken became our main offering. That little, forty-seat place became a mighty seed planted in the name of Paschal and 837 West Hunter Street, a mighty fortress of Paschal progress and plenty.

Robert continued growing mountains of what was fast becoming his famous golden brown, crispy, picture-perfect chicken. In just a few years, we had become noted for serving the best tasting, marinated, most crunchy, most flavorful fried chicken sandwiches to be found anywhere. First, it was Atlanta...then the South...and then all across America.

After we had worked, saved, and expanded the "shack" into Paschal's Restaurant, our clientele reached as far away as inside the DC Beltway. Robert's culinary creativity grew out of what he had inherited from our mother's rich, diversified palate pleasers. The two of us simply combined birthright, hard work, and God's will to guide us into knowing what we truly wanted. Our daddy always said:

Don't let no white man or anybody else put no big rocks in your pathway. If they are little rocks, just kick 'em out of where you want to go. If they are big ones, step over 'em. If they are giant sized, call for help, pray, and roll 'em out of your way. Just remember, you must keep pushing and rollin' things out of your way to get to wherever you wanna go.

We never forgot. Finally, our history just took us over. Almost before we knew it, the Paschal brothers were owners of a noted restaurant, nightclub, and luxury hotel. Now, on March 11, 2002, nearly fifty years later, I stood in the historic restoration of Atlanta's Castleberry Hill, in front of a new Paschal's Restaurant.

I felt so deeply blessed and honored this beautiful, bright Monday morning. At 11:00 AM, I joined a crowd of well-wishers on the steps to the entrance of the restaurant/lofts complex for the formal ribbon-cutting ceremony. The new Paschal's at Castleberry Hill eased into history.

I had not totally left the food service business since Robert's death. I had no desire to leave the business, which had been our source of overcoming. Robert would not have wanted me to quit just because he was no longer by my side. I was comfortable with my Atlanta airport connection to Concessions International. However, businessman Herman J. Russell approached me to partner with him in a new venture, "the total rebirth of a Paschal's Restaurant." I talked with my wife and several close friends. All enthusiastically pushed me onward.

When word finally came that our new venture was taking shape, hundreds of well-wishers bombarded me. They made telephone calls, paraded by the location, and encountered Phyllis and me at church and social gatherings. It was both encouraging and comforting that so many wished for one more return to, as they said, "The Paschal's of yesteryear."

As the doors to the new restaurant were officially opened, Atlanta's newly elected mayor, the Honorable Shirley Clarke Franklin, was among those present. Mayor Franklin, Atlanta's first female mayor and a black woman, joined my partner, Herman Russell, and me at the podium. Numerous elected officials, dignitaries, family members, and friends shed proud, joyful tears. I could feel Robert's presence.

The Reverend Dr. Dwight D. Andrews offered the prayer of blessing and thanksgiving for Paschal's at Castelberry Hill. My wife's pastor, he is senior minister of Atlanta's historical First Congregational Church United Church of Christ, a nationally acclaimed jazz musician, composer to noted playwright

August Wilson, and a professor of music at Emory University. Dr. Andrews' prayer offered reverent words of encouragement, praise, and uplifting spiritual sustenance.

Before this formal opening event, Herman Russell and I had orchestrated a full week of festive happenings. Friday, March 8, was especially exciting. Georgia's governor, the Honorable Roy Barnes and his wife, Mrs. Marie Barnes, spent an enjoyable evening at the new Paschal's. They first dined and then engaged in lively, friendly table hopping, visiting with the appreciative crowd that had filled the main dining room to overflowing. Along with our wives and family members, there were invited friends and associates with whom we had nurtured and enjoyed long-standing relationships. There were noted politicians, business leaders, educators, ministers, community leaders, dignitaries, and other professionals. The new Paschal's at Castleberry Hill had dutifully kicked off with great promise. I knew this was perhaps the last great Paschal dream realized.

Here I was, approaching my eightieth birthday. God had mercifully spared me to take yet another giant step in continuing our Atlanta legacy. As I stood at the top of the front entrance steps and looked over the large gathering, I reflected on the sheer magnitude of the venture. I wanted to reach out, touch, and hug each person in the huge, diverse crowd. Through the years, because of the continued faith and support of some of these same people, their ascendants, and their offspring, my brother and I had been able to set and maintain our high standards of love, respect, service, and giving.

Herman Russell leaned over and whispered, "What do you say? Wonderful, isn't it?" He and I have vowed to continue the Paschal level of service. We are combining our business know-how and remaining energies to perpetuate our special brand of Southern hospitality and elegance. We have histories and promises to keep.

On the opening day, I could not help but glance northward up Northside Drive and then westward toward AU Center, what is now Paschal's Center at Clark Atlanta University. In 1995, a little more than a year before Robert's passing, we sold the original Paschal's to Clark Atlanta University. Mentally, I reviewed that decision and the opening at Castleberry Hill. I realized an incredible closeness of Robert's spirit and presence. At once, a warm and chilly feeling of perfect, expanding accomplishment and gratitude seemed to engulf my whole body.

As I turned to walk away, having spoken the last words of my brief welcoming remarks, I felt an irresistible and, increasingly, irrepressible urge. I

Castleberry Hill **155**

knew then I had one more river to cross. I had to complete the telling of the Paschal story.

The voice of the publisher of the *Atlanta Daily World,* Ms. Alexis Scott, brought me back to the moment, "Mr. Paschal, will you please tell us about the unique architectural design of the building?" Several reporters and staff persons accompanied her. We turned and entered the doors to the new Paschal's. Situated less than two blocks from Atlanta's Georgia Dome, home of the Atlanta Falcons football team, the restaurant calls to the public. I was excited about conducting yet another tour. As we walked, I talked:

> Our two-story, red brick restaurant soars. It is loftlike in design, offering an atmosphere of what Herman and I enjoy calling industrial elegance. Under the guidance of our energetic and creative interior design firm, Jackson Studio Architect Designers, we took great care to make sure the inner walls would show off the same red brick as the exterior. The first floor, also housing a large bar and lounge area, easily seats 200 patrons for breakfast, lunch, or dinner. An upper dining balcony, accessible by either elevator or an attractive, suspended, sturdy, muted steel stairway, comfortably seats fifty. Herman and I collaborated to select the colors, which are bright, vivid earth tones. The interior includes the 150-seat banquet hall and a thirty-five-seat meeting room. Over the main dining room, hanging eloquently from the high loft ceiling, two large, metal chandeliers appear as if suspended from bunched brooms of wire. Each light sports a circular sunburst of red-tipped bulbs. They hang extended on long, steel pipelike fixtures. Every detail offers the eyes a complete picture of an elegant, contemporary loft. Herman and I are pleased with the uniqueness of the design and the very positive public response. Robert would have loved how we have moved and swung with the times.

And They All Came Back

Sunday, April 15, 2002

If disbelief or doubt had sought refuge within, they were instantly obliterated and transformed into spiritual abundance. The scene was deeply moving and rewarding. Fellowship and love spilled from every table. People poured into Paschal's at Castleberry Hill from Northside Drive with cars were backed up, north and south, waiting to enter.

Then they came, the Paschal veterans, the new, young, and not so young. They were the after-church crowds. They were families with their children, all dressed to perfection. They were all there, including friends, patrons, associates, and acquaintances. Each one was happily, attentively, and comfortably seated. They moved downstairs and upstairs. In a short time, they were even spilling over into the spacious banquet room. The building was alive with soft laughter, joyous smiles, and hugs and kisses.

Andrew Young, and his wife, Carolyn, were seated in a booth. He was nattily attired in dark blue. His wife wore a white knit suit and matching white hat. Andy and Carolyn were having their after-church conversation and Sunday meal. It was almost like old times. Andy and his late first wife, Jean, were among those who gave life to "stopping by Paschal's." Andy and his family had regularly joined all the other civil rights soldiers for Sunday dinner at Paschal's. Paschal's in Atlanta is once again alive, prospering, growing, and continuing to fulfill the Paschal dream in full swing. I can think of no situation or circumstance that could make me happier. It is like the music and poetry of the spirit, repeated many times and made real.

Once again, I cannot resist the depths of longing for Robert—the cotton picker, the cook, the business tycoon, and the philanthropist—to have been able to witness this most wondrous event. But I feel his presence. I am not alone.

Every year since the late 1800s, most black folks in Atlanta and some whites turn their attention to the commencements held the third week in May in the AU Center. Spelman, Morris Brown, and Morehouse Colleges as well as Clark Atlanta University and the Interdenominational Theological Center (ITC) are in close proximity to one another. For the most part, they share their beautiful campuses. Black folks from all over the United States (after the blessings of the Civil Rights Movement, black, white, and other folks of color from around the world) come to the AU Center. Commencement celebrations have continued to draw hundreds of notables, many of whom are alumni. They come by plane, chartered buses, and motor vehicles. They arrive ready to reunite, reflect, party, see the new sights, and just hang out with former classmates, relatives, and friends. Hanging out at Paschal's was one of the most treasured of all the commencement traditions. All have dined, enjoyed jazz, and, after we built the hotel, often occupied every room available. Of course, our local high school commencement ceremonies follow not too far behind. Many of those who came back in 2002 could not resist talking about Mr. Bob.

A large number of educators in the Atlanta Public Schools system are products of the AU Center schools. If you add them and their families and friends to the huge numbers who travel, often from afar, to be in Atlanta during this happy springtime onslaught, you have quite a conclave. I expected the 2002 graduations would result in me seeing numerous old friends and acquaintances. However, I could never have been prepared for what actually happened. The presence of so many old Paschalites, happy remembrances, thanks for times gone by, and shared histories combined to make me want to throw my arms around the armies who collected. These scenes still fill my heart.

Although the new restaurant is well-staffed, it remains my practice, even at my age, to spend time there daily. Robert's and my credo always remained: "Keep your head out of the clouds. Be there with your feet solidly planted and your arms outstretched. Stay in the midst of and in touch with those you are blessed to serve."

This notion rang loudly in my thoughts as I looked forward to the coming gathering. I could just feel it.

It must have been less than thirty minutes after the last note of dismissal had sounded for the Morehouse commencement. I was standing near the entrance when the first busload pulled in. All of the riders began standing and moving toward the door of the bus. At the same time, numerous cars waited in line to turn into the entrance. Other cars were waiting to get in line. Bus riders had begun climbing down from the bus. Though years had passed and some were on crutches and several were using walkers, I could recognize these aging friends of Paschal's. By the time they had exited from the bus and four loaded cars, I had counted sixty-three people. I stepped out of the entrance doors to greet them.

"There he is!"

"James Paschal!"

"Lord, is it good to see you again in life!"

"James, it has been almost ten years since I have seen you!"

"God! This place is beautiful!"

Several ladies threw their arms around my neck and planted kisses on my cheeks. Ladies and men were asking me to take pictures with them. It was a heartwarming gift of reunion and nostalgia. I stood at the door and welcomed them, one by one. As each large group finished their meal, others continued coming in to take their place. Stopping by Paschal's is being happily heard once again.

To quote one of my old acquaintances, "Revival time is here! The souls of the movement can once again gather for revival and renewal! We can once again return to 'The Place.'"

Mother, Lizzie Paschal and two young cousins-on the porch of the better home the family moved into in the town of Thomson, Georgia.

Mother, Lizzie Paschal, Gussie's son James Grant, niece Robbie Lee Gammage and another young relative—outside the house in McDuffie County, Georgia—"The Country...".

Father Henry Paschal and Co-Worker "Stergis" standing outside the Knox Hotel where they worked—Thomson, Georgia.

THE PASCHALS OF ATLANTA

Selling Southern hospitality
pays off for hard-working brothers

"IF SOMEONE had told me a few years ago that I'd be planning the layout for the world's largest airport, I wouldn't have believed it," muses James Paschal. Neither would anyone else.

True, the names James and Robert Paschal, owners of Paschal Restaurant and Motor Hotel in Atlanta, have long been synonymous with business acumen and Black enterprise. Their procurement of a million-dollar loan in 1959 for the establishment of a restaurant and nightclub, and the subsequent construction of a 120-room hotel in 1967 were early inspirations for Black businesses struggling for a foothold in the Atlanta market.

Still, when the brothers and Dobbs House Inc., the world's largest airport terminal operator, last year inked a contract with the city for joint operation next year of all retail operations in the new Atlanta airport—a deal expected to put a whopping $1 billion into the coffers of Paschal and Dobbs House over the next 15 years—the resounding question in the board rooms of the nation's business moguls was, Paschal who?

The answer to that question lies just two blocks away from the Atlanta University Center where the brothers' highly successful food and hotel business has been operating for the past 32 years. Starting in 1947 with the few coins James had saved as a Pullman Porter,

home newspaper route and pharmacy job, they opened a tiny restaurant serving sodas and sandwiches.

"The place was so small that we didn't have a kitchen," recalls James, who like Robert still puts in 14-hour days. "All the food had to be prepared at Robert's house and sent up by cab because we didn't have a car." In 1959, they moved across the street to their present location, and a year later opened La Carrousel lounge, a nightclub which over the years has featured such performers as Aretha Franklin, Lou Rawls, Ramsey Lewis, the Modern Jazz Quartet and Dizzie Gillespie. La Carrousel opened with the distinction of being one of the few places to openly violate one Atlanta law. "Our license was for 'coloreds only,'" James chuckles, "but our clientele was 60 percent white."

Seven years later the hotel's doors swung open, and before long visitors flocking to the city were taking home stories about the Black hotel with good rooms, fantastic fried chicken, and "that nice hostess, Mrs. [Ombell] Sherman." For Atlantans, however, Paschals has long meant much more than good rooms and great food.

For example, every morning for the past 20 years, Black elected officials, political candidates, would-be candidates and various power brokers from Mayor Maynard Jackson on

Brothers James (l.) and Robert Paschal, owners of Paschals Restaurant and Motor Hotel in Atlanta, have lots to smile about, considering their new deal with Dobbs House Corp. in which the two companies will jointly manage all retail operations in the new Atlanta airport, the world's largest, next year. The venture is expected to gross over $1 billion in next 15 years.

An excerpt from Ebony Magazine in November 1979.

The sign announcing the truck's cargo has been attached...the 5,000
Paschal's chicken lunches are on their way to Lakewood Park.

Robert and James join Mayor Ivan Allen in breaking ground for the new motor hotel.

Entrance to the beautiful La Carrousel Lounge.

A Young Hugh Masekela blowing away…

The Jimmy Smith Trio.

One of many integrated jazz groups to appear at Paschal's.

KALIL MADI   ANDY SIMPKINS   GENE HARRIS
DRUMS   BASS   PIANO
"THE THREE SOUNDS"

The Three Sounds - One of the many Jazz groups which played at the La Carrousel

The Three Sounds

HE YOUNG HOLT TRIO

The Young Holt Trio

James at home, still at work, discusses plans on the telephone.

James and Robert show of many awards.

Ramsey Lewis

Above Left: James and Robert
Above Right: James at the entrance of Paschal's

Robert and James reviewing a business plan.

Robert with a drawing of the hotel.

Reviewing an artist's rendition of the planned hotel.

James and Robert pose with Mayor Allen on the site of the new Motor Hotel.

James' younger sister, Claudie.

James and his young son Curtis.

Phyllis' sister Marian Johnson.

Phyllis dressed for "an evening out".

James and "Phil".

The brothers pose outside the front entrance of La Carrousel.

Phyllis's mother, Mrs. Edith Johnson.

Mrs. Edith Johnson, Phyllis and Marian's mother.

Robert and James in their first restaurant.

THIS IS PASCHAL'S MOTOR MO-
TEL, which was founded and is operated
by two Atlanta, Ga., brothers, Robert
and James Paschal. It is a five-story, 120
room luxury motel that is an elegant addition to Atlanta's business world.

Negroes Are Making Great Strides
In Business World of Atlanta, Ga.

An article about the Paschal brothers.

ESTONE BUSINESS ACHIEVEMENT

eaking Ceremony For Paschal's Motor Hotel

r Ivan Allen, Jr. and Vice Mayor
Mr. & Mrs. James Paschal and
fficial ground breaking ceremon-

Shown above Mayor Allen and Paschal Brothers break-
ground as Vice Mayor Massell, Alderman Cecil Turner
and others look on.

An article about the Paschal brothers.

The Paschal Brothers, James and Robert.

5,000 chicken lunches—packed and ready to go!

A tractor-trailer truck waits to be loaded with an order of 5,000 Paschal's fried chicken lunches. The order was placed for an entertainment event at Lakewood Park in Atlanta.

Robert Paschal fried his famous "copper brown, crisy, succulently delicious" fried chicken until he could fry no more. Only his brother James knows the secret family recipe. And he's not telling.

James greets ambassador Andrew J. Young.

James and his beloved "Phil".

Curtis and wife Tonya.

James with legendary entertainter Jayne Mansfield at the La Carrousel.

Mrs. Coretta Scott King (left) and James Paschal (right) receiving a check for $25,000.00 from Billy Brooks (center) official of Dobbs House, Inc. The donation was made to advance the work of the Civil Rights movement for nonviolent social change.

While Phyllis rests, James takes an exploratory stroll around the beautiful grounds of their Bahamian Resort hotel.

Mayor Ivan Allen lifts the shovel to unearth the first soil on which the new Motor Hotel will stand. Mayor Allen is joined by Senator Leroy Johnson, Robert's wife Florine, Robert, James, and James' wife Phyllis.

The Paschall Dream

JAMES PASCHALL

Luxury hotel dominates the skyline of Atlanta

The Paschall brothers had a dream . . . a dream they have made come true.

From a small start to a million-dollar luxury hotel is a long step. It took 15-hour work days, and seven-day work weeks, but Robert and James Paschall made it.

Check Atlanta's skyline today. An ultra-modern, motor hotel has risen to take its place among the finest, most beautiful structures in the city. Now standing majestically beside Paschalls' Restaurant and Paschalls' La Carousel Night Club, is the all new Paschalls' Motor Hotel that represents an investment of more

atmosphere was the setting for nights of great jazz music featuring a carousel of America's most renowned jazz artists.

Jimmy Smith, Cannonball Adderly, Ramsey Lewis, Horace Silver and the others found a special rapport, a warmth, a feeling of complete comfort which made them look forward to performing for La Carousel audiences as much as jazz connoisseurs looked forward to hearing them play. Today "La Carousel" enjoys the reputation of being one of the leading night clubs for "Le Jazz Extraordinaire" in the south.

ROBERT PASCHALL

ranean parking area that can easily accommodate 165 cars.

Paschalls Motor Hotel is strategically located at 8__ Hunter Street, S.W. near Atlanta's business, cultural, religious and recreational centers. It is a short bus ride from downtown Atlanta yet far enough away to escape the hub-bub of a thriving metropolis.

But one needn't go downtown to find most any kind of goods or service. Nearby are gasoline stations, bank, a post office, drug store, variety store, barber shop, beauty shop.

An article about the Paschals.

THE PASCHALS OF ATLANTA

Selling Southern hospitality
pays off for hard-working brothers

"IF SOMEONE had told me a few years ago that I'd be planning the layout for the world's largest airport, I wouldn't have believed it," muses James Paschal. Neither would anyone else.

True, the names James and Robert Paschal, owners of Paschal Restaurant and Motor Hotel in Atlanta, have long been synonymous with business acumen and Black enterprise. Their procurement of a million-dollar loan in 1959 for the establishment of a restaurant and nightclub, and the subsequent construction of a 120-room hotel in 1967 were early inspirations for Black businesses struggling for a foothold in the Atlanta market.

Still, when the brothers and Dobbs House Inc., the world's largest airport terminal operator, last year inked a contract with the city for joint operation of all retail operations in the new Atlanta airport—a deal expected to put a whopping $1 billion into the coffers of Paschal and Dobbs House over the next 15 years—the resounding question in the board rooms of the nation's business moguls was, "Paschal who?"

home newspaper route and pharmacy job, they opened a tiny restaurant serving sodas and sandwiches.

"The place was so small that we didn't have a kitchen," recalls James, who like Robert still puts in 14-hour days. "All the food had to be prepared at Robert's house and sent up by cab because we didn't have a car." In 1959, they moved across the street to their present location, and a year later opened La Carrousel lounge, a nightclub which over the years has featured such performers as Aretha Franklin, Lou Rawls, Ramsey Lewis, the Modern Jazz Quartet and Dizzie Gillespie. La Carrousel opened with the distinction of being one of the few places to openly violate one Atlanta law. "Our license was for 'coloreds only,'" James chuckles, "but our clientele was 60 percent white."

Seven years later the hotel's doors swung open, and before long visitors flocking to the city were taking home stories about the Black hotel with good rooms, fantastic fried chicken, and "that nice hostess, Mrs. [Orabell] Sherman." For Atlantans, however, Paschals has

Brothers James (L) and Robert Paschal, owners of

An article about the Paschals.

Congressman John Lewis and other political, business, and religious persons gather with members of Concerned Black Clergy for a "Get Out The Vote" Rally at Paschal's Restaurant. -- Atlanta Journal Constitution...

A Get Out the Vote rally at Paschal's

Vice President Al Gore visiting Paschal's.

AJC - Tues. 8/21/01

Herman Russell (left) and James Paschal discuss plans for the new **Paschal's Restaurant**, part of Russell's Castleberry Hill project near the original Paschal's, which was sold to Clark Atlanta University in 1996.

HISTORIC PASCHAL'S RETURNING TO ROOTS

Famous Atlanta restaurateur teams with developer to bring historic eatery to Castleberry Hill project.

By SHELIA M. POOLE
spoole@ajc.com

Paschal's Restaurant will once again dish up its famous fried chicken and sweet potato pie in the shadow of downtown Atlanta.

NEW LOCATION

Paschal's Restaurant on Martin Luther King Jr. Drive opened in 1947 and was a center of gatherings for civil rights leaders through the 1960s and 1970s. Now, Paschal's is planning to dish up its soul food again this winter at the new Paschal's Restaurant at Castleberry.

Morris

An article from the Atlanta Journal-Constitution.

Breakfast
at Paschal's (personal reflections)

by Hal Lamar

To me $4.26 seemed like a heck of a lotta money to pay for 2 eggs, grits, wheat toast with no butter and coffee. And the cronies at my table also bellyached over their bills. We vented our spleens to Mary Buchanan, our waitress with double the patience of Job and we all took a vow not to set foot again in this high priced bistro.

We've been making that vow now for about 5 years. We know we will never keep it. In fact, one or all of us will be back that way in a few hours for lunch, and at least one of the throng has a standing dinner date there.

What place is this which seems to have us in its clutches?

Paschal's.

I've broken bread at that place since I was a kid. I had my first date there, circa 1980 following an elementary school prom. We dined on the fried chicken which made them famous, early June peas and a salad amid soft lights which two 12 year olds could scarcely appreciate.

Over the years, my money and I have parted company at Paschal's. The name is synonymous in Atlanta. Three years in military service and a broadcast/print couldn't free me from the clutches of the eatery started by James and Robert Paschal back in the year of our Lord 1947.

In a military mess hall in Vietnam, thousands of miles from Martin Luther King, Jr. Drive (then called Hunter Street), a fellow GI sitting across from me remarked that the fried chicken being served up that evening was pale in comparison to the "chicken I ate at Paschal's when I visited Atlanta one summer."

What keeps us locals coming back for more, bypassing other cheaper, closer places from where we work or dwell is a question that may forever beckon a straight answer. Part of my reasons are purely self-serving.

As a reporter, I learned a long time ago that Paschal's is the place for scoops. It's an oasis usually avoided by my colleagues which is just fine with me. On any given hour of the day, there is no telling who might have their

Civil Rights Activist Jesse Jackson and former state representative Julian Bond confer over breakfast at Paschal's Restaurant, c. 1968. Courtesy Skip Mason/Digging It Up Archives.

feet parked under one of Paschal's' tables.

If I need to track down a politician playing duck and dodge, the chances are pretty good I'll find him or her at Paschal's (eventually). For entertainers, Paschal's is tantamount to a Brown Derby in LA or Toots Shaw's in the Big Apple. The late Robert Kennedy set up an office in one of the meeting rooms during Dr. Martin Luther King Junior's funeral in 1968. King was a frequent diner who frequently dialogued with regulars and visitors in the restaurant's famed front room. Such lively conversations among the knows and don'ts said that starlet Jane Mansfield once frequented the restaurant. Jesse Jackson dines there when in town, and politicos like Julian Bond, John Lewis, Hosea Williams and Maynard Jackson launched careers there one day over

chic en salad.

Over the last 8 years Concerned Black Clergy holds meets there every Monday morning which attracts a lot of newsmakers. I seldom leave Paschal's wanting for a good story or exclusive twist to a current one.

In 47 years, the Paschal Brothers restaurant and the La Carousel Lounge and hotel added in the early and late 60's respectively has benefited from a lot of word-of-mouth advertising. It's as much an attraction or thing-to-do in Atlanta as taking in a Braves game, riding the MARTA rail, visiting the King Center or touring Underground Atlanta.

For a guy like me, it means a daily sojourn for the morning meal and conversation with Jake the Mechanic, Al the preacher, Henry the lifelong politician, Johnson the dry cleaner and other assorted characters. We'll size up the

new mayor, rip up the old mayor, toast the waitress about a husband, boyfriend or a bad attitude, gripe about the bacon that's old, the sausage that's too hot, the hotcakes that got cold too quick or the coffee that might have been fresh two hours ago.

But after about 2 hours of that and occupying a booth that we should have long since given up, we reach deep, tip our servers generously and bid each other the best day of our lives.

In 24 hours, we'll see one another again.

Such is life which would not be complete without breakfast at Paschal's.

Hal Lamar, news anchor, reporter and talk show host for WAOK WVEE Radio in Atlanta, is a native who loves Paschal's no matter what he says about it.

Hal Lamar reflects on the Paschal dining experience.

Paschal brothers: A legend honored

Restaurant was haven for civil rights leaders

By Gail H. Towns
STAFF WRITER

Hundreds of people decked out in their Sunday best listened intently as former Mayor Maynard Jackson began to divulge the secret "recipe" that made Paschal's Restaurant's fried chicken so famous.

"It took a little touch of justice, a pinch of freedom and reaching out to help," said Jackson during a Tuesday evening tribute to James Paschal and his late brother Robert, owners of the landmark Atlanta restaurant and hotel where freedom fighters felt at home.

The $30-per-plate dinner came nearly a year after the late Robert Paschal and his brother, James, sold the restaurant to Clark Atlanta University for $3 million. Robert, the mastermind behind Paschal's legendary fried chicken, died Thursday at 87.

"Mister James" checks on Paschal's about once a week and manages the family's snack bars at Hartsfield International Airport.

The old neon sign on Martin Luther King Jr. Drive announcing "Paschal's Restaurant and Motor Hotel" has been replaced by one proclaiming it Paschal

Center at Clark Atlanta University. It serves, in part, as a 70-room dormitory for graduate students and 44-room hotel for guests of the Atlanta University Center.

Regulars say the famed restaurant is much more inviting these days. An $800,000 renovation shut it down for a few months last spring as Clark Atlanta University removed asbestos, painted, redesigned corridors, replaced wiring and installed fire alarms and sprinklers. The heavy dark drapes have come down and the weathered red carpet has been replaced.

Students who live at Paschal Center like having private rooms with private baths but say security is a problem. They've reported car break-ins and strangers wandering in the halls.

"It's not an ideal living location for graduate students," said Jerome Farquharson, a CAU student government leader.

The university has begun around-the-clock foot patrols to better guard the area and access to the residence hall has been tightened.

Despite the problems, it's an honor to live there, says Devin White, graduate student body president. "It feels likes you're

FRANK NIEMIER / Staff

Community asset: James Paschal (center) is greeted by Louise and Donald Hollowell.

living in a part of our history — you're living in a place where our great civil rights leaders once slept and ate," he said.

Political leaders, community activists and Atlanta's black clergy continue to use the center's Matador Room for weekly meetings. Former city officials, university professors and retired teachers sip sweet iced tea in the dining areas.

Paschal's is still "the heart and soul of black Atlanta," said NAACP veteran Earl Shinhoster. "It's still the place to be seen and to find out what's going on. It will

remain a part of the culture."

Since January, the center has served 4,116 people in the banquet halls and restaurant. President Clinton dined at the restaurant last fall while on the campaign trail.

Bill Ezell, who heads Cornerstone Management, the company CAU hired to operate the center, retained and retrained about 70 percent of the original staff.

"The biggest challenge has been having the community understand that we're still open to the public," Ezell said.

In February, the restaurant began serving Sunday brunch. A marketing plan will be rolled out this spring. Famed Paschal's hostess "Miss Orah Bell" Sherman — who's 80, and still going strong after at least 35 years there — says the restaurant will be fine.

"Folks just got the wrong understanding. Some people thought it was just going to be a dorm, but it isn't," she said. "It's the same as when the Paschals were here, with a lot of improvements. The food is the same, darling."

An article from the Atlanta Journal-Constitution.

Paschal's Motor Hotel and the La Carrousel Lounge.

Epilogue

The memories stay in my mind, happily surrounding me. They will not let go. I will not let go.

Our lives still amaze us. Phyllis and I thank God daily for each other, and I never stop thanking God for my mother, father, sisters, brothers, and, especially, his gift to me, my beloved brother, Robert. That we could become keepers of our dreams and pass on blessings and benefits to so many others is truly a miracle. I shall be eternally proud of this miracle.

These days, my wife constantly intimates her concern for my health. Our doctor has ordered me to slow my pace. I smile and declare my plans to watch my step and cushion my blazing schedule. I do consider the idea of bringing on additional assistance. When Phil reminds me that she is waiting for the day when that "Paschal assistant" walks through our door, I simply respond, "Yes, Mrs. Paschal."

While my life has been one of nonstop work and nonstop blessings, Robert and I always knew (and tried to show we knew) we were never alone. We could never have reached anywhere near the top rungs of any of the success ladders without understanding and cherishing the roles so many have played. Without the unforgettable, consistent individuals who came to Paschal's from across Atlanta, our country, and, indeed, around the world, there could never have been a Paschal's. For the rest of my life, I shall remain deeply and humbly grateful. I sincerely wish I could remember every name, detail, and situation that brought Paschal's into being. However, my heart holds nothing but eternal love for all who came our way.

Through the years, there were the loyal friends, staff members, patrons, celebrities, vendors, and "just people." All strengthened us and, to borrow a phrase sometimes used by politician Henry Dodson, so many of you kept us "propped up." At Paschal's Restaurant, many were members of the Concerned Black Clergy, the Coffee Club, SNCC, NAACP, and SCLC. There were politicians, sororities, fraternities, clubs, organizations, college students, teachers, administrators, musical and visual artists, church members, and even strangers. In addition, so many parents brought their children. Poor and rich people came. Black, white, yellow, red, and brown people came. The precious memories shall never perish. If there is a Paschal history, the people have made it so. Forgive me if I have not given all the credit where it is surely due. My heart is full of love for each and every one who has passed our way. Moreover, for my now-deceased and beloved brother, Robert, I still sincerely—and will forever—hold onto my deepest love, honor, and appreciation.

So many of you have shared your love with us. Along the way, you taught us much and reconfirmed much of what we already knew. Your love has added—and continues adding—depth and new dimensions to whatever we may have known. Some basics can never be forgotten or destroyed. They are planted solidly on the pages of time and will forever shine light on the heads of others as they blaze their own pathways to success.

The Paschal Formula for Success

- If you do not set out always determined to do your best in everything you undertake, then simply do not set out.

- When your best is done, never quit! Your best is only one step toward moving you upward to doing even better than what you have just called your best.

- Never engage in underhanded behavior. The hand that takes the lead in engaging in unclean acts can never be cleaned again, no matter how hard you scrub.

- Hard work as well as belief in God, self, and your fellow human beings all pay off.

- When you truly love people, you do not have to try to impress anyone with false attitudes and behaviors. Most people can spot a phony when you first drive up.

- Success only pays off when success takes root in your own mind, not in the mind of someone who wants you to be successful.

- When you are willing to learn, your mind remains open to life and all of its great possibilities.

- Productive dreams do not wither away and die. Rather, they grow and grow and grow. As your dreams grow, so do all the unlimited powers of your creativity. Never stop dreaming or working toward your every dream.

Dreaming should never end. Fulfilling your dreams is a journey into desire, trust, belief, faith, hope, hard work, and then blessed fulfillment. However, that journey must be approached in an arena where fear does not exist. Profound, continuous belief in your own capabilities will give you the strength and perseverance necessary to emerge victorious. Never stop thinking and believing that magical things will happen in your life, no matter your age.

I will share a recent example: As Herman Russell and I began our purposeful deliberations around plans to establish a new Paschal's Restaurant in Castleberry Hill, we heard all of the yeas, nays, whys, and a considerable number of wows. The "Wow!" added music to our positive perspective. There were (and perhaps still are) some who question whether we still have the will, energy, and all else it takes to see our ideas come into successful fruition, given our advancing ages.

I truly believe that pursuing one's dreams should not be stunted by one's age, race, birthplace, or present location in this universe. Because I am now eighty-two years of age, that does not mean I have lost my desire to dream or my ability to think. I will not ever lose my will to move into action when I am smitten by continuous waves of "dreaming without ceasing." Pursuing dreams has been my life's blood. Dreaming and pursuing dreams, I have no doubt will keep my "soul anchored in the Lord" and his will for me until death.

In the absence of such deeply embedded beliefs, I feel Robert and I would have never been graced to share in the receipt of what, for us, was some unforgettable honors. In 1984, Morris Brown College conferred an honorary doctor of laws degree on me. That heartfelt recognition tearfully humbled Robert and me:

> ...the business perspicacity of the shoeshine boy from Thomson, the proprietor of James' Place, the restaurateur par excellence, and the executive vice president of Dobbs-Paschal Midfield Corporation. Thus, two sons of Henry and Lizzie Paschal of Thomson, Georgia, the entrepreneur and the chef, through their work ethic, determination, vision, deliberate decisions, teamwork, and support from their families were able to realize their dream for bigger business. Their parents would have been proud. We, their friends and associates, are not only proud. We are also grateful to them for what they have given our community.

While some of the awards, including the proclamations, plaques, pictures, and newspaper and magazine articles may singularly reference my name, you and I know, without Robert, there would have never been a Paschal's, nor would there have been any honors, many of them firsts. Rarely, anyone who speaks to me of memories of Paschal's fails to include Mr. Robert.

Whatever we Paschals may have contributed—or continue to contribute—to the pages of history grew out of lives firmly grounded in the basics of hard work, trying to live right, and offering human service. The joys of living, the satisfaction of contributing to the fulfillment of others, the ability to aid in building minds, and creating a passion for life in others have been our goal. We can only say, "Thanks be to God!"

My wife and I as well as our entire family feel privileged, blessed, and reinforced by God's bountiful, continuous showers of blessings. We have been generously able to share in God's love and share that love with so many others. As a family, we have been able to remain faithfully strong in our devoted love to each other, our families, and the thousands of others whose lives we, according to so many, have been blessed to enrich.

Your every dream has a possibility for being transformed into reality, but only *you* can make it so! Your mind and your body are gifts from God. Let nothing and no one inhibit your progress toward fulfillment. You have total responsibility for the development, training, and application of God's gifts to you.

God bless all of you, forever and ever.

Reflections

"They are two men who are doing something!"
**Norris B. Herndon, president of Atlanta Life Insurance Company, in 1959.
Son of Alonzo Herndon (1858–1927), founder of Atlanta Life Insurance
Company, Atlanta's first black millionaire**

"Robert and James Paschal were something else!" They did something truly
unique! They were not college-educated men, but anytime you can take a
damn lowly chicken and do what they did with a chicken…that's one hellavu
damn chicken, isn't it?
"Lady" Tanya Freeman, FOX 5 News Atlanta (July 28, 2003)

Just utter the name Paschal and an internationally diverse crowd will chime
back, "Robert's fried chicken," "service with a smile," "Mrs. Ora Belle Sherman," or "La Carrousel." For fifty years in Atlanta, Georgia, James and Robert
Paschal demonstrated how hard work as well as a loving, kind, and, at times,
firm and deeply rooted passion for offering exceptional services could achieve
profitable outcomes. The decades of the Paschal brothers of Thomson and
Atlanta form an unforgettable and colorful mosaic of living black history.

In the decades encompassing 1947 to 1995, "stopping by Paschal's" was the
regular, common declaration throughout much of Atlanta. Each with his or
her own special flavor played a major part in giving life to the Paschal history
in Atlanta. Jack and Jill mothers and fathers took their children to Paschal's to
see living examples of black middle-class life and culture. Many people found
the love of their life at Paschal's.

The Paschal brothers had an almost overwhelming impact on their patrons,
friends, students, and staff. The impact has not only been expressed in the
loyal following accumulated in the nearly sixty years the Paschal enterprise has
existed in Atlanta, but it has also been shown in the many tributes paid to

them in the media, at gatherings, and in many writings over the years. Portions of a few of those letters, tributes, and other remarks illustrate the depth of appreciation so many have felt for Robert and James Paschal.

Mrs. Anne Nixon Cooper, Centenarian (103 in January 2005), Community Volunteer

From 1922 to 1938, I lived on Mayson-Turner Avenue, a few blocks from Hunter Street. There, young Robert Paschal worked at Jacob's Drug Store at the soda fountain. Before long, he was also selling foods and snacks. Robert became so popular in the community that we were all calling him "the mayor of Hunter Street." He was so kind [and] helpful. He would see about anyone in the neighborhood. Then, when James came to town, we all fell in love with him, too. Those two Paschal brothers, from the start, won over the hearts of everybody, black and white.

When the brothers opened their first little place on West Hunter Street, we were all so glad. When they made it possible for us to be able to sit at a table where we could have sodas and ice cream, we could hardly contain ourselves. From that little beginning, across the street grew the great restaurant, nightclub, and hotel. I just want you to know that I watched all of it grow, and I watched their rise to the top. I am proud of it!

Mrs. Lucy A. Davenport, Former Paschal's Staff Member, Decatur, Georgia

During early Fall 1959, I was a young lady of nineteen years of age. I had the pleasure of eating at the famous Paschal's Restaurant. At that time, the restaurant was located across the street from its present location.

Eating at Paschal's was very exciting to me, being from a family of fifteen children. We had moved from the rural south (country) only four years prior. My father and mother were not able to ever let us eat in a restaurant.

This was during the segregation times. The joy one felt after having an opportunity to dine in a clean, well-kept restaurant owned and operated by black people was like the exciting feeling one experienced when seeing black people on television for the first time.

For us, being able to eat at Paschal's was a great, special feeling. Paschal's, we had been told, was a place for the rich, famous, very important, and business people. Soon after, I began working at Paschal's. For a short while, I learned Paschal's was really a place for any[one] who wanted to dine, eat, enjoy, or work. There was even a young white lady who worked at Paschal's.

In the spring of 1963, I was working as a waitress at another local restaurant, which was also owned by another black businessman. On one of my days off, I decided to go to the new Paschal's Restaurant. As I sat enjoying my favorite, a fried chicken sandwich, another black businessman, Mr. Henry Dodson, a photographer, a politician later on, saw me. Knowing I was a waitress at Beamon's, he asked if I was going to apply for a job at Paschal's. I told him no. I was just out for lunch. Mr. Dodson said, "You wait right here. I'll be right back!"

He came back with Mr. Robert Paschal and his brother, Mr. Gilmer Paschal, in tow. I later learned Mr. Gilmer Paschal was also on staff, in a managerial position. Mr. Dodson had told the brothers I was a very good waitress and was the kind they should have working in their business. Mr. Robert asked when could I report for work. I was hesitant to answer because I had no reason to leave Beamon's. But, after a few days, I began working at Paschal's and continued to work at Beamon's. Working at Paschal's became one of the greatest opportunities of my life. Not only did I enjoy my work and felt fairly paid, but I met so many famous people. I met people from the musical and entertainment fields; the political, business, educational, and religious fields; as well as well-known persons from private life.

It was mandatory that all of their employees had to be well-trained and had to greet every customer in a polite, respectful manner. No excuses. All the service and wait staff personnel were required to offer quick, courteous, friendly service to every customer. The staff had to be always well-groomed and dressed in their appropriate, clean uniforms, except for Mrs. Sherman [the hostess]. It did not matter which of the dinning areas anyone chose to be served in. All customers had to be treated with the same respect. China, silverware, and glassware were always used in every eating area.

The Paschal brothers were a team like you had never seen before. They were respectful to each other. If an employee would approach one of the brothers about a perceived employee problem or a business-related matter at any time, the response would always be, "My brother and I will get with you on that." And they would. You could count on it. I never heard the[m] expressing any differences they may have had about anything in public. They were always pleasant and respectful to each other, their employees, and the customers.

The day of Dr. Martin Luther King Jr.'s funeral, we started serving breakfast at 7:00 AM. At 10:00 AM, Mr. James Paschal said, "In honor of Dr. King, we will serve no one else until after the funeral service was over." Mr. Paschal placed television sets in various eating locations so the employees, customers, and others who chose to do so could stay at the restaurant and watch the service.

I am so glad I had the opportunity to work for the Paschal brothers. The memories will always be with me, and I will always be appreciative and thankful to God for that great experience.

Mrs. Earlene Ammons Harris, Educator and Community Volunteer, Atlanta

Mr. James is formal in his approach. He always says, "Yes, ma'am" and "No ma'am," without regard to age. He is very dignified in his carriage—impeccably groomed, well-shod and well-suited, and calm in his demeanor. He does not raise his voice or behave in a high-handed manner when speaking with others. He is deliberate in his actions and a gentle businessman.

Mr. Robert was the opposite of Mr. James in many respects. Mr. Robert's domain was the kitchen. His presence assured quality control. He was always dressed in his kitchen whites—white pants, white shirt, and white apron. If things were going the way he wanted them to go, he was often found sitting on two crates, one step away from the deep fryer. Mr. Robert was small in stature. He hardly looked like he was 100 pounds, soaking wet. Because he was so frail, I worried about his health. About this time, he was known to leave the hospital and go straight to the kitchen, hospital bracelet and all, and start frying chicken. On one occasion, after he had proudly shown me his hospital bracelet, I asked him when was he going to retire and take better care of himself. He laughed aloud and replied, "Honey, these young Negroes don't know how to fry no chicken."

The first Sunday after moving to Atlanta in 1988, my husband, J. Jerome Harris, and I ate at Paschal's. J. Lowell Ware, then publisher of the *Atlanta Voice*, invited us to dine with him and his wife, Alyce. I had fried chicken, collard greens, and corn with sliced tomatoes and onions on the side. I washed all of that down with sweet tea. Mr. Ware had the same thing, except he ordered buttermilk. How many restaurants would be able to fulfill that request? The next Sunday, I was back at Paschal's. We soon abandoned the formality of the dining room and started taking our meals in one of the booths in the lunch counter area.

During the summer of 1989, we were guests of a well-known publishing company who hosted a grand affair at Paschal's. Everyone attending was able to sit in La Carrousel and enjoy jazz music while having drinks. When we were ready to move to the dining room, everyone was ushered in so we all could pause beside what I called Paschal's Wall of Fame, pictures of all the heroes of the Civil Rights Movement.

I asked Mr. James if he would honor us by saying a few words of welcome and giving a little of the history of Paschal's. Mr. James was reluctant, but he finally agreed to do so. He warned me that Mr. Robert never liked the lime-light. Therefore, he would not speak to us. Never one to be deterred, I begged and pleaded with Mr. Robert. At the very last minute, he came through!

He started by telling us how old he was and how Paschal's was established. I was grateful, as were all our guests. I felt really special. From that day forward, I never went to Paschal's without looking through the door of the kitchen to see if Mr. Robert was there. If he was, I would go in and chat with him. He was just that kind. My husband often told me, "Earlene, you're not supposed to go into the kitchen." I paid him no attention. If Mr. Robert was there, I knew it was quite all right.

John Ingersoll, Associate Vice President, Arts and Sciences Development, Emory University, Atlanta

I met my wife, Vivian Rippy, in the La Carrousel Lounge in broad daylight amidst a most serious crowd of people, the faculty of Spelman College.

President Albert Manley or one of his advisors thought it would be refreshing to hold the first faculty meeting of the 1968–1969 academic year off-campus. I [was] an assistant professor of history. During the social hour, I saw the lovely new hire for the German department, instructor Vivian Rippy, fresh from a year in Germany on the Middlebury College program.

We did not go out on a date until the following March 7, but we made up for lost time by getting married on June 21. B/V (before Vivian), I had eaten countless times at Paschal's. I already had a special fondness for the place. But A/V (after Vivian), Paschal's assumed the dimensions of a shrine, and I have never driven past that historic site without uttering a thankful prayer for its fried chicken, its brave support of the Movement, and especially its hospitality to the Spelman College faculty one August afternoon thirty-three years ago.

Mr. Howard F. Mills Sr., President/CEO, L'BERTA Enterprises

I had been advised of a black-owned hotel in Atlanta, Georgia, that had about 100 rooms. The early part of 1970, I had the pleasure of making a site visit to see the property. Many of the other hotels I visited were older and usually not the type in which I could comfortably place some of our customers.

I arrived in Atlanta and went to Paschal's Hotel. I was surprised to see a new hotel with restaurants, meeting rooms, and a first-class lounge for upscale entertainment during the evening hours. I was greeted warmly at the front desk, and the bellboy escorted me to my room. I could not wait to put my bags down so I could check out the remainder of the facilities.

I usually made my site visits during the evening hours to catch everyone off guard and without an escort to talk to staff and other customers. One group [was] praising the facility and was telling me how often they brought people to Paschal's. One man mentioned how the chicken was the best. He introduced me to Mr. James Paschal.

Mr. James Paschal, and his brother, Robert, were two of the most modest, low-key, and eager-to-please gentlemen I had ever met. I had the great pleasure later in the evening of meeting with both of the Paschal brothers. I had not heard the word "sir" used so much in my entire life. They were more interested in treating their customers correctly and with respect than anything else. At no time did I ever get the feeling that money was their primary goal.

I remember one situation that truly measured the character, integrity, discipline, and true professionalism of the brothers. Whenever the National Urban League held its conferences, we would seek out African-American facilities to convene a heavy reception for a group of 225 executive directors and board members and executive staff. I was determined to use Paschal's, even though many other places had been identified as beautiful as well as having space, caterers, decorations, and whatever we needed.

Paschal's Matador Room was not large enough to accommodate our needs. I suggested using the Matador and Sherwood Rooms. I felt, by putting up a temporary wall, we would be set. Mr. James told me my idea would violate the city's fire code. We certainly could not block off the big lobby. That would deny free access to hotel guests needing to move freely around the hotel, including the dining rooms.

Finally, Mr. James Paschal said, "Mr. Mills, my brother and I really appreciate you bringing this big piece of business to us. However, we do not believe we can do this function to meet your specifications. Therefore, we would suggest you take it to a facility that will give you what you want with less headaches."

I respectively requested that Mr. Paschal allow me to work it out. I assured him that our guests and I would be pleased. We held a marvelous, beautiful affair. Even the Paschal brothers were very pleased with their accomplishments. To add a note of their unselfishness, they recommended a small, local African-American baker to assist us with some of the desserts.

Mrs. Malinda King O'Neal, Owner/CEO, MKO Graphics & Printers

Not only did the Paschal Brothers afford me an opportunity to get to know many Atlantans, they were like family. I am still reaping the benefits of my forty-six years of relationship with the Paschal brothers—James, Robert, and Gil.

For fifteen years, I have hired college students as receptionists in my printing business, just as Paschal's hired me and so many other college students. I have tried to pass on the Paschal brothers' legacy of reaching out to the community.

Mrs. Bette Graves Thomas, Retired Educator and Secretary of First Congregational Church United Church of Christ

As child[ren] of two schoolteachers who were paid very modestly, my sister and I looked forward to payday. After school and a trip to the bank, Mama would take us to Paschal's, where each of us was allowed to order a chicken sandwich of our choice: chicken, tomato, and lettuce for fifty-two cents, or chicken, French fries, or potato salad for fifty-seven cents. Although this may seem very meager [now but], it was indeed a real treat for us. This memory, coupled with [the memory of] the fried shrimp dinner my boyfriend bought me for six dollars the day after my prom still bring pleasant thoughts to mind.

Judge Gail S. Tusan, Superior Court of Fulton County

Paschal's has offered a safe haven for several African-American professional groups. In the mid-1980s, Justice Robert Benham formed a networking group for African-American judges from across the state. At that time, there were not very many of us, and we needed an organization that would support us in our professional capacities.

Because we were new and not many in number, funds were scarce. We turned to Paschal's for our organization's first annual dinner. As usual, the Paschal brothers and their staff received us with open arms. Mrs. Sherman and the other staff members treated us so well. They were all so attentive to our needs. We will always be indebted to Paschal's for helping so many of us get our start.

There were other professional groups who also benefited from the Paschal love. These included the Georgia Association of Black Women Attorneys and the Gate City Bar Association.

Mrs. Lottie Watkins, President/CEO, Lottie Watkins Enterprises, Community Volunteer

All of Atlanta quickly learned to love Robert and James Paschal, and they quickly became our miracle men of West Hunter Street.

Quotes from "An Evening Honoring Robert and James Paschal"

Bryant Bass

"I will miss Paschal's Restaurant because I was there the first day they opened in 1947, the last day they were open in 1996, and just about every day in between."

Julian Bond

"No morning was ever complete without a meeting of the Paschal's Precinct, a gathering of wannabe politicos, has-beens, might-bes, and is-toos!"

Arthur Bronner

"The Paschal brothers have been an inspiration, and Paschal's fried chicken was a treat to everyone who ate there. And I ought to know because I was one of the regulars!"

Tyrone Brooks, State Representative, Former Civil Rights Volunteer

"Mr. James and Mr. Robert are two creative, innovative, and revolutionary businessmen who truly have made everlasting contributions to the African-American community."

Ben Brown

"Robert and James Paschal are two men who brought an institution into being, which will live to serve generations to come in the name of the Paschal Center."

W. L. "Bill" Calloway

"Fifty years ago, I negotiated the lease on the building for the Paschal brothers' first restaurant. I am proud to have played a small part in their pioneering spirit."

Albert M. Davis, MD

"Congratulations, Robert and James Paschal, for your phenomenal success in satisfying the souls and appetites of Atlanta citizens for many years!"

Charles Goosby, DDS

"The exalted dignity of the chicken achieved a new level of respect because of the Paschal brothers."

Bishop Cornelius Henderson

"The history of the Civil Rights Movement was significantly impacted by this Southern landmark and the Paschal brothers with their special hospitality."

Attorney Donald and Louise Hollowell

"For fifty years, Robert and James Paschal, progressive visionaries, demonstrated courtesy, honesty, service, and satisfaction to their customers and the entire community."

Curtis Mayfield (deceased), Artist/Entertainer (via telecon)

"Mr. James and Mr. Robert Paschal were very strong forces in my life. Mr. James probably does not even remember, and he is too modest to confess, if he did. He probably saved me from going to jail one time. He may have even saved my life. One time, I thought a brother had done me wrong. Mr. James, in his soft, but firm, way, literally took me by the arm and talked me out of getting in the face of this brother. I will never forget him. I am sure Mr. James kept me out of serious trouble."

Phyllis Paschal (Passed away on October 3, 2005)

"I don't know of any morning he [James] left home for work without an eager expression on his face."

Ora Belle Sherman (Passed away on January 16, 2004)

"For thirty-five years on the job at Paschal's, working with Mr. Robert and Mr. James and meeting new people and old friends every day has been just like therapy for me!"

Lewis Slaton (Former District Attorney)

"After thirty-five years of friendship and association, I can truthfully say that Robert and James Paschal are twenty-four karat!"

Harvey B. Smith, DDS

"Robert and James, I miss you both, but I miss the chicken hash and grits the most!"

Juanita Sellers Stone

"Robert and James Paschal epitomize a true team spirit, steadfastness of pace, supportive sharing, and a work ethic extraordinaire."

Roswell O. Sutton

"Simply stated, fifty extraordinary years of entrepreneurship epitomizes the life and work of Robert and James Paschal."

Richard Thomas Jr., Former Paschal Employee

"Thank God I am one of their entrepreneurial offsprings. When I truly was in need, they allowed me to work in their kitchen. There was always Mr. James, the personification of a solid, gentlemanly, soft-spoken, smiling, always nattily attired man in total fullness. You just knew Mr. James truly cared, but he was taking no mess. [He] can twist your arm off to the next joint to head you in the right direction, but he makes sure you feel no pain as he did it. You just knew you had to do what he said because you just knew the man was right."

Full Text of Articles and Remarks

Article from the March 5, 1997 edition of the *New York Times*
Robert H. Paschal, restaurateur, dies

Business played role in civil rights struggle

ATLANTA—Robert H. Paschal, the Atlanta restaurateur and entrepreneur whose perfectly seasoned fried chicken sustained the civil rights movement, died Thursday at his Atlanta home. He was 88.

His younger brother, James, said the cause was cancer. They were partners for fifty years in a business that started as a lunch counter and grew to include a hotel, restaurant, nightclub, and lucrative airport concession.

Because it was one of the few black-owned eating and meeting establishments in the city, Paschal's became a natural home for the civil rights struggle. Among its regular patrons were the Rev. Martin Luther King Jr., Andrew Young, Rep. John Lewis, Julian Bond, Adam Clayton Powell Jr., Stokely Carmichael, the Rev. Joseph Lowery, the Rev. Jesse Jackson, and Maynard H. Jackson.

Lewis, who now represents the congressional district that includes Paschal's, recalled Monday that he ate his first meal in Atlanta at Paschal's after arriving from Alabama to work for the Student Nonviolent Coordinating Committee. He also remembered the last time he ever saw King was at Paschal's, about two weeks before King was assassinated.

"Some of the decisions that affected the directions of the country were made in that restaurant," Lewis said.

To some extent, civil rights strategists were drawn to Paschal's by necessity. Until the sit-ins of the early 1960s, many of which were planned at Paschal's, public accommodations in Atlanta were segregated, and there few other places that black Atlantans could gather to share thoughts and a meal. But they also were drawn by "Mister Robert's incomparable fried chicken, candied yams, early peas, collard greens, and other Southern delicacies."

Even though the brothers sold the hotel and restaurant last year to Clark Atlanta University for about $3 million, Atlantans still salivate at the mere mention of Paschal's chicken. It was crispy, tender, spicy, and always delivered steaming hot to the table.

"If Robert had been a little bit lighter and if capital had been available, we wouldn't know about Colonel Sanders," Lowery said Monday. "It would have been Colonel Paschal's."

Paschal was happy to leave the company's business dealings to his brother while he took charge of the kitchen. He was remembered Monday as a quiet, gentle man who impressed people with his generosity and his tenacious work ethic.

"Paschal was the ultimate role model in terms of the dignity of work," Lowery said. The story of the Paschal brothers is, in many ways, the story of black entrepreneurship in the second half of the twentieth century.

After moving to Atlanta as young adults from Thomson, the brothers opened their lunch counter in 1947 in west Atlanta near the campuses of the city's historically black colleges. After serving thousands of chicken sandwiches, they moved their business across Hunter Street (now renamed Martin Luther King Jr. Drive) to a larger building. They eventually opened a hotel and lounge called La Carrousel.

As the city's first black-owned hotel, Paschal's was a source of pride in the black community. La Carrousel drew integrated crowds to see headliners like Aretha Franklin and Ramsey Lewis.

During the civil rights movement, the Paschal brothers provided food and meeting space for free for planning sessions preceding the Atlanta sit-ins, the March on Washington, and Mississippi Freedom Summer. When King was killed, the restaurant drew so many mourners that the brothers had to close the doors.

As black Atlantans became the city's preeminent political force, Paschal's remained an important meeting place for power brokers and candidates, starting with Maynard H. Jackson's first mayoral campaign in 1973.

Soon, the place became a mandatory stop for white politicians, whether candidates for district attorney or president, seeking validation among blacks.

Reverend Dr. Joseph Lowery
Eulogy for Robert Paschal

Bob [was] a vibrant, energetic, creative, culinary artist. Whenever you would challenge Bob about the origin of some of the delicacies from the Paschal's kitchen, [he] would laughingly reflect about how he gave his mother some of the credit for his own conjured up recipe.

Bob's cooking capabilities really came about as the result of his poking around in the kitchen alongside his mother, Mrs. Lizzie Paschal, and his learning experiences after he arrived and remained in Atlanta. He learned well, and he taught well all of those whom he trained. Of course, that did not include his brother, James. Brother James handled the management section of the business. James was never accused of being blessed with a mind to cook. Bob was satisfied to let his younger brother handle the business end of their partnership.

When you really got to know him, Bob Paschal could make you split your sides laughing. He could literally make you cry. He could tell you some not-so-tall tales about growing up poor and black, on the low down, back sides, and the mean front ends of Southern sharecropping in McDuffie County, Thomson, Georgia. How he and his brother James, their parents, and other brothers and sisters toiled and struggled. About how they traveled up the lowly, dark, and rough sides of the mountains. How he and his brother James climbed, worked hard, and fought many enemies in the early days to make Paschal's what it was, what it became for many, what it is today, and what it shall forever remain. The names Robert and James Paschal will never, never die. Why?

Because those of us who have been the beneficiaries, those of us who know the truths about how deep are the roots of the legacy of James and Robert Paschal, those of us here today, those of us who are spread around the globe who enjoyed even a taste of the offerings of the Brothers Paschal, must vow, here and now, to spread that history. We must call to the attention of our children and our grandchildren how deep a debt we all owe to James and Robert Paschal. We must tell the truth! They need to know, down through the generations, that if you were black and many times white and lived through and withstood the pain of the regular hell and damnation rained down upon our heads just trying to be free, that James and Robert Paschal stood tall. They were beside us—around us. We often had to rest our tired, weary, jailed, and beaten bodies in the beds of their Paschal Hotel. They were indeed under us.

We must tell generations about the old West Hunter Street and the new Martin Luther King Jr. Drive.

Oh, Bob could tell you, oh so vividly, how they wrestled in the dark and vicious pits of prejudice and jealousy, white jealousy, and yes, sometimes even black jealousy. How the sharp and painful fangs of racism often tore into the depths of their hearts. How the white bank officials must have laughed at Robert and James for having the unmitigated gall to seek big bank loans so they could push and strive to seriously join the ranks of Atlanta's business moguls. How these men must often have had to blaze, face first, through the stinging fire and blizzards of denial of their requests to borrow money, which would have helped them advance their businesses, businesses that would have offered jobs and possibilities, not just for blacks, but for persons of any hue. How just some money could have helped them, before they pressed forward, and made it happen anyway. But no, they probably had to fight denials because they had been born with faces that were undeniably black, though some said "mixed with a bit of Caucasian." But the Paschal brothers were of genius and solid quality.

The more they were denied, the harder they fought. Oh, thanks to a mighty God, their battles were sweetly and victoriously won. These disciples and servants of God's goodwill and giving have duly earned any and all of our treasured reflections. These two hard-working boys to men have truly spoken to the world. They have given to us all fifty years of seeing and enjoying what good sense, hard work, fairness, honesty, good food, and, yes, managing your money can bring. They taught us all how love will win out over anger, hatred, and racism. They showed us how to shove off one's back the heavy burdens of being denied your rights in a racist society. They have shown us what it means to reject anger and show love when anger would almost seem justifiably the choice of the moment.

The Paschal brothers rose to where they kept company with some of the world's most famous and most powerful. Yet, neither ever, ever lost the common touch. Bob loved all kind of folks, but he truly held a deep, deep, abiding love and respect for his business-headed brother, James. That is, except when he wanted to show old James, who is right dapper himself, how he, Bob, could outdress his right spiffy younger brother.

Andrew Young, former UN Ambassador, Mayor of Atlanta
"An Evening Honoring Robert and James Paschal"

In spite of an absolutely daunting flight plan, I knew I simply had to be here. Because I, like so many others of you in this room, owe much of the richness, meaning, success, and safety of the Civil Rights Movement and my own success to the overflowing generosity and love of James and Robert Paschal.

The Paschal brothers were there for me when I ran for and won the 5th District Seat for the United States Congress. They were there for me each time I ran for mayor of the City of Atlanta and for governor of Georgia. Ralph David Abernathy said, "No doubt, the walls of America will be changed in Paschal's."

James and Robert Paschal brought everything it took to help make a great Atlanta even greater with them to Atlanta. All that could possibly have been given has been given. Every year, after our marches, we would gather at Paschal's for our family meals. Coretta would invite various celebrities, and they would come. We started out, and our gatherings numbered about fifteen or twenty. Our crowd soon grew to over 150. We could all feel that deep, inner spirit. Robert and James Paschal poured forth from their broad, loving hearts, a special kind of bravery, love, and compassion as well as a sincere and public kind of caring that this city had never seen before from two brothers, black, or white. And they never asked for—nor did they expect—anything in return. But they did not stop with Atlanta.

You can travel all over America, even to some foreign countries, and say the words, "Paschal's of Atlanta." And someone will eagerly tell you a story of either eating, educating, lovemaking, meeting, soaking up the world's greatest jazz, the transformation of civil rights, or some other uplifting human epic in the pure Paschal style. The story will be either the savory and delectable succulence of Robert's fried chicken and the many whose hungry bellies were filled for free. Or, they will tell you about the comforts and joys of love defined or intimately discovered, or rediscovered, at Paschal's hotel. Or, there are many, many others who will share how James and Robert so often spent their own money to make life so much better for so many others. Many times, these were people they did not even know. But they warmly took them in on the words and confidence of others. What a blessing they have been.

I simply must share this soulful piece of Negro history. After the brutal assassination of Martin King, Coretta spent time at Paschal's writing her book. These two brothers perhaps bonded more folks out of jail, fed more hungry folks, and schooled more poor black folks and some white folks with Paschal money than any other black folks with money that I know of. These brothers made personal choices, which made them, as two stalwart black men, infinitely more accessible to those who needed their sweeping benevolence and giving spirits. The full range of their eclectic brilliance transcended any human obstacles that might have slowed their sharing of the blessings that God had so generously bestowed upon them. Now, if that ain't love, culture, Christianity, and caring for one's people, all people, and history made whole, tell me what is. I was there. I was a part. I know whereof I speak.

Jesse Hill, Atlanta Businessman, Retired Head of Atlanta Life Insurance Company
"An Evening Honoring Robert and James Paschal"

Anyone in the hall who truly knows me know[s] how the Paschal brothers were a cosmic power in my own self-actualization. When the climate of downtown Atlanta was filled with racial divisiveness and when downtown Atlanta was a heatedly unwelcome territory for our black brothers and sisters, Robert and James Paschal always stepped forward as our two great Hannibal warriors of our time. They often had to help us keep cool heads and fearless hearts.

What for many of us were fearful and trembling times, Robert and James Paschal stood bravely there. With arms outstretched, they were steadfast beacons of love, hope, and black power. They were examples of colorless power. It was these stalwart, humble, two, strong, black brothers who offered themselves and their place, Paschal's. What was to become nationally known and recognized as "The Place," Paschal's was a courageous, open, resilient citadel, a safe haven in Atlanta for blacks. And then, there were also those whites who, at such a time, owned the courage to assemble, to meet together prayerfully and politically with black folks.

It was there, at Paschal's, that we would plan our next steps for fighting in the struggle to make certain that Atlanta would fulfill its destiny to become the lighthouse for its own loving, interracial actions, for clearing its pathways and building, nurturing, and sustaining its foundation and the will to become "the city too busy to hate." While we are not totally there yet, thanks to Robert and James Paschal, we are certainly farther along on our way. We are not where we were before Paschal. These two humble men persisted in refusing to acknowledge or accept their designated status as legends in their own time. They have been modest to a fault.

The students of the nonviolent arm of the Civil Rights Movement and the Paschal regime could form legions. They are the poor, the now rich and famous, the politician, the preacher, the sinner, the saved, the black, the white, the brown, the red, and the yellow. It is true. Almost any and all who came the way of Robert and James Paschal found outstretched arms and horns of plenty. This affair this evening is a classic example. Look around us. We are, this evening, business and industry, corporate and small. We are politics, religion, society, education, law, medicine, finance, technology, and the arts. We are here from all parts of Atlanta and the nation. But most importantly, we are family. We are all here, one family of humankind, black, white, red, yellow, and brown, poor and wealthy. We are here simply to say a real, long overdue and grand thanks to Robert and James Paschal.

Mrs. Coretta Scott King, Widow of Dr. Martin Luther King Jr.

Though we, all of us who dearly love Robert and James Paschal, deeply mourn the loss of Robert Paschal, I commend the decision to proceed with this richly deserved tribute to the Paschal brothers.

They have given so much to our community and the people of this nation. I will always remember Robert Paschal as one of the warmest, kindest people I have ever known. He had a beautiful, gentle spirit, and he loved people, just as he loved life.

His beloved brother, James Paschal, is also one of the most caring, compassionate people I have ever had the privilege of knowing. James has not only been a great, beloved brother to Robert. He has also been a brother to us all, and we salute his loving spirit on this day as well.

Together, Robert and James Paschal have been among the most successful entrepreneurs in the history of Atlanta, black or white. Through sheer hard work, determination, and business expertise, the Paschal brothers have built magnificent enterprises that are admired across this nation.

I will always treasure warm memories of dinner at Paschal's, where the King family, including Daddy King, Mama King, and all the rest of the King family, ate every Sunday for many years. We loved Paschal's cooking and all of the good people who worked there. They always made our family feel like we were right at home.

But today, I want to salute Robert and James Paschal for their outstanding example of compassion, caring, and social responsibility as businessmen and citizens. Paschal's Restaurant was the meeting place of the Civil Rights Movement and the site of many historic events during our freedom struggle.

Paschal's was the only public place in Atlanta where racially-integrated groups could meet and dine together until the desegregation of public accommodations. After James and Robert opened Paschal's Hotel, it became the hotel of the movement, the place where black leaders and freedom fighters could call home when they were in Atlanta. The freedom fighters paid high and lasting tribute to the hospitality they always received at Paschal's.

My husband, Martin Luther King Jr. and his staff at the Southern Christian Leadership Conference held many planning meetings, strategy sessions, and press conferences at Paschal's Restaurant. It was at Paschal's that Martin officially announced the Poor Peoples' Campaign on March 10, 1968.

Robert and James Paschal have provided their resources to support SCLC, the King Center, other civil rights groups, and a host of deserving causes, which have helped people in need. The brothers have lifted up our community.

And though today, March 4, 1997, we mark Robert Paschal's passing with a deep and abiding sadness, we thank God for his life and that of his beloved brother, James, who continues to serve our community with selfless devotion.

And so, it is with deep respect, admiration, and gratitude that I join in this tribute honoring Robert and James Paschal. I add my words of appreciation for their remarkable contributions.

Mrs. Mignon Lackey Lewis, Spelman Graduate of the 1940s

May 1947. My mother had traveled to Atlanta from Ardmore, Oklahoma, to attend Atlanta University to study for her master's degree. We lived on the campus of Clark College. The walk to Paschal's was not too far. Soon, we began to make many, many trips to indulge in the fun chatter and [to eat] your famous fried chicken and trimmings. Although I and my family had eaten plenty of fried chicken in Oklahoma, none was as delicious as Paschal's chicken.

Months later, I entered Spelman College, and my trips to Paschal's were limited only because of the strict rules of students leaving Spelman's campus unsupervised. [But] my boyfriend would make a welcomed delivery to the campus with fried chicken sandwich in hand in brown paper bags, the going "wrapper" at that time.

But Mr. James, you and your brother offered more than delicious fried chicken with all the trimmings to so many thousands of us. It was a cherished era of increased social and political awareness for so many of us students. Paschal's became a vital part of our growth. Your restaurant became our place of learning, believing, and understanding. Even though, so many times, we students may have done more socializing than engaging in serious thought about our educational, social, and economic predicament, we learned. And we shall never forget!

As the years passed and I married, each time my husband and I traveled to Atlanta to escort each of our daughters to college, our first visit, after unloading bags, was to hurriedly make our way to 830 West Hunter Street for an exciting, anticipated visit to Paschal's Restaurant. Each of our daughters was introduced to both you and your brother. We wanted them to know these two black brothers who, by the 1940s, were already known to be two of the most giving, successful, and humble black men we knew.

Mrs. Sara Mitchell Parsons, First White Woman to Run for Election to the Atlanta Board of Education on an Integrationist Platform from *Southern Wrongs to Civil Rights* (1998)

Those beautiful, loving, Paschal brothers overflowed with compassionate service. They were never groveling, no drivel, never boastful, just filled with equanimity of heart to all those dedicated fighters who were in pursuit of freedom for all.

Robert and James Paschal welcomed me to their place of business. I attended many, many meetings and made many of my lasting political and social friends, allies, and alliances at Paschal's. Now let me tell you this. We whites were not crazy. We knew we were not treating black people as we should. We were not dumb. Blind to truth and fairness, maybe. But we knew we were wrong. We knew we were not paying our help enough. We overworked black people and paid them far below what was right for the amount of work we required them to do. It was wrong, wrong, wrong.

Afterword

Hallelujah! It was a must that the Paschal past be told and recorded. The power of the story became even more evident to me during two memorable experiences. First was "An Evening Honoring Robert and James Paschal." The presence of more than 1,400 adoring, beautiful people from all walks of life and places in America made a profound statement of love and deep respect for the lives of James and Robert Paschal. That gathering of friends in the Tom Murphy Ballroom of the Georgia World Congress Center in downtown Atlanta was an unbelievable and breathtaking phenomenon.

Five years later, the late Honorable Maynard Jackson said it far more eloquently during our conversation in the latter part of 2002, with the promise to meet again the following year:

> It will haunt us forever, if those of us who were there, who were a vital part of this rich legacy, leave to our children the task of having to excavate and shake off the dust from the glowing records of James and Robert Paschal. It will be nothing short of an act of negligence.
>
> Varied multitudes passed the way of Robert and James Paschal. Many were drawn in by the compassion, caring, and protection of these two brothers. Everyone who paused was blessed for having done so. Not only were these brothers men of honor, but also sincere, hardworking, and giving. Atlanta's history and the history of our nation have been forever blessed by the lives of these two men. Robert and James Paschal are forceful examples of black intelligence and guidelines for success and self-designed systems for earning and sharing personal wealth.

As my basic research continued and began broadening, evidence rapidly mounted supporting Maynard's position and that of hundreds of others. What makes the story of James and Robert Paschal so unique, historical, demanding, and lasting?

Listening to the experiences and engaging in interviews and conversational exchanges was moving and convincing. So many leaders, writers, editors, and educators have placed James and Robert Paschal in a unique place in history. The many who helped to shape the times have said they know of no other comparable history, including the late Dr. Benjamin E. Mays and the imminent historian, Dr. John Hope Franklin, who, when he visited Paschal's, remarked to Mr. James Paschal, "You brothers owe history a favor. Record your story."

> Historians may well recall that Paschal's Motor Hotel was used often as the war room for nonviolent revolution. Paschal's establishment has been the center for more than a decade of a glorious campaign to build a new America, an America free of racism, war, and poverty. An establishment described by his friend, Julian Bond, as simply, 'The Place.'[1]

Often, the Paschal brothers had to face down those who doubted their capabilities. There were the vicious threats that crawled in from white racist ghosts too timid to take human form. There were the jealous stares and sly comments of disbelief from our own people. If their detractors had given themselves a chance, surely they would have been transformed by the grace of God and his two servants, the Paschals. But the brothers sailed on, full steam ahead. They continued braving any overt or covert deeds of greed, attempts at deceit, and the ruthlessness that can often dominate the world of business.

James and Robert Paschal are different. They have shown themselves to be brothers of one mind, one purpose, one determination, and one belief in the triumphant possibility of success. Their unique teamwork was formed out of a spirit of love and beauty.

Growing up in Thomson and McDuffie County, Georgia, they saw clearly one white world and one black world. They had seen the inequities in the two worlds. Early on, these exploitive conditions, this state of total servitude of a people, pulled without ceasing at their heartstrings.

As they journeyed onward toward manhood, all of the vicissitudes and devastations wrought by being poor in a world of riches, snarling racism, and hatred became all too real. But they could not let go of their dreams. They

---

1.   Dr. Ralph David Abernathy, quoted in "The Place," by Gene Stephens, *Pride*, 1972.

made lasting promises to themselves, and the power and depth of these promises touched thousands of lives.

From the very beginning of the undertaking of this work, it was obvious the Paschal name holds deep meaning for so many. The brothers are still held close to many hearts and deeply cherished, valued as strong symbols of authentic Atlanta history, black history, and hope and inspiration.

Requests to share personal experiences of the Paschals came in from across the country. All agreed that, during the late 1930s and the ensuing decades and continuing to this time, you could not easily escape this history. If you were born in, lived in, moved into, became educated in, read about, or just heard about black life in Atlanta, Georgia, you had to know the name Paschal. Atlanta and the Paschal brothers were synonymous with black wealth, good living, and a growing opportunity for black success. So many people are convinced their own personal liberations have indelible roots in the Paschal garden.

One member of the Church of God in Christ, Paschal's Restaurant neighbor, said, "We just could not get over the Paschal brothers. Have you ever seen anyone, black or white, who expressed their love for so many? They did not just say, 'We love you.' Mr. Robert and Mr. James showed their love by doing so much, so freely. I know because I was one of those students they helped. They freely shared their abundance with so many."

A young man standing beside her said, "I just want to say this. If Robert and James Paschal, coming out of the mean, gritty, rural sharecropping dirt of McDuffie County, Georgia, [did] what they did, God, what is wrong with the rest of us!"

There were so many other tributes. Expressive voices and letters of congratulations and sentimental journeys at Paschal's poured in.

The Paschal historical quilt contains every imaginable pattern and patchwork of an almost mystical human legacy. That unique history cozily covers almost the length and breadth of the scale of human possibilities. The Paschal brothers were destined to become bridges over troubled waters for many, otherwise lost, soldiers.

Many people believe James and Robert Paschal are the first brothers of color in the United States who can legitimately lay claim to such an empowering epic. The passionate recognition of the significance of the Paschal story and the pleas for its placement in the historical records are not new. One such letter to the brothers is more than thirty-five years old. Dated February 7, 1967, Mrs. Margaret Davis Bowen, wife of then retired Bishop J. W. E. Bowen, implores Robert and James:

Please commission someone to write a book about your families and share your success story with the world!! This is not only Negro history, but American history!

Though swimming against turbulent tides, James and Robert Paschal still managed to emerge as the glue that held life together for so many others, many of whom they hardly knew. These brothers took many great leaps of faith and blazed trails for so many to show so many unlimited dream-making possibilities. Out of their experiences, they spoke softly, forcibly, and prophetically and with a quiet eloquence to future generations.

Respected, rich, and famous by the ages of thirty-eight and forty-seven, these two men truly exemplified role model in the strictest sense. An article about them hints at the need for replication of the Paschal system and laments the seeming lack of support by blacks of black-owned restaurants:

> For some three decades, Paschal's restaurant on Martin Luther King Jr. Drive was the epitome of white tablecloths and fine dining in the African-American community. Paschal's was a place where preachers, business leaders, civil rights activists, and other power brokers gathered for business, pleasure, entertainment, conversation, and, of course, good food. Paschal's was the place for black folks to go for dinner, says Warner Hayes, a lawyer. 'I haven't seen too many other black restaurants appear in the city since Paschal's that was on that level of support and significance. It just has not happened.' Dwight Miller, general manager of Sylvia's [restaurant] said, 'Paschal started the whole trend in Georgia; we're trying to claim their fame.' With an almost reverent demeanor, some still dare, happily, to admit they must return, if they seek to learn, to the feet of the masters of the craft.[2]

Mae Armster Kendall

---

2. Maynard Eaton, "The Fire This Time," *Atlanta Tribune, The Magazine*, September 2001, 25–32.

Selected Bibliography

King, Rev. Martin Luther King Sr. *Daddy King: An Autobiography.* New York: William Morrow & Company, Inc., 1980.

Lewis, John. *Walking with the Wind: A Memoir of the Movement.* New York: Harcourt Brace & Company, 1998.

Pomerantz, Gary M. *Where Peachtree Meets Sweet Auburn.* New York: Scribner, 1996.

Young, Andrew. *An Easy Burden: The Civil Rights Movement and the Transformation of America.* New York: HarperCollins, 1996.

Index

A

Abernathy, Ralph David, description of Paschal's, 11, 103
adoption of Curtis Paschal, 111–112
Allen, Ivan, Jr., on Paschal's Motor Hotel, 129–130
Andrews, Dwight D., 153–154
anger, Paschal family rejection of, 72, 84, 142, 151
army service of James Paschal, 84
aspiration
    of James Paschal, 43–44, 46, 55, 63–64, 90
    Paschal Creed, 99–100
    taught in Paschal family, 33, 36–37
    taught in school, 38
Atlanta
    Black-owned businesses of, 98, 102–103, 115, 129–130, 215, 232–233
    centers of Black cultural life in, 102, 103, 130
    race relations in, 130
Atlanta Action Forum, 138
Atlanta Life Insurance Company, 129, 215, 232
Atlanta University Center, 103, 130
    and Paschal's restaurant, 117–118, 156
    See also Clark Atlanta University
Auburn Avenue, 102

B

Banks, Carolyn Long, 125–126
baptism, 54–55
Barnes, Roy, 154

Bass, Bryant, on Paschal's Restaurant
Beatty, Susan, first white waitress at Paschal's, 134
Black Muslims, and Paschal's Restaurant, 134–135
Black-owned businesses of Atlanta, 98, 102–103, 115, 129–130, 215, 232–233
Bloody Sunday, 126
boll weevil, effects of infestation on Blacks, 30–31
Bond, Julian, 109
    on Paschal's Restaurant, 223
Bowens, Margaret Davis, 112–113
Breakfast at Paschal's Club, 110
Bronner, Arthur, on Paschal's Restaurant, 223
Brooks, Tyrone, on the Paschal brothers' legacy
Brown, Ben, on the Paschal brothers' legacy, 224
Brown, H. Rap, 135, 136
Bryant, Robert T., 141
Bunche, Ralph, 136
business management
    principles of James Paschal, 65–66, 76–77, 79–80, 83, 84, 142, 150
    networking, 87–88
    Paschal Creed, 99–100, 157
    See also work

C

callin' pole, 22
Calloway, W. L., on Paschal's Restaurant, 224
candy store, first large business of James Paschal, 80–83
Carmichael, Stokely, 136
Carne, Jean
Carson Pirie Scott, 140–141
Castleberry Hill. *See* Paschal's Restaurant at Castleberry Hill
Christmas celebrations in the Paschal family, 63
church
    baptism, 54–55
    cultural importance in African American life, 48, 51–52
    revival meetings, 52–54
Citizens Trust Bank, 98, 115, 129
Civil Rights Act, 128, 130

Civil Rights Movement, 72–73
  in Atlanta, 104
  gaining momentum, 116, 133
  interracial nature of, 14
  legal cases, 103–104
  and Paschal's, 11, 12, 14, 107, 116, 124–128, 133–135, 136, 227, 229,
    231–235, 238
  white involvement with, 14, 110
  white reaction against, 126, 128, 134
Clark Atlanta University, 156
  purchase of original Paschal's Restaurant, 154
Clinton, Bill, 104
Concessions International, 141
Congress of Racial Equality, 127
Cooper, Anne Nixon, on Paschal's Restaurant, 216
cotton picking, 18, 27–29
  difficulty of, 30–32
creed, Paschal, 99–100

D

Davenport, Lucy, on Paschal's Restaurant, 216–218
Davis, Albert, on the Paschal brothers' legacy, 224
determination
  of James Paschal, 74, 76–79, 90, 212
  Paschal Creed, 99–100
  taught in the Paschal family, 32, 36, 73, 76–77, 153
Dobbs House Inc., airport contract of, 10, 138
Dobbs-Paschal Midfield Corporation, 139–141
dreams, James Paschal's thoughts on, 211–213

E

Easley, Purvis, 132
Easter celebrations in the Paschal family, 63
education
  balancing with work, 81
  for Blacks in the 1920s and 1930s, 37–39

importance of, 25, 32
valued by Paschal family, 38–39
Emory University, 219
eulogy for Robert Paschal, 3
An Evening Honoring Robert and James Paschal, 1–2, 4–9, 13–14, 125–126, 237
   notable guests at, 5–6
   quotes from, 223–225
   speeches at, 7–8, 231–235

F

fairness, Paschal Creed, 99–100
faith
   Paschal Creed, 99–100
   taught in the Paschal family, 20, 23, 32
family
   and food, 46–48
   unity of, 58–59
fashion
   cultural importance for African Americans, 49
   professional attire, 75
food
   cultural importance of, 22–23
   importance of in family life, 46–48
foundry, James Paschal's work in, 86–87
Fountain Drive neighborhood, 112–113
Franklin, Shirley Clarke, 153
Freeman, Tanya, on the Paschal brothers, 215
fried chicken
   praise of, 215, 224, 227, 228
   Robert's creation of recipe, 13, 97

G

generosity, 95, 101, 135
   Paschal Creed, 99–100
Georgia Restaurant Association, 137
goat, and James Paschal's first business venture, 44–45

Goosby, Charles, on Paschal's Restaurant, 224
Gore, Al, 104
gratitude, 95, 209–210
    Paschal Creed, 99–100
Great Depression, 24–25
    and race relations, 25
Griffin, Marvin, 121

H

Hartsfield-Jackson International Airport, 139
    honors the Paschal brothers, 142
Harris, Earlene Ammons, on Paschal's Restaurant, 218–219
hatred
    warning against, 21, 63, 72, 84, 99–100
Henderson, Cornelius, on the Paschal brothers' legacy, 224
Herndon, Norris B., on the Paschal brothers, 215
Hill, Jesse
    on the Paschal brothers' legacy, 232–233
    praise of Paschal's, 8
history, importance of studying, 16
Hollowell, Donald Lee, 103–104
    on the Paschal brothers' legacy, 224
Holmes, Hamilton, 104
hospitality industry, 88–89, 101, 157, 215, 218
    Paschal Creed, 99–100
hotel. *See* Paschal's Motor Hotel.
Hunter, Charlayne, 104

I

integration, 96, 116, 119, 104, 119, 135, 137, 141–142
Interdenominational Theological Center, 156
Ingersoll, John, memories of La Carrousel, 219

J

Jackson, Jesse, 109
Jackson, Maynard, 109, 137
    on the Paschal brothers' legacy, 7, 237

Jacob's Drug Store, influence on Paschal brothers, 67–68
James's Place, 80–83
Jeptha Street, 130
  renamed Paschal Boulevard, 100
Johnson, "Blind Willie," 34
Johnson, Edith (mother of Phyllis Paschal)
  death of, 146
  relationship with Phyllis, 144
  as single mother, 91–92
  youthful spirit of, 144
Johnson, Marian (sister of Phyllis Paschal), 91–92, 146
Johnson, Phyllis. *See* Paschal, Phyllis
Johnson family, extended, 92
Jordan, Vernon, 104

K

Kennedy, Robert F., 109, 136
Keystone Corporation, 70
King, Coretta Scott, on the Paschal brothers' legacy, 233–234
King, Martin Luther, Jr., 109
  death of, 130, 218
  dream for America, 124
  at Paschal's restaurant, 123, 127, 136, 234
King, Martin Luther, Sr., 123–124
King family, 6
Knox family, 36
Knox Hotel
  Henry Paschal's work at, 71–72
  James Paschal's lessons learned from, 72–77, 79–80
Ku Klux Klan
  and Paschal's, 126, 128
  violence in the South, 32

L

La Carrousel
  atmosphere of, 122
  beginnings of, 118

memories of, 219
performances at, 120, 228
political role of, 122
unifying influence of the arts, 119
Lamar, Hal, on Paschal's restaurant, 108–109
Lewis, John, 109, 136
on Paschal's restaurant, 227
Lewis, Mignon Lackey, on the Paschal brothers' legacy, 234–235
life
of abundance, 146–148
finding success in, 15
love
Paschal Creed, 99–100
taught in the Paschal family, 21, 23, 62
Lowery, Joseph, eulogy of Robert Paschal, 229–230

M

Maddox, Jim, 100
Maddox, Lester, 130
Mansfield, Jayne, 109, 120–121
March on Washington, 127–128
Martin, Clarence T., 100
Martin Luther King Jr. Drive. *See* West Hunter Street
Mayfield, Curtis, on the Paschal brothers' legacy, 224
Mays, Benjamin Elijah, tribute to Paschal brothers, 151
McDonald, Timothy, on Paschal's Restaurant, 136
McDuffie County, Georgia, 20, 34
Mills, Howard F., Sr., on Paschal's, 220–221
Mitchell Street, 130
Moore, Howard, 104
Morehouse College, 156
Morris Brown College, 94, 156
honorary doctor of laws degree conferred on James Paschal, 212
The Movement. *See* Civil Rights Movement.
Mt. Carmel Baptist Church, 51. *See also* church

N

National Urban League, and Paschal's Motor Hotel, 220–221
nonviolence, taught in the Paschal family, 23, 72, 96, 142
numbers racket, and Paschal's Restaurant, 134

O

O'Neal, Malinda King, 5–6
    on the Paschal brothers' legacy, 221

P

Pace, Kate, 74
Parsons, Sarah Mitchell, on the Paschal brothers' legacy, 235
Paschal, Annie Mae, 58
Paschal, Claudie, 58
Paschal, Curtis
    adoption of, 111–112
    adulthood of, 149
    as business partner, 140
Paschal, Effie, 48
Paschal, Florine (wife of Robert), 95
Paschal, Gilmer, 49–50, 66
Paschal, Gussie, 48, 58
Paschal, Henry (father of James and Robert), 17, 18
    decision-making process of, 55
    determination of, 153
    education valued by, 25
    family unity valued by, 58–59
    failing health of, 71
    life of, 40–43
    picking cotton, 28
    relationships with whites, 62, 73
    values of, 40–41, 43
    work ethic of, 19, 71–72
Paschal, Hodges, 66–67

Paschal, James
    army service of, 84
    aspirations of, 43–44, 46, 55, 63–64, 90
    baptism of, 54–55
    and basketball, 77, 81
    birth of, 17
    business management, 65–66, 70–71, 79–80, 83, 142, 150, 218
    business networking of, 87–88
    business sense of, 49, 71, 75, 83
    candy store, first large business of, 80–83
    Christian principles of, 55, 84, 213
    conversion experience of, 53–54
    after death of Robert, 153, 154, 156
    determination of, 74, 76–79, 90, 212
    on dreams, 211–213
    early home life of, 18–19
    education of, 37–39
    entrepreneurialism as defiance, 78–79
    first business venture of, 44–45
    first restaurant of, 97
    foundry work, 86–87
    gratitude of, 209–210
    honorary doctor of laws degree, 212
    in hospitality industry, 88–89, 157, 215, 218
    James's Place, 80–83
    later life, 209
    "life of abundance," thoughts on, 146–148
    parenthood, 112
    past and future, reflections on, 209–210
    and Phyllis Paschal, 92–95, 143, 145, 149
    picking cotton, hatred of, 29, 31, 46, 64
    principles of, 151
    professional attire, importance to, 75
    Pullman porter work, 87–90
    reasons for writing, 14, 15–16
    reliance on Robert, 212
    respect for ailing father, 75–76
    selling vegetables, 64–66

spirituality in business management, 76–77, 80, 84
travels of, 147–148
work ethic of, 72, 74–75, 81–82, 209, 225
See also An Evening Honoring Robert and James Paschal; Paschal brothers
Paschal, Lizzie (mother of James and Robert), 17, 18–19
cooking, 23–24
death of, 84
gardening, 65
homemaking work of, 60–61
picking cotton, 28
Paschal, Phyllis (wife of James), 143–145
college career of, 93–94
early life of, 90–92
extended family of, 92
homemaking skill of, 144, 145, 149–150
and James Paschal, 92–95, 143, 145, 148, 149
learning to cook, 146
and Marian Johnson (sister), 91–92
parenthood, 112
physical description of, 145
relationship with mother, 144
spiritual life of, 144
travels of, 147–148
on work ethic of James, 225
Paschal, Robert
aspirations of, 45–46, 66, 68
in Atlanta, 49–50, 66–67, 96, 216
cooking and business, 142, 229
creation of fried chicken recipe, 13, 97, 229
death of, 2
ethics of, 142, 151, 157
first restaurant of, 97
funeral of, 3, 229–230
gratitude of, 209–210
interactions with customers, 219
obituary for, 227–228
physical description of, 218
picking cotton, 28, 31, 53, 64

sawmill work, 45
work ethic of, 53, 67–68, 97, 218, 228
See also An Evening Honoring Robert and James Paschal; Paschal brothers
Paschal Boulevard, 100
Paschal brothers
    legacy of, 215–216, 221, 223–225, 229, 231–235, 237, 239–240
    overcoming obstacles, 238–239
    overcoming prejudice, 230
    praise of, 215–240
    reliance on each other, 212
    teamwork, 238
Paschal Creed, 99–100
Paschal family, 21
    aspirations of, 18, 33, 36–37, 49–50
    Christian faith of, 20, 32
    Christmas celebrations, 63
    church community and, 51–52
    determination taught by, 73
    Easter celebrations, 63
    education valued by, 25, 32, 38–39
    ethics of, 142
    extended, 46
    farming, 42–43
    food and family life, 46–48
    garden, 46
    home, 33
    home remedies, 63
    house in Thomson, Georgia, 57–61
    hunting, 42
    and Knox family, 36
    move to Thomson, Georgia, 55, 57–58
    nonviolence teachings of, 23, 96, 142
    pride in dress, 49
    relationships with whites, 62–63
    swing incident, 58
    unity of, 58–59
    values of, 36–37, 62–63, 72, 84, 211
    work ethic of, 45, 46, 68–69

Paschal Gang, 110
Paschal's Center at Clark Atlanta University, 154
Paschal's Concessions Inc., 139
Paschal's Motor Hotel
    accommodations of, 131–132
    and Civil Rights Movement, 11, 132, 238
    groundbreaking of, 129
    manager Purvis Easley, 132
    Mayor Ivan Allen on, 129–130
    and National Urban League, 220–221
    opening of, 131
    plans for, 130–131
"Paschal's Precinct," 223
Paschal's Restaurant
    airport contract of, 10
    and Atlanta University Center, 117–118, 156
    awards and honors won by, 133
    beginnings of, 97
    Black Muslims and, 134–135
    Civil Rights Movement and, 12, 14, 104, 116, 124–128, 133–135, 136, 227,
        229, 231–235
    cultural importance of, 102–103, 131, 215–216
    David Abernathy's comments on, 11
    diversity of clientele, 209–210
    Dobbs House, joint venture with, 139–141
    employees of, 100, 117–118, 121, 134, 216–218, 221, 225
    ethics of, 99–100, 101, 118, 142, 157, 211
    expansion of, 105–106, 110, 114–115, 116–117, 118
    famous visitors of, 109, 120, 121, 123, 125, 128, 136, 227, 228
    fried chicken sandwich demand, 107
    gratitude, 209–210
    growth of, 101
    history summarized, 152, 227–228
    initial obstacles to, 98, 100
    integration of, 119, 133, 134, 135, 137, 141–142
    legacy of, 157
    and Martin Luther King Jr., 123, 127, 136, 218, 234
    media attention, 108, 118

memories of, 215–240
and the numbers racket, 134
opening of, 12
as opportunity to help others, 101, 105
popularity of, 106–110
praise of food served at, 228
and race relations, 235
service valued at, 215
and student life of Atlanta, 117–118, 156–157, 221, 234–235
See also La Carrousel; Paschal's Motor Hotel; Paschal's Restaurant at
    Castleberry Hill.
Paschal's Restaurant at Castleberry Hill
    continuing Paschal legacy, 157
    description of, 155
    opening of, 153–154
    popularity of, 155–156
The Pickrick, 130
Poor People's Campaign, 128
prejudice, overcoming, 230
professional organizations for African Americans, supported by Paschal
    brothers, 221–222
Pullman
    description of cars, 88
    James Paschal's work as porter, 87–90
    lives of porters, 88–89

R

race relations
    in Atlanta, 130
    during Civil Rights Movement, 14
    and the Depression, 25
    entrepreneurialism as defiance, 76, 78–79
    integration, 96, 104, 116, 119, 137, 141–142
    overcoming prejudice, 230
    and Paschal's Restaurant, 235, 238
    pre-Civil Rights Movement, 20–22, 24, 29, 32, 34–36, 73
    segregation, 37–38, 61–62, 91, 96

during sharecropping, 17
in Thomson, Georgia, 36–37
unifying influence of the arts, 119
racism, James's thoughts on, 16, 78
religion
in African American culture, 51–53
baptism, 54–55
conversion experience of James Paschal, 53–55
See also church
revival meetings, 52–54
Robie, William T., 110
Russell, Hermann, 141, 153

S

segregation, 61–62, 91
in education, 37–38
ending of, 96
See also integration
Selma marches, 126, 128, 136
service, 157, 215. *See also* hospitality industry
settling up, 31
sharecropping, 17, 19
difficuty of, 18, 20–22, 27–29, 30–32
settling up, 31
women and children, 24
Sherman, Ora Belle, 6, 109, 121
on working at Paschal's Restaurant, 225
Slaton, Lewis, on the Paschal brothers' legacy, 225
slot machines, 83
Smith, Harvey, on Paschal's Restaurant, 225
Smith, W. H., 115
Southern Christian Leadership Conference, 127
Spelman College, 156, 234
Stone, Juanita Sellers, on the Paschal brothers' legacy, 225
student life, and Paschal's restaurant, 234–235
Student Nonviolent Coordinating Committee, 127, 135

success, 142
   finding, 15, 211
sugarcane, 47
Sutton, Roswell, on the Paschal brothers' legacy, 225
swing incident, 58

T

Thomas, Bette Graves, on Paschal's Restaurant, 221
Thomas, Richard, on the Paschal brothers' legacy, 225
Thomson, Georgia, 20, 34
   beauty of, 36
   Paschal family's house in, 57–61
   race relations in, 36–37
Tusan, Gail S., on Paschal's Restaurant, 221–222

U

unity, valued by Paschal family, 58–59

V

violence
   Paschal family's opposition to, 23, 32, 72, 84, 96, 142
   and racism, 32, 34, 96

W

waitress training, 117
Ward, Horace, 103–104
Washington, Alice, on the Paschal brothers' determination, 73
Washington, March on, 127–128
Watkins, Lottie, on the Paschal brothers' legacy, 222
West, Clara, 38
West Hunter Street, 102, 103, 130
   central to Civil Rights Movement, 104
whites
   Civil Rights Movement involvement of, 110
   treatment of blacks, 17, 34–36, 62–63, 73
Williams, Hosea, 109

work
    balancing with school, 81
    ethic of James Paschal, 72, 74–75, 81–82
    Paschal Creed, 99–100
    Robert Paschal's thoughts on, 53, 67–68, 97
    valued in the Paschal family, 19, 45, 46, 68–69, 71–72
World War II, 84–85

Y

Young, Andrew, 156
    on the Paschal brothers' legacy, 231–232
    praise of Paschal's, 7

978-0-595-67503-6
0-595-67503-4

Printed in the United States
46719LVS00004B/106-510

9 780595 675036